CAMBRIDGE LIBRARY COLLECTION

Books of enduring scholarly value

British and Irish History, Nineteenth Century

This series comprises contemporary or near-contemporary accounts of the political, economic and social history of the British Isles during the nineteenth century. It includes material on international diplomacy and trade, labour relations and the women's movement, developments in education and social welfare, religious emancipation, the justice system, and special events including the Great Exhibition of 1851.

The Christian and Civic Economy of Large Towns

This three-volume study by the Scottish churchman and social reformer Thomas Chalmers (1780–1847) is a revealing work of Christian morality as applied to urban economic theory. Having moved to Glasgow in 1815, Chalmers was given a free hand in 1819 for an experiment in urban ministry at the new parish of St John's in the poorest district of the city. His reforms improved education and reduced the need for institutional poor relief by dividing the area into manageable 'proportions' that were closely looked after by parish elders and deacons, reviving a traditional community spirit and promoting self-help. Although sometimes severe, Chalmers' system and this influential work reflect Enlightenment optimism regarding human nature, suggesting the need for the Church of Scotland to respond actively to problems of urban industrialisation. Volume 2, published in 1823, investigates the nature of pauperism in Scotland and England and the ways in which Parliament and the parish can work towards its abolition.

Cambridge University Press has long been a pioneer in the reissuing of out-of-print titles from its own backlist, producing digital reprints of books that are still sought after by scholars and students but could not be reprinted economically using traditional technology. The Cambridge Library Collection extends this activity to a wider range of books which are still of importance to researchers and professionals, either for the source material they contain, or as landmarks in the history of their academic discipline.

Drawing from the world-renowned collections in the Cambridge University Library and other partner libraries, and guided by the advice of experts in each subject area, Cambridge University Press is using state-of-the-art scanning machines in its own Printing House to capture the content of each book selected for inclusion. The files are processed to give a consistently clear, crisp image, and the books finished to the high quality standard for which the Press is recognised around the world. The latest print-on-demand technology ensures that the books will remain available indefinitely, and that orders for single or multiple copies can quickly be supplied.

The Cambridge Library Collection brings back to life books of enduring scholarly value (including out-of-copyright works originally issued by other publishers) across a wide range of disciplines in the humanities and social sciences and in science and technology.

The Christian and Civic Economy of Large Towns

VOLUME 2

THOMAS CHALMERS

CAMBRIDGE
UNIVERSITY PRESS

CAMBRIDGE UNIVERSITY PRESS

Cambridge, New York, Melbourne, Madrid, Cape Town,
Singapore, São Paolo, Delhi, Mexico City

Published in the United States of America by Cambridge University Press, New York

www.cambridge.org
Information on this title: www.cambridge.org/9781108062367

© in this compilation Cambridge University Press 2013

This edition first published 1823
This digitally printed version 2013

ISBN 978-1-108-06236-7 Paperback

THE

CHRISTIAN

AND

CIVIC ECONOMY

OF

LARGE TOWNS.

BY

THOMAS CHALMERS, D.D.

MINISTER OF ST. JOHN'S CHURCH, GLASGOW.

VOL. II.

Glasgow:

PRINTED FOR CHALMERS AND COLLINS;

WAUGH AND INNES, EDINBURGH;

R. M. TIMS, DUBLIN;

AND G. AND W. B. WHITTAKER, LONDON.

1823.

CONTENTS.

THE

CHRISTIAN AND CIVIC ECONOMY

OF

LARGE TOWNS.

CHAP. IX.

ON THE RELATION THAT SUBSISTS BETWEEN THE
CHRISTIAN AND THE CIVIC ECONOMY OF LARGE
TOWNS.

BEFORE proceeding farther, it may be useful to
offer a short summary of the principles which have
already been expounded about a right ecclesiastical system for great towns; and then to eluci-
date the bearing which a good Christian, has upon
a good civic, economy: discriminating, at the
same time, between the peculiarities which apper-
tain to each of them.

There is a sure experimental alliance between
the defect of Christianity among a people, and
the defect of certain human arrangements that
conduce to its growth and preservation;—and
one most palpable defect of the latter sort is, that
the population of cities have been permitted so far
to outgrow the means of their religious instruction. There are many towns in our empire, where

the Establishment has not provided room in churches for one tenth of the inhabitants; and the inhabitants, when thus left to seek out Christianity for themselves, have shown how feeble the native demand of the human mind for it is, by their not supplementing, with chapels and meeting-houses, beyond another tenth, this enormous deficiency of the Establishment. It is clear, in these circumstances, that the vast majority must be left to wander without the pale of Christian ministrations, and Christian ordinances, altogether—where they have settled down into a mass of heathenism, which, to the eye of common experience, looks completely irrecoverable. There is a very general feeling of helplessness and despair upon this subject, as if the profligacy and ungodliness of cities were elements in every way as unconquerable as is physical necessity itself: and thus it is, that any serious or sustained attempt to make head against this sore mischief, is ranked, by many an incredulous observer, with the Quixotism that goeth forth, on some region of wild adventure, to reclaim a hydra, that scarcely admits of being softened, and will certainly never be subdued.

To make the recovery in question still more hopeless, there is no denying of the fact, that were churches to be built at this moment, up to the full accommodation of all our city families, it would have almost no perceptible influence on the habit into which they have degenerated. It is not at the sound of a bell, that they will consent to relinquish the sordid or profane gratifications wherewith they fill up that day of rest, which they have turned into a day of rioting and lawless indulgence. New churches might be built, and, if well appointed, new churches might be filled, but rather by a transference of sitters from the old churches, than by any large or extensive drafts on a still unmoved population. So that this one expedient which has been so much talked of, and to which even the eye of national wisdom has lately been directed, may, in itself, be utterly powerless, as to the object of making any sensible advances on the heathenism of our people,—all serving to confirm the general hopelessness that there is upon the subject, and to afford a plausible warrant for the contempt wherewith schemes of philanthropy are so apt to be regarded by the more secular and sober minded of our citizens, who feel satisfied with things as they are, nor want their quiescence to be at all disturbed by any suggestion or demonstration, whatever, of things as they should be.

This sluggishness of the population, in respect to Christianity, has led us to advert to the difference, in point of effect, between their being left to seek it for themselves, and their being aggressively plied with the offer of its ministrations and its lessons. It is a difference which we conceive to be well exemplified by the advantages which a local, has over a general Sabbath school. The teacher of a general Sabbath school draws to him those pupils, chiefly, whose parents have a predisposition for the instructions of the gospel; and so, may he be instrumental in perpetuating Christianity where it is, but not in reviving it where it is not. The teacher of a local Sabbath school, on the other hand, feels himself charged with all the families that are to be found on the face of his assigned territory; and, by the mere force of moral suasion, does he find himself able to compel nearly all the children to come in: and thus, instead of a mere process of attraction, which ever operates only on minds already possessed of some kindred quality to religion, does he set up an active process of emanation, whereby he operates on minds that are indifferent, or even hostile to the cause; and the cheering experience is, that under this local system, the attendance of the young is more than tripled beyond what it was under the general system,—thus pointing out the way in which a population might have been preserved from degeneracy, had it been adopted sooner; and the way in which, if adopted now, a population might still be recalled from it.

For, what is true of Sabbath schools for the young, is also true of churches for the whole population. Let a church draw its sitters from the city at large, and it is by the feeble process of attraction, and by this alone, that it secures their attendance. A minister cannot charge himself with so wide a field of superintendence as the whole city. He cannot take cognizance of all its families, or pay such week-day attentions to them as might induce their Sabbath-day attendance upon himself. Meanwhile, the population increases, and outgrows the room that there is in churches for their accommodation; and many are the families that fall without the reach of all ministerial cognizance whatever, and who without the habit of church-going, are also without the taste for it: and thus, it is not only true that the number of places of worship is greatly beneath the necessities of the people, but the demand of the people themselves, for new places, is also greatly beneath these necessities;—so, that if by a sudden movement of patriotism, many new churches were speedily made to arise to the view of the citizens, the mortifying result were, that the citizens, still unmoved out of their long acquired and firm habits of non-attendance, would leave the churches to stand unoccupied, and so stamp the charge of temerity and impotence on the whole speculation.

It is on this account that we hold it indispensable, for the restoration of a Christian habit in our cities, to give to churches the benefit of the same principle of locality, that has been found so signally efficacious in bringing Sabbath schools into contact with the whole population. Every church in the Establishment should be as exclusively connected with its parish, as a local Sabbath school is with its assigned territory. The week-day attentions of the minister, instead of being generalised over the whole city, in which case they are sure

to be languid, and heartless, and ineffective, should
be as much concentrated, and as frequently reiter-
ated as possible, in the smaller and more manageable district, over which he has hitherto had little
more than a bare nominal superintendence. Were
he permitted to recruit his church from his parish,
as far as his parish might be disposed to furnish
him with hearers, this would soon translate him
into a far more intimate and endearing relationship
with its families, than by all his other attempts he
could possibly attain. The circumstance of having a thousand hearers in his parish, instead of a
hundred, would give him a weight and an ascendency convertible to the best Christian, and collater-
ally bringing along with it the best civil and economical purposes that ever were contemplated by
the eye of patriotism. All the bland, and kindly,
and civilising influences of a parochial system
could thus be brought into play among the dark
and crowded recesses of a city. And little is it
known, how much the cruel disruption of the minister from his parish, by a system of seat-letting
that ought instantly to be abandoned, has contributed to that degeneracy which looks at present
so hopeless and irrecoverable.

But, there is a way of acting, upon this suggestion, which must be attended to. The substitution of a local, for a general congregation, should
not be attempted by an instantaneous dismissal of
all the extra-parochial sitters, and the offer of
their vacant room to the inhabitants of the parish

where the church is situated. This, independently
of its being an act of violence to individual feeling, were an act of impolicy, even for the purpose
that is meant to be accomplished by it. The
strong existing habit of alienation from all ordinances, on the part of those who have long lived
in ease and comfort without them, must be adverted to: and, such in fact is the inveteracy of this
habit, that, were a thousand sittings vacated in the
church of one of our plebeian parishes, for the
sake of extensively accommodating the parishioners, it is likely that not more than a hundred of
these sittings might be inquired after. It is not
enough that room be provided—the renovation of
a new habit must be brought about: and, it were
positively throwing away the accommodation that
we have, if pews were emptied for the people,
faster than the people came forward with their
demand for the pews. This points to the conclusion, that a parochial, can only come in the place
of a general attendance, not by an immediate, but
by a gradual substitution of the one for the other.
And there is no law of graduality that seems better adapted for the purpose, than simply to hold
forth, to the preference of parishioners, all those
vacancies which are created by the death or the
removal of present occupiers. There is no offence
given to any actual sitter by such an arrangement:
and the vacancies which, in a congregation of fifteen hundred, will not take place at above the rate
of a hundred in the year, will not exceed the rate

at which the demand for them may be stimulated, by the ordinary labours and attentions of any city minister, in the parish which has been assigned to him; and every new seat-letting extends his interest in his own local territory, by adding to the number of his Sabbath hearers who reside within its bounds; and thus the ties of reciprocity between him and his people, are every day becoming closer—till at length, but for the extent of his population, the relationship would be as affectionate on his part, and as cordial on theirs, as is that which obtains between the worthy minister, and the simple natives of a parish in the country. This is a consummation which never can be reached, under the present system of seat-letting; and it were vain to attempt the speeding of it forward by any sudden or desultory shift in the distribution of the sitters,—although we have no doubt that, by the method now recommended, (while nothing striking or visible could be produced in a single year), the whole effect would be surely and quietly realised in less than the space of a single generation.

The power which a local Sabbath school teacher has, in virtue of that peculiar arrangement under which he operates, to draw out a full attendance, of the juvenile population of his district, on that seminary over which he presides, is the very power that, under the same arrangement, might be exercised by the minister of a city parish. Not that he would suddenly call forth the attendance of his whole population on the church where he preaches,—for he has the habits of manhood and of established life to contend against,—but that he would do it gradually and surely. Let his people be only aware of their right of preference for the vacant sittings of their own church—and he will find his progressive, but certain way to the desirable result of a Sabbath audience, the great bulk of whom are composed of the residenters upon his own territorial vineyard. He has it so much in his power, within the limited district of a parish, to make himself the object of recognition among its families. He can so easily, by his week-day attentions, obtrude himself and the business of his profession upon their notice. He can so naturally become the object of their Sunday preference, by becoming the object of their gratitude for his practicable labours among the young, and the sick, and the dying. He can withal, by the institution of a good Sabbath school system, so readily fill up the vacancies in his congregation out of its seminaries, by the very likely transition that would take place among the youth on the borders of manhood: when, after leaving the schools that he had provided, so many of them would most naturally find their way to the church in which he preached. It is thus, that, as the fruit of his concentrated attentions through the week, on a parish, the minister might recruit and sustain the attendance, with a facility which can never be experienced by him whose loose and general relationship to the whole

city leaves him no other chance for a congregation, than the unfostered demand of people who
are in a great measure beyond his reach, and with
whom he can never come into close and recurring
contact in the way of household ministrations.

We are the more earnest upon this point, because we are aware of no other method by which
a demand can be excited for additional churches,
at all commensurate to the moral and religious
necessities of our population. Under the present
system, there may, by the mere increase of people,
be such an increase of the demand, in our second
rate towns, as shall ensure the addition of one or
two churches in half a century, or in such a period
of time as may have witnessed the accession of as
many families as could fill a dozen of churches.
And thus it is, that profligacy and profanation so
rapidly outstride all the counteractions which have
been raised against them; and which, however it
may have escaped observation hitherto, have in
truth lost their efficacy, by the utter neglect of
the principle of locality, as applied to the churches
and parishes of a city. It may only be by the
countenance and good will of magistrates, that the
indispensable article of churches, for the accommodation of the people, can be provided. But it
is only by the assiduity of ministers, with all the
advantages for local and parochial cultivation upon their side, that the no less indispensable article
can be provided, of a demand, on the part of the
people, for this accommodation. Give to such a

minister the power of meeting this demand with vacancies as they occur. Let him be able to satisfy the inquiries of his people, by the assurance of disposeable room for them, and for them only, at the next term of seat-letting. Save both him and them from the discouragement of beholding that room taken possession of, through the partiality of city administrators, by interlopers from without; and then, by very ordinary exertion indeed, under this amended system, could the demand of the people be so excited, as not merely to fill, but to press on the existing accommodation. In this way too, the demand would clearly announce itself—and, from the intenseness of the competition for places, could there be gathered the distinct and satisfying intimation, when it was that new erections might safely be adventured on—and, greatly beyond the power of accommodation in his own church, might each minister create occupiers for future churches, whose united voice would clearly indicate the time for old parishes being divided, and new ones formed out of shares and detachments from contiguous parishes.

We fear that without this expedient, the increase of churches will follow tardily and sluggishly in the rear of a far more rapidly increasing population; and, that thus, from one year to another, there will be a decay of proportional means for the arresting of vice and profligacy in our land. It is not, as we have often averred, with Christian instruction for the supply of our spiritual wants, as it is with any given commodity for the supply of our bodily wants. In the latter case, there is no strenuousness required to call forth a demand: so, that upon the simple offer of the commodity, we may be sure, that it will be as much sought for, and as much used, as is good for the interest of our species. But the case is widely different with the lessons of Christianity. To raise a demand for them, is a work of as great or greater difficulty than it is to provide the supply of them. And, it is only by the clergy of the Establishment, each keeping up an intensely parochial operation within his own sphere, instead of dissipating his influence over the wide superficies of a whole city—it is only thus, we apprehend, that much more of Sabbath accommodation will come to be provided, because it is only thus that much more of it will come to be either called or cared for.

The mode of parochial seat-letting, as now laid down, we regard as by far the most important suggestion that can be offered to our city administrators, for the purpose of forwarding a right Christian economy in our great towns; and we shall deem their compliance with it to be the very best contribution which they could render to the cause. And yet, we speak the language both of apprehension and experience, when we profess ourselves to be not very sanguine, either of their speedy adoption of this mode, or of their faithful and persevering execution of it. It requires a force, of no ordinary momentum, to shift the rou-

tine of municipal business; and no where is there
more devout homage rendered to the omnipotence
of custom, than in the office of city clerks or city
chamberlains; and there, as in a secure and impregnable fastness, will she continue to hold her
imperial sway—alike regardless of promises that
are not remembered, and of principles that are not
understood. It is not, that in the required line of
proceeding there is at all any difficulty: for nothing more patent, we should think, than simply, in
the disposal of vacant places, to grant a preference
to parochial, over extra-parochial applications.
And were any thing like a striking or visible result to come *soon enough* out of this arrangement,
we should not despair of a more ready compliance
with it. Could the final benefit be so placed before the immediate eye of our civic practitioners,
as to force itself upon their observation, it is likely
enough that, on their part, there would be a more
punctual adherence to this great law of parochial
equity. But the operation of the law is so gradual—and, when bidden to look through the vista
of half a generation, for the full and salutary effect,
it then appears to be so much a matter of speculation, and so little a matter of sense, that any argument which can be addressed upon the subject
has but a feeble influence, when it has the mighty
power of old use and old authority to contend
against. It is thus, we fear, that with all those
advantages of the principle of locality, which an
Establishment naturally possesses—it may be long

ere in towns, she shall come completely to realize them; and, meanwhile, that the unordained or dissenting teachers of religion may, by the assumption of what is tantamount to parishes for themselves, earn that superiority of usefulness which our regular clergy, while the existing methods are perpetuated, will vainly and hopelessly aspire after.

Should one hundred applications from the families of a poor city parish, for seats in their own parish church, come into competition with a hundred applications from families in the wealthier and more fashionable side of the town, we know not in what terms to brand or to depreciate the impolicy that would set aside the former, and give preference and acceptancy to the latter. Such a forthcoming for seats, on the part of our operative population, were just the commencement of a process, which, of all others, it were most desirable to help and to encourage forward: nor can we conceive an object on which either serious principle or enlightened patriotism ought to be more intently set, than that of opening and multiplying all possible facilities for this best of all popular movements. The intelligence of the first year's success would call forth a host of expectancy from neighbours, for the vacancies of the second year, and thus would the matter make progress, so as that with the infection of a new taste, there should be the spread of a new habit, in that very quarter of society which is now so wofully overrun both with political rancour, and with personal worthlessness. The appearance of a parochial demand for seats, from artizans and labourers, is just that initial tendency to what is good which ought to be hailed with delight, and met with the readiest alacrity, by all who have any presiding influence in the management of our public affairs. And when, instead of this, the tendency is discouraged, and driven back again to the dormancy out of which it had arisen—when the hand that ought to have fostered this approximation inflicts upon it the check of a mortifying repulse, made as offensive as possible, by the preference of a rich man who is out of the parish, to a poor man who is in it—when, disheartened by repeated failures, the attempt is no longer made, because the galling experience of this sordid and ungenerous partiality has at length convinced parishioners that the attempt is altogether hopeless,—the conclusion is, that philanthropy may often be thwarted in her likeliest designs, not because of the natural impediments which lie in her way, but because her best and dearest interests happen to lie at the disposal of men, who have neither the heart to care for the success of a generous enterprise, nor the talent to appreciate it.*

---

* It may be right to mention, that in Glasgow, where the public functionaries are so alive to every consideration of the public welfare, the rule of parochial seat-letting has been virtually conceded to, at least, one of the parishes, though, at the outset of its operation, the old habit which wont to obtain in the executive department of this business may, for a time, be a little uncontrollable.

It is much better, for the right Christian economy of a town, when the rule of parochial equity, in seat-letting, tends to the disappointment of capitalists than to the disappointment of labourers. By the former disappointment, an effective interest is created in behalf of more churches; and the inconvenience of a limited accommodation is made to fall upon those who are most able to remedy and to extend it; and these wealthy outcasts can form into a powerful body of application for an additional church—so that to reject the applications of the wealthy, in favour of the poor, is to walk in that direct line which leads to the increase of our ecclesiastical provision in great cities. Whereas, to reject the applications of the poor, in favour of the wealthy, is just to reverse this process. It is to make irrecoverable outcasts of those who are without the means of at all helping themselves. It is to damp, into irrecoverable apathy, the whole class of society to which they belong. It is to extinguish the first hopeful symptoms of a revival, throughout that mass of human beings, whose estrangement from all the sanctities of Sabbath observation, is of such deadly import to the well-being of a community. It is to stifle that incipient voice which arises from among the poorer orders themselves; and, by listening to which, a healing influence would have come back upon them, and restored to soundness that great foundation of a country's prosperity and peace—the virtue of its people. It is thus that men, who are the very first to tremble at the outbreakings of radicalism, may lie the most deeply chargeable with the guilt of having fed and sustained it in its principle; withholding, as they do, the best counteraction to all the brooding elements of a fiery and mischievous fermentation.

Of all the outrages, either felt or fancied, on the rights of the people, this is the one which is followed by the surest retaliation; and that, not so much from its present influence, in swelling the tide of discontent, as from its final result in the more confirmed irreligion of our city populace. It forms the addition of at least one real, to the whole previous list of their imaginary grievances, and leaves upon its aspect such a glaring expression of preference to the desires of the wealthy, over the righteous demands of the poor, as not only to furnish one topic of substantial provocation, but as to impart a plausibility to all the others. This, however, does not constitute the main soreness of that cruel and unfeeling policy which we have endeavoured to expose, and which lies in the effect that it has to perpetuate the depravity of the multitude, and that too, in the face of a willingness, on the part of the multitude, to be set on the path which leads both to tranquillity and to righteousness.

We deem this topic, of seat-letting, to be of sufficient importance in itself, for justifying all the amplitude of remark and argument that we have bestowed upon it: and, we think, it may farther be employed for the purpose of illustrating a distinction, which we shall find most closely and essentially applicable to many other particulars connected with the Christian and Civic Economy of towns; and which the reader would do well to apprehend and to fix in his remembrance, more especially, throughout the whole of our intended lucubrations on the subject of pauperism. We advert to the distinction between what may be called a natural and a political difficulty in the way of any given reformation. There is no natural difficulty in the way of certain benefits that would accrue from a right arrangement of matters as to seat-letting. But there is a political difficulty in the way of initiating and maintaining the arrangement itself. Grant the simple enactment of a preference for parishioners to all vacant places in their own parish church, as the vacancies occur, and a faithful adherence to this enactment; and, *in the nature of things,* there is no let or hindrance in the way of a very great improvement on the economy of our cities; and that, with little more to do, than just to wait the operation of this new method. Vacancies will, by deaths and removals, occur, as a matter of course. Other things being equal, parishioners will, by the mere influence of juxtaposition, aided, as it generally is, by the influence of connexion with their minister, on other grounds, prefer accommodation in their own, to accommodation in other churches. If there be any thing in the very superior attractions of one, or more, of the city clergy, to disturb this preference, this will operate within his parish, as well as beyond its limits, and secure an overwhelming superiority of competition for seats from his own parishioners; so as to give to the favourite minister all the surer chance of at length realising a parochial congregation. This, in the very order of nature, he will sooner or later arrive at; and we should then, upon the whole, behold, under such a system of management, the ministers of a city having each a compact and concentrated influence over his own separate portion of it—an influence that would be inconceivably augmented, from the very circumstance of such a number of families, with whom he stood parochially associated through the week, being now his stated hearers on the Sabbath—and an influence, which the whole operation of the principle of locality would enable him to wield with tenfold greater facility and effect than he ever can do over the hearers of a general congregation. There may be artificial impediments in the way of setting up this arrangement, but there are no natural impediments to it: for, after it is set up and acted on, the nature both of individual man and of society affords nought but openings and facilities in its favour; and, without more than the ordinary strenuousness of average and every day people being farther concerned in the matter, the benefits that would flow from it are altogether incalculable. Nature would soon unpeople a parish church of its present sitters.

Nature would more incline parishioners than others to fill up the vacancies. Nature would put into the breast of each clergyman a far more lively interest in a parish where he had a thousand, than in one where he had only a hundred hearers, and would vest him with a far more useful ascendency over it. Nature would prompt him to the exertions of a more willing activity, in a field that was crowded with the members of his own congregation; and even should his natural habits, as in some cases it undoubtedly is, be not labour but indolence, the reformed economy would, at least, render any slender week-day attentions which he was disposed to bestow, ten times more effective than they ever can be under the existing economy. So, that in respect of natural difficulties, or such difficulties as attach inherently and essentially to the subject of management, there are none, but the contrary, in the way of bringing about a desirable result; and whatever difficulties we have to contend with, in this matter, are altogether factitious or political,—appertaining, not to the constitution of the thing to be managed, but to the constitution of what may be called the managing apparatus—not to the subject that we want to be operated upon, but to the agency who now work it.

For example, the difficulty, in the present instance, lies not in the parish where we should like the arrangement, that we are now pleading for, to be carried into effect, but it lies among the ar-

cana of city business and city committeeship. It
is not a natural but a political difficulty. It consists in a kind of *vis inertiæ*, whereby it is so hard
to move any municipal body out of its old tendencies. The field of contest is not the population, but among the heads and rulers of the population; and the mighty resistance that is to be
overcome, nearly all arises from the rust and the
tardiness which adhere to the ponderous machine
of a city corporation, that obstinately perseveres
in its wonted cycle, and whose subordinate committees as obstinately persevere in their wonted
epicycles. The way to overcome this, no doubt,
is by the force of persuasion, addressed to the present and the living administrators of this superintendence. But, without meaning the slightest
disrespect to these individuals, who, to say the
least of them, must, in regard to intellect, be on
the fair level and average of humanity, there is,
perhaps, no class of men who are better entitled
to a sensitive dislike and jealousy of all innovation. They are incessantly assailed, and upon all
hands, with counsel and criticism; and full many
must be the crudities of undigested speculation
that are submitted to their notice; and the very
labour of separating the precious from the vile of
the suggestions, wherewith they are plied, must be
oppressive to men who are already overborne; and
it is no wonder that they should feel the disturbance of any change whatever, in their accustomed
routine, to be harassing and vexatious; and the

public are really not aware of all the indulgence
that is due, upon these grounds, to men who make
such important surrenders of time and of convenience to the well-being of the community: so,
that it was not with a view to advance any charge,
but with a view to impress what we deem a distinction of capital importance, that we have given
way to the train of our present observations.   A
natural difficulty is that which is encountered on
the field of direct and immediate management,
and after we have obtained an actual occupation
of the field, in the way that is desired.   A political difficulty is that which is encountered previously to taking this occupation, and, generally,
on the road to it; and is often of a nature so impracticable, that the operation, out of which a
good result was promised, may never be begun.
The natural difficulty lies with the thing to be
managed, and is a let or hindrance between the
operation and the result.   The political difficulty
lies with the existing managers, and is a let or
hindrance anterior to the operation, and often preventive of it.   The operation of the rule of seat-
letting would most surely lead to the result that
we anticipate, and have attempted to explain; because there is no natural impediment among our
men of private condition in parishes, but the reverse, in the way of such a consequence.   But,
among our men of public office in corporations,
there is a very strong political impediment in the

way of establishing, and practically abiding by, the rule.

The truth and importance of this distinction will come to be more fully recognised when we treat of Pauperism. The example of nearly all Europe, with the exception of England, proves, that there is no natural difficulty in the way of a population being subsisted, without almost the single case of an individual perishing by want; and that, without any legal or compulsory provision for the poor. But now, that such a provision has been established in this country, and that the great unwieldy corporation of the state must be moved, ere any step can be taken towards the abolition of it, and that the subordinate courts of administration, in every parish, have sunk and settled into the obstinacy of an old practical habit, in all their proceedings, there is a host of political difficulties that must be met and overcome, not ere it can be proved with what certainty the people, when left to themselves, will find their own way to their own comfort and independence, but ere the measure shall be carried of actually leaving the people to themselves. We think that there is no natural difficulty which stands in the way of the success of such an experiment, *if tried;* but we feel that there are many political difficulties in the way of putting the experiment to the trial. We hold it a practicable thing, to conduct any parish, either in a city or in the country, to the old economy of a Scottish parish, on the strength of an arrangement which we shall afterwards endeavour to set, in more detailed exposition, before our readers; and that there is no impediment on the parochial field, which is the real theatre of the experiment, in the way of final and looked for success. The struggle is not with the population, for obtaining the success of the arrangement—but the struggle is with our legislature and our municipalities, for obtaining the arrangement itself. The place of most formidable resistance is not in the outer, but the inner department of this business, and the occasion of it is, when, in the hall of deliberation, the attempt is made to break up our existing artificial economy, and thus to prevail over the dislike and the prejudices of hacknied functionaries, and to carry that nearly impregnable front, wherewith all novelty is sure to be withstood, by the clerks, and the conveners, and the committee-men, of an old establishment. The battle is not with the natural difficulties of the problem, but with its political difficulties—not with the laws of human nature, as to be found in the parish where the experiment is made, but with the tendencies of human nature, as exhibited on that arena of public discussion and debate where the experiment is proposed. In the work of abolishing legalised charity, the heaviest conflict will not be with the natural poverty of the lower orders, but with that pride of argument, and that tenacity of opinion, and all those political feelings and capacities which obtain among the higher orders. In short, we hold that there is nothing in the condition of the people which opposes a barrier against the abolition of all legal and compulsory pauperism, but that there is a very strong initial barrier in the condition of our laws, and courts, and long established usages. In the practical solution of the question of public charity, the recipients will not be found so difficult of management as the lawgivers and administrators. There is a method by which might be effected, and almost without difficulty, the abolition of public charity among our plebeians—but the consent of our patricians must be obtained, ere we are free to put the method into operation: and what we affirm is, that it is a greater achievement to obtain leave and liberty for using the method, than to obtain success for the method itself; or, in other words, that the great impediment to the removal of this sore national distemper, lies not among the plebeians, but among the patricians of the commonwealth.

But there is another distinction, which we must labour to impress—even that which obtains between the way in which a Christian, and the way in which a Civic good is rendered to the population of cities, by the establishment of a good ecclesiastical system amongst them.

We should not call that a Christian benefit to any individual, which conduces not either to his security, or to his preparation, for an inheritance in heaven. Ere he is Christianly the better, for the labour that has been bestowed upon him, there must be wrought in his soul that change of principle and of character, without which, he will for ever remain an outcast from the abodes of a blissful eternity. We shall not, nor is it necessary to dogmatise, at present, about the precise nature of this change. We shall only suppose, that some change or other must be made to pass upon every human heart, ere he who owns it has passed from the state of an heir of condemnation, to that of the heir of a glorious immortality. Any benefit short of this, is not entitled to the denomination of a Christian benefit, and it is just by the number of individuals who receive this distinct benefit, each for himself, that we would estimate the amount of Christian good done to a population.

Now, there is no doubt that this good would be promoted, by the arrangement which we have suggested, by a full parochial attendance of the people upon acceptable ministers, and by the labours of those ministers, now rendered greatly more effective, in virtue of that more strict parochial relationship which we have ventured to recommend. And, yet it is not to be disguised, that even in those congregations which are reputed to be the most prosperous and flourishing, the number of actual converts may bear a small proportion, indeed, to the number even of steady and interested hearers—that, in respect to the whole auditory, they may constitute a very little flock, and stand forth a peculiar people, in the midst of the many still sunk in the lethargy and unconcern of nature—that, as the fruit of the labour, and close earnestness, of a lengthened incumbency, all that a most assiduous pastor shall leave behind him may be a mere fraction of his parishioners, turned, through his means, to the genuine faith and discipleship of Christianity. This is what will most readily be admitted, by those who rate Christianity according to the high standard of the New Testament—who demand, as tests of the reality of conversion, those lofty and spiritual characteristics that were so current in the early churches, however rarely exemplified in modern days—who require, for eternity, a devotedness of heart, as well as a decency of external observation—and are not satisfied with any transition of habit, short of that thorough regenerative process which sanctifies the affections as well as reforms the external history, and by which man becomes a new creature in Jesus Christ our Lord.

Now, if this spiritual renovation, to the feelings and the principles of peculiar Christianity, be an event of such exceeding rarity—if it but occur at distant intervals, to cheer and to reward the labours even of our most devoted clergymen —if, in the best attended ministry, and under the busiest application of powerful and persuasive influences, it still holds true, that though many are called, yet few are converted,—then it but leads us again to the conclusion, that let churches be built, and parishes be organized, and the wisest

and fittest arrangements be adopted, the quantity
of Christian good which is in consequence done,
may be in very minute proportion, indeed, to the
number of human beings among whom it is attempted; that a very handful out of the untouched mass may be all the harvest that is reaped, and
that too, by a machine of which we are required
to enlarge the compass and the magnitude, so as
to make it commensurate to the whole population.
And thus, both with enlightened Christians, who
are aware of the extreme paucity of that faith
which is unto salvation, and with mere secular
philanthropists, who can, at the same time, perceive how little, even under the most close and
diligent administration of the ordinances of the
gospel, the real sacredness of the gospel is ever
diffused throughout the general bulk of any congregation;—with both, may there be an impression, as if the effect that we promised, from the
setting up of a right Christian apparatus in cities,
was most sanguinely overrated—with the former,
who are most thoroughly, and, as we think, most
rightly convinced, that, without a special and sanc-
tifying influence from above, no engine of human
contrivance is at all available to the conversion of
a human soul—and, with the latter, who will feel
that, if all which is gained be but the bringing
down of some mysterious and preternatural influence from heaven, on a mere scantling of the
population, then the labour of raising so vast a
spiritual organization is not only thrown away

upon an inadequate object, but upon an object that is only prized by a few unintelligible fanatics, with whom they can feel no sympathy, and will hold no fellowship.

We refer the former of these two classes to the first chapter of this work, where we have attempted to demonstrate the good and the necessity of a terrestrial apparatus, for the distribution of that living water, or that spiritual influence, which cometh from above: and we have only farther to remind them, that even though a few more of the whole human race be thereby snatched from the common ruin of our nature, and be recovered to a blissful immortality, it is not from them that we should expect any complaint of the inadequacy of such a result, to the means or to the labour that may have previously been expended. And, besides, it is to be presumed that the extended means of Christian instruction which we have ventured to recommend, would, at least, be productive of as great a proportion of additional Christianity, as the present means are of the Christianity that is now actually produced. And would they, because so little is produced, set aside the means that are already in operation? Would they discontinue the expense of all the existing churches, because in almost every church, it is still the fearful minority, we have reason to apprehend, who are brought under the saving power of the gospel, and so are raised, by spiritual education, into a meetness for paradise? The truth is, that when-

ever a more copious descent of the Holy Ghost
shall come down upon us, it will pass through all
the channels of conveyance that have been furnished for it in the land; entering into pulpits,
and then spreading itself over congregations, and
finding its way, most readily, through the most free
and frequented pathways of communication that
have been opened up between the ministers of religion and the people among whom they expatiate.
By subdividing parishes, we just multiply these
pathways; and by localising parishes, we just
make the pathways shorter, and more convenient
and accessible, than before.   We do not set aside
the doctrine of a spiritual influence; for we believe that it is this which will be the primary and
the essential agent in that great moral regeneration that awaits our species.   But just as in the
irrigating processes of Egypt, the reservoirs are
constructed, and the furrows are drawn, and every
field on the banks of the Nile is put into readiness
for the coming inundation—so we, knowing that
the Spirit maketh its passage into the human heart,
by the word and the ordinances of the gospel, are
just labouring at a right process of spiritual irrigation, when we provide such arrangements as
will bring the greatest number of human beings
into broadest and most recurring contact with this
word, and with these ordinances.

  But, at present, we have it still more at heart
to propitiate the latter class, or our mere civil
and political philanthropists, to the cause of a

right ecclesiastical system for cities. And the
argument we would urge upon them is, that, under such a system, the civic benefit which they
most care for, is both anterior, in regard of time,
and greatly more extended, in regard of diffusion,
than the Christian benefit about which, we fear,
they are much less solicitous. The fact admits
of being explained, but we have only time, just
now, to announce it,—that the preacher who, by
his doctrine, is best fitted to convert the few, is
also best fitted to congregate the many,—that he
who is the most powerful, in respect of the saving
influence which he causes to descend on the very
little flock, is also the most popular, in respect of
the attractive influence wherewith he assembles
the multitude around his stated ministrations: in
a word, that he who is most qualified for the Christian good, of turning some from darkness to spiritual light, is also most qualified for the civic
good, of turning many from their habits of Sabbath riot, and Sabbath profanation, to, at least, a
personal attendance on the services of Christianity.
It is certainly a question, full of interest, what that
is, in the lessons of an orthodox minister, which
draws the crowd around his pulpit, and yet falls
short of reaching an effective Christian influence
to more, perhaps, than a very small proportion of
them. Without resolving the question, we would
turn to this fair application the undoubted fact
upon which it is founded; we would bid our philanthropists mark the distinction which obtains be-

tween the Christian and the civic good that may be rendered to a population. The one extends but to the select few, who have been reclaimed from the love of the world, to the love and the spiritual services of him who made the world. The other may extend to the whole of a crowded congregation, reclaimed from the outlandish heathenism of their old practices, to the decencies of Sabbath attire and Sabbath observation. There is a humanizing, that is far short of a Christianizing, influence. There is a soberness of habit to which a general population may be trained, and that, under the very process which conducts a few of that population to spirituality of heart. The very practice of church going would make a more orderly and pacific society on earth, even though it should fail of preparing more than a very few of that society for heaven. It is thus, that, by a deed of acceptable patronage, the magistrates of a city may confer a temporal benefit on the community, that shall be felt extensively, and almost instantaneously, even though the minister of their appointment may have to labour most strenuously for years, and yet be the instrument of a Christian blessing to but an exceeding small number of families. The fact is melancholy to those who are engrossed with the considerations of death and judgment, and the various concerns of the imperishable soul. But we now address those who are taken up with the mere accommodations of the fleeting journey of this world's existence—whose demand, as the rulers of a town, is more for quiet citizens, than for holy and regenerated believers— who should like men to be so far moral as to be manageable, whether or not they shall also be so far spiritual as to be heavenly—who want, at all events, to have a commonwealth free from the profligacy that leads to turbulence on earth, however short its vast majority may fall of that piety which leads to triumph, and to a rich inheritance in paradise. Now, what we affirm is, that on the higher ground of Christian usefulness, a right ecclesiastical system may only reclaim from the evil to the good, its tens or its fifties, out of the teeming multitudes of a city parish; but that while it is doing so, there is also a collateral influence, by which it reclaims its thousands and tens of thousands, from what is evil, to what is good, on the lower ground of civic usefulness.

To estimate the Christian good done to an individual, made pious, through the labours of a devoted clergyman, we have only to compute the difference between a ruined and a blissful eternity. To estimate the civic good done to a town, the majority of whose people stood estranged from the ordinances of Christianity, but are now, by the multiplication of churches, and the right exercise of patronage, reclaimed to attendance upon them, we must bethink ourselves a little of the many substantial influences, upon the general character, which such a habit will necessarily bring along with it. Conceive, then, one family, in hum-

ble and operative life, trained, though it may only
be to the outward regularities of a Christian Sabbath; and taking respectable occupancy of its own
pew, where it exhibits the domestic group of well
doing parents and well disciplined children—each
exchanging, on that day, the garb of citizenship
for the becoming holiday attire, which thrift and
management have enabled them to provide; and
retained in constant attendance on the lessons of
a minister, from whom, if they do not inhale the
vital spirit, they will, at least, imbibe, though perhaps insensibly, somewhat of the sedate and moral
tone of Christianity, and be strengthened in their
taste for the decencies of even-going citizenship.
May we not read, on the very aspect of such a
family, the indications of virtue, and order, and
industry, through the week, and a manifest superiority, in all these attributes, over another family,
that spends its Sabbath recklessly and at large?
It is certainly not from families of a right Sabbati-
cal habit, that popular violence will draw the aliment by which it is upholden; for it is a habit
which holds no alliance, whatever, with dissipation, or idleness, or discontent. And, therefore,
could a right exercise of patronage simply induce
a greatly more general attendance of the lower
ranks upon divine service—then, far more readily
and extensively than the spread of thorough conversion among the people, would there be the
spread of such secondary virtues as should amount
to a civic good that were altogether incalculable.

If in pure Christianity, which we have attempted to prove is popular Christianity, there be an initial charm to draw the people around its ministrations, and that greatly beyond its final effect, in turning them from the children of this world, to the children of light; and if it be farther true, that the very habit of Sabbath regularity stands associated with all the other habits of sober and pacific citizenship, then, though the great majority of a congregation, so attracted and detained, shall still continue to be of this world, yet are the virtue and tranquillity of the world greatly promoted, even by the more superficial transformation which they have thus been made to undergo. So, that by every deed of acceptable church patronage, though small be the accession which may thereby be gained to the kingdom of heaven, yet a mighty accession will be made to the stock of good civic accomplishments and properties upon earth. Nor is there another way by which our municipal rulers could more effectually mark the wisdom of their policy, or do so much to meliorate the distemper of a vicious and disorderly population, than by the appointment, to their vacancies, of such Christian ministers as are best suited to the taste of the labouring classes, and who of this hold out the most authentic and palpable testimony, by the simple fact of their overflowing congregations.

The distinction between the Christian and the civic good that is done to a community were still more apparent, did the minister localise upon a given territory, and as he went from house to house, in week-day visitations, meet, at every turn, with the greetings of affectionate recognition from the members of his now parochial congregation. Throughout the whole of this progress, he might rarely meet with the heirs and expectants of a blessed eternity—yet, who does not see, that beyond the limits of a circle so select and peculiar, he bears about with him a humanizing influence that may be felt in almost every habitation? It is a sad contemplation to him whose heart is occupied with the weight and reality of eternal things, that out of so vast a population, a mere handful of converts may be the whole fruit of a lengthened and laborious incumbency. And yet it is an experimental truth, that in respect of temporal and immediate good, the whole population may be sensibly bettered, by the ever recurring presence of an affectionate pastor in the midst of them. The primary impulse, it is true, on which he sets out among his people, is the good of their immortality; and, in the occasional fulfilment of this high errand, he finds his encouragement and reward. But he scatters abroad, and far more largely, among the families, another good, which, though but of secondary and subordinate importance in his eyes, is enough to stamp him, in the estimation of every civil and political ruler, as by far the most useful servant of the community. There is a substantial, though unnoticed, charm in the visit of a superior. There is a felt compliment in his attentions, which raises an emotion in the breast, the very opposite of that disdainful sentiment towards the higher orders of society, that is now of such alarming prevalence amongst our operative population. There is a real contribution made to the earthly moralities of the poor man, by the consciousness of that friendly tie which unites him in an acquaintanceship that is ever growing with the minister of his parish. The very aim that is made, by the people, to afford him a decent reception, in the cleanliness of their houses, and the dress of their children, is not to be overlooked, in our estimate of the bland and beneficial influences that accompany his frequent reiterations over the face of his allotted vineyard. There is, in all these ways, and in many more, a most effective, wholesome, and widely spread influence, coming out of the relationship that subsists between a local clergyman, and the families that reside within the limits of his superintendence— an influence which, in respect of its amount upon the individual, may come far short of that Christian good that issues in everlasting blessedness, but which, in respect of its diffusiveness, tells throughout the whole host of his parishioners, and issues in the important earthly or civic good of a better habited population—an influence that will, at least, reach so far as to reduce their profligacy, and to quiet their turbulence, and to soften all their political exasperations, and to beget a kindly amalgamation of the various classes with each other, and, if not to secure their eternity, yet altogether to shed a comfort and a virtuousness over the pilgrimage which leads to it.

It both serves to spread this moral cement, and forms a mighty addition to its quantity, when the minister, by means of a well-appointed eldership, can multiply among his people the number of their Christian friends, who enter their abodes, and take a kindly interest in their families. Even with such an apparatus, we might expect the amount of Christian good to be only fractional, in respect to the whole population; yet this would not prevent a civic good, which, in a very few years, might be almost universal. Only let that monstrous coalition be broken up, in virtue of which the office of a spiritual labourer has been so wofully neutralised, by the duties and the dispensations of pauperism being laid upon it—let the jealousies and the heart-burnings incidental to such a business, be conclusively done away from all the ministrations of Christianity—let the clergyman have coadjutors who, like himself, may go forth among the families, on the single errand of Christian advice or Christian consolation—let them watch their best opportunities, and, in an especial manner, never neglect those openings of advantage, where sickness paves the way for the welcome admittance of a religious visitor, or the death of some near and beloved relative makes his sympathies and attentions so inexpressibly soothing—let them, perhaps, in addition to the influence of their sincerity and worth, be a little raised, as they generally are, above the mass of the commonalty, in respect of fortune and intelligence,—and the effect of such an order of things, in attempering the social fabric, and in multiplying the links of confidence and good will between man and man, were altogether incalculable. A certain portion of good Christianity would, in all likelihood, come out of this arrangement; but a far greater proportion of good citizenship would, most assuredly, come out of it: and we repeat it, that all those who take a greater interest in the latter object than they do in the former, are still in the most direct way of advancing their own favourite cause, when, through the medium of the former, they attempt to reach the latter; or, when in devising for the temporal welfare of that community, with whose concerns they are entrusted, they do their uttermost for improving the ecclesiastical system of great towns, by the multiplication of churches, and the appointment of acceptable and efficient clergymen.

And here it may not be out of place to remark, how much it serves to divide and to weaken the force of popular violence, when the vast and overgrown city is broken down into separate parochial jurisdictions—where each is isolated as much as possible from the other, by its visible landmarks, and its own distinct and busy apparatus of management; and where the people, instead of all looking one way, to the distant and general head, and forming into a combined array of hostile feeling and prejudice against it, are, in virtue of a local economy, which possesses interest enough to have formed a sort of *esprit de corps* among the inhabitants of every subordinate district, habituated to look several ways to that nearer and more interesting *regime* by which they are respectively surrounded. In a great town, where the parishes are little better than nominal, and there is no affecting relationship between administrators and subjects, all the public and political tendencies of the popular mind run towards one point, and may form into one impetuous and overwhelming surge against the reigning authority of the place. The more that this else unmanageable mass is penetrated and split up into fragments, and that the effervescence which is in each is made to play around a separate machinery of its own, the more safe will be the leading corporation from any of those passing tempests, by which the multitude is often thrown into fierce and fitful agitation. A parochial economy is not the less effectual, for this purpose, that the jurisdictions which it institutes, instead of being of a legal, are rather of a moral and charitable character. The kindly intercourse that is promoted between the various classes, under such an arrangement as this, is the best of all possible emollients, in every season of political restlessness. It is the distance between the ruler and his subjects, which, whether

in the unwieldy state, or in the unwieldy metropolis, leaves room for those dark and brooding
imaginations that are so apt to fret and infuriate
into a storm. The more that this distance is alleviated, by the subdivisions of locality, the more
do the charities of common companionship mingle
in the commotion, and exude an oil upon the
waters, that assuages their violence. They are
the towns of an empire, which form the mighty
organs of every great political overthrow; and if
a right parochial system in towns would serve to
check, or rather to soften, the turbulence that is
in them, then ought the establishment of such a
system to be regarded by our rulers as one of the
best objects of patriotism.

There is no class of philanthropists who ought
to be more aware of the distinction between a
Christian and a civic good, and of the way in
which the one is outstript by the other, than the
teachers of Sabbath schools. A very few months
of discipline, in these seminaries, will witness a
very palpable transformation on the manners, and
habits, and general appearance of the young pupils. The cleanliness, and the docility, and the
scholarship, and the decency of demeanour, and the
friendliness of regard towards their instructor—
these may all be induced, in a short time, on the
great majority of attendants; and they are all so
many important contributions of civic good rendered to that community, in the business and concerns of which they are afterwards to partake.

The direct consequence of such juvenile training, is to rear them into better members of society than they would otherwise have been; and yet there is not a more familiar exhibition than that of a visible growth, in these secondary accomplishments, on the part of almost all the learners, while, perhaps, not a single individual can be quoted, as having been the subject of a sound and scriptural conversion during the period of his attendance. It is the part of a Christian labourer to persevere in his assiduities with diligence and prayer; and though only one, out of many, should be turned from the darkness of nature to the light of the gospel, to think not that such a result is too insignificant for the big and busy operation of many years. And far less, ought the mere secular philanthropist to grudge the expense or the magnitude of such an apparatus, for he may reckon on a greatly more abundant crop of that fruit which is unto social prosperity here, than of that fruit which is unto immortality hereafter. His objects, at least, will be extensively promoted by the diffusion of Sabbath teaching among the outcast and neglected families of a city population. He is not to measure the extent of civic, by the extent of Christian good that may emanate from a right ecclesiastical system; and however languidly the mere theologian may lend his concurrence to an economy of means, on the ground of their slender efficacy in regenerating the souls of men—yet may the municipal functionary be very sure that, for the earthly good which he aspires after, no more likely expedient can be devised, for humanizing the lower orders, and adding to the stock of those virtues which go to strengthen and uphold a commonwealth.

And we must not, when on this subject, omit the fine remark of Wilberforce, respecting the power of Christianity to elevate the general standard of morals, even in countries where it has failed of positively converting more than a very small proportion of the inhabitants. The direct good which Christianity does, is when it stamps the impress of its doctrine on the few whom it makes to be the living epistles of Christ Jesus. But they are epistles which, to use the language of holy writ, may be seen and read of all men. Society at large may not be able to appreciate the hidden principle of the evangelical life; but they can, at least, peruse the inscription of its visible graces and virtues, and can render them the homage, both of their full esteem and of their partial imitation. It is thus that Christians are the salt of the earth; nor is it known how much they contribute to the general healthfulness and preservation of that community, throughout which they lie scattered. The presence of but one Christian individual in a city lane, may tell, by a sort of reflex and secondary influence, on the general tone of his vicinity. His example may not be of force enough to regenerate the hearts of his acquaintances; but it may be of force enough to induce a certain reformation upon their habits: and whether the fire of sacredness shall pass or not, from one bosom to another, that light, by which the outward history of every genuine disciple is irradiated, may be borrowed and sent back, though with fainter and duller brilliancy, from all his associates. It is thus that, through the medium of few Christians, many may be moulded into better citizens; and notwithstanding the exceeding rarity of conversion, yet, by that sort of repeating process, wherewith it acts on the social habits and earthly moralities of the species, may there emanate from the very little flock a real, though unacknowledged blessing, over the whole face of a world that lieth in wickedness.

We hold it necessary to have expatiated thus much on the relation that subsists between the Christian and the civic good that may be rendered to a town population, because we are aware of a certain feeling, wherewith the whole speculation is shrewdly and sagaciously looked to, as if it were at best a sanguine, though plausible romance, that could never be realised. And, among this class of sceptics, we have to rank some of our soundest theologians, who, aware of the extreme paucity of conversion, even under means of the likeliest devising, are led to anticipate therefrom a corresponding paucity of reformation in the social and secular habits of the people. Now, we altogether defer to their judgment, in regard to the paucity of conversion; and we most thorough-

ly concur in their affirmation, that few are the
people who now walk on the path which leadeth
to life everlasting; and, acceding to the justness
of their demand, for a Christianity as strict, and
lofty, and spiritual, as that which is pourtrayed in
the New Testament, and conscious, at the same
time, how rarely it is exemplified in our days, we
hold with them, that a right machinery may be
erected, and put for years into busy operation,
and yet that a few additional gleanings, out of a
field teeming with imperishable creatures, may
form the whole amount of what is thereby secured
and gathered in for the kingdom of heaven. But,
with our eyes perfectly open to this melancholy
likelihood, we are still, and even on Christian
grounds alone, desirous of the machinery. It has
its indispensable uses, as we have already attempted to show, even in the season of most copious
descent of living water from above; and if, ere
that day of refreshing shall arrive, it be instrumental in adding, though only one, to the number
of the saved, we think that, on the high count and
reckoning of eternity, the profit of the apparatus
far outweighs both the labour and the expense of
it. But it is on civic ground, we think, that such
a machinery would earn the triumph of its earliest
and most conspicuous achievements; and we have
to entreat the attention of our mere ecclesiastics
to the way in which the one influence may be diffused over the whole extent of humanity, while
the other remains circumscribed within those bar-

riers which can only be forced by the weapons of
a higher warfare—ere they shall resolutely give
up the cause of civil and economical improvement,
as alike inaccessible, by ecclesiastical means, to all
the efforts of human strength, and to all the devices of human policy.

But it were an object of more immediate and
practical importance to overcome the incredulity
of our civil functionaries upon this subject; to the
imaginations of many of whom, we fear, there is,
in the peculiar walk of clergymen, something ca-
balistic, and mysterious, and remote from the
whole business of ordinary affairs. The direct
aim of a spiritual labourer is to work in his people a spiritual regeneration of character; and this
is a matter that may, to the eye of clerks and
council men, stand too much aloof from the scenes
and transactions of our every day world, to have
any intelligible bearing on the department which
they occupy. When the argument is addressed
to a man of common official experience, by which
the civic good of a population is linked and limited with the operation of a high evangelical influence, that he does not comprehend, then the
whole anticipation that is founded upon it, will
bear to him very much of an ideal character: and,
when he is farther told of the exceeding few who
are saved and sanctified by the truth as it is in
Jesus, he will very naturally conclude, that the
specified cause, and the predicted consequence,
are alike insignificant; and that the result of an

improved ecclesiastical system, in cities, will be as
paltry, in point of extent, as it is aerial, in point
of speculation. If Christian regeneration be as
rarely exemplified in actual life as poetical romance is, then it may be thought, that after all,
the promise of any great sensible good to be done
to society; is just as unlikely of fulfilment from
the doings of a priesthood, as from the dreams of
poetry. These form some of the elements of that
indisposition which obtains among our rulers to
the erection of city churches, and the subdivision
of city parishes; and, therefore, it is the more necessary to expose those more palpable human influences, on which hinges the dependance between
a vigorous and well filled up Christian economy,
on the one hand, and a great popular reformation,
on the other, in all the virtues of good neighbourhood, and good citizenship. It is the minister,
after all, who most urges the spiritualities of
Christian faith and holiness, that most attracts the
multitude to congregate into a stated audience,
and thus to exchange a former looseness of habit
for the decencies of Sabbath observation;—and
it is he who is generally found to be most assiduous in week-day ministrations;—and it is he who
will most readily obtain the zealous co-operation
of others, to mingle in all the charities of intercourse along with him, among the families of sunk-
en and neglected plebeianism;—and though the
work of grace, for another world, be still restricted
to a small minority of his parish, yet a sure colla-

teral attendant upon his labours is, that a work of converse and cordiality is carried abroad throughout the mass of his people, which tends to heighten the aspect, and to improve the whole economy of the present world. This is a process, the *rationale* of which might be obvious enough, even to a mere earthly understanding; and so might the power and charm of locality; and so might the effect of one Christian's example, in raising the standard of morality among many who are not Christians; and so might the tendency of Sabbath schooling, both to induce a more orderly and civilized habit among the young, and to strengthen the tie of kindliness between the teachers and the taught, or between the higher and lower ranks of the community. There is nought surely of the mystic or unsubstantial in any of these influences; and if nevertheless, they be the most faithful stewards of the mysteries of God, from whom they are most ready to descend on the families of our general population, there ought to be an indication here, to our men of political ascendency, whether in the state or in the city corporation, of what that is which forms our best and cheapest defence against the evils of a rude, and lawless, and profligate community.

CHAP. X.

ON THE BEARING WHICH A RIGHT CHRISTIAN ECO-
NOMY HAS UPON PAUPERISM.

We are able to affirm, on the highest of all authorities, that the poor shall be with us always—
or, in other words, that it is vain to look for the
extinction of poverty from the world. And, yet
we hold it both desirable and practicable to ac-
complish the extinction of pauperism: so that between the state of poverty and that of pauperism,
there must be a distinction, which, to save confusion, ought to be kept in mind, and to be
clearly apprehended.

The epithet poor has a far wider range of application than among the lower orders of the community. We may speak, and speak rightly, of a
poor nobleman, or a poor bishop, or a poor baro-
net. It is enough to bring down the epithet on
any individual, that out of his earnings or property he is not able to maintain himself in the
average style of comfort that obtains throughout
the class of society to which he belongs. The
earl who cannot afford a carriage, and the labourer
who cannot afford the fare and the clothing of our
general peasantry, however different their claims
to our sympathy may be, by being currently termed poor, are both made to share alike in this designation.

To be poor is primarily to be in want;—and
even though the want should be surely provided
for, by the kindness of neighbours, yet is the
epithet still made to rest on the individual who
originally wore it. The aged female householder,
who is both destitute and diseased, may, in virtue
of the notice that she has attracted, be upheld in
greater abundance than any occupier in the humble alley of her habitation. And yet it may with
truth be said, that she is the poorest of them all—
poor in respect of her own capacity for her own
support, though comfortable in respect of the support that is actually administered to her. She,
even after the charitable provision that has thus
been attached to her lot, is always termed poor,
and in this sense do we understand the prophecy
of our Saviour, that the poor shall be with us always. She, in the midst of her comforts, still exemplifies the prediction; and we doubt not, that
there will be such exemplifications to the end of
time. She is poor, and yet she is not in want.
The condition of poverty, arising from a defect of
power or of means on the part of him who occupies it, will ever, we apprehend, be a frequent
circumstance in society; while the wants of poverty, arising from a defect in the care of relatives,
or in the humanity of friends and observers, will,
we trust, at length be exclusively done away. So
that even after the charity of the millennial age
shall have taken full possession of our species,
may the prophecy still find its verification under

an economy of things where the state of poverty shall be at times exemplified; but where the sufferings of poverty, from the vigilance and promptitude of such sympathies as are quickened and kept alive by the influence of the gospel, shall be for ever unknown.

It was with the benevolent purpose of hastening so desirable a consummation, that poor rates were instituted in England. A fund is raised in each of the parishes, by a legal and compulsory operation; out of which a certain quantity of aliment is distributed among those residents who can substantiate the plea of their wants, to the satisfaction of its administrators. A man is, or ought to be poor, and that referably too, not to any of the higher classes of society, as a poor clergyman or a poor gentleman, but referably to the labouring classes of society; or, he ought, in respect of his own personal means, to be beneath the average condition of our peasantry, ere he is admitted upon the poors' fund. When so admitted he comes under the denomination of a pauper. A poor man is a man in want of adequate means for his own subsistence. A pauper is a man who has this want supplemented in whole or in part, out of a legal and compulsory provision. He would not be a pauper by having the whole want supplied to him out of the kindness of neighbours, or from the gratuitous allowance of an old master, or from any of the sources of voluntary charity. It is by having relief legally awarded

to him, out of money legally raised, that he becomes a pauper. We are just now occupied with
the mere business of definitions, but this is a business which is often necessary: and we therefore
repeat it, that the state of poverty is that state in
which the occupier is unable of himself to uphold
the average subsistence of his family; and the
state of pauperism is that state in which the occupier has the ability either entirely, or in part,
made up to him out of a public and constitutional
fund.

But the truth is, that the invention of pauperism, had it been successful, would have gone to
annihilate the state of poverty as well as its sufferings. A man cannot be called poor, who has
a legal right, on the moment that he touches the
borders of indigence, to demand that there his
descending progress shall be arrested, and he shall
be upheld in a sufficiency of aliment for himself
and his family. The law, in fact, has vested him
with a property in the land, which he can turn to
account, so soon as he treads on the confines of
poverty: and had this desire been as effective as
was hoped and intended, a state of poverty would
have been impossible. A man may retain the
designation of poor, who has been relieved from
all the discomforts of want, by the generosity of
another; but this epithet ought not to fall upon
any, who can ward off these discomforts by means
of a rightful application for that which is constitutionally his own. So that had this great politi-

cal expedient been as prosperous in accomplishment as it was mighty in promise, there would have remained no individual to whom the designation of poverty had been applicable—and the wisdom of man would have defeated the prophecy of God. But though the wisdom of man cannot make head against the state of poverty, the charity of man may make head against its sufferings. The truth is, that pauperism has neither done away the condition of poverty, nor alleviated the evils of it. This attempt of legislation to provide all with a right of protection from the miseries of want, has proved vain and impotent; and leaves a strong likelihood behind it, that a more real protection would have been afforded, had the case been abandoned to the unforced sympathies of our nature—and had it been left to human compassion to soften the wretchedness of a state, against the existence of which no artifice of human policy seems to be at all available.

We have already abundantly remarked on the slender influence of a right Christian apparatus, in regard to the very small number that may be Christianized by it out of the whole population—while, at the same time, its influence may be immediately and extensively felt, in regard to the very great number that may be civilized by it. The same relation, of which we have attempted to demonstrate the existence, between the Christian and the civic good that may be done under a right economy in towns, obtains, and in a stil more remarkable degree, we think, between the proper Christian effect that is accomplished in a city parish, and the effect not merely of arresting, but even of driving away its pauperism altogether. Were the conversion of the many an essential step towards the overthrow of pauperism—then by some would the latter effect be regarded as a romantic, and, by others, as a fanatical anticipation. But in like manner as the same economy which works but a minute Christian, may work a mighty civic good; so, while it only does away the blindness and depravity of nature from a very few individuals in a parish, may it, at the same time, do away a corrupt and corrupting pauperism from all its families. We think, that the political achievement of emancipating all from pauperism may be sooner arrived at, under a system of means which has for its main object the Christianity of the people, than the spiritual achievement of emancipating a twentieth part of them from the power of the God of this world, and calling them out of darkness into the marvellous light of the gospel. Our readers, we trust, are sufficiently familiarized, from the remarks and reasonings of our last chapter, to the compound effect of a good parochial economy over the families among whom it is instituted; and can now clearly perceive, how while there is one influence addressed by it to the spiritual principles of our constitution, which may only tell on a select and scanty peculium from among the general mass—there is ano-

ther influence addressed by it to the natural principles of our constitution, which tells widely and
suddenly on the vast majority of the people. Now,
connected too with the question of pauperism,
there are certain strong and urgent natural principles; some of which are powerfully operated
upon by the Christian local economy that we
would recommend, and all of which tend to hast-
en the extinction of pauperism, at a rate of far
greater velocity than the progress of essential
Christianity among the people. So much, indeed, is this our feeling, that while we look on a
good Christian economy, as eminently fitted both
to sweeten and to accelerate the transition from
the charity of human laws to the charity of human kindness, yet we do not think it indispensable
to this effect; but that on the simple abolition of
a compulsory assessment for the relief of new applicants, there would instantly break forth from
innumerable fountains, now frozen or locked up
by the hand of legislation, so many refreshing
rills on all the places that had been left dry and
destitute, by the withdrawment from them of
public charity, as would spread a far more equal
and smiling abundance than before over the face
of society.

The first, and by far the most productive of
these fountains, is situated among the habits and
economies of the people themselves. It is impossible but that an established system of pauperism
must induce a great relaxation on the frugality

and providential habits of our labouring classes. It is impossible, but that it must undermine the incentives to accumulation; and, by leading the people to repose that interest on a public provision, which would else have been secured by the effects of their own prudence and their own carefulness, it has dried up far more abundant resources in one quarter than it has opened in another. We know not a more urgent principle of our constitution than self-preservation; and it is a principle which not only shrinks from present suffering, but which looks onwards to futurity, and holds up a defence against the apprehended wants and difficulties of the years that are to come. Were the great reservoir of public charity, for the town at large, to be shut, there would soon be struck out many family reservoirs, fed by the thrift and sobriety, which necessity would then stimulate, but which now the system of pauperism so long has superseded;—and from these there would emanate a more copious supply than is at present ministered out of poor rates, to aliment the evening of plebeian life, and to equalise all·the vicissitudes of its history.

The second fountain which pauperism has a tendency to shut, and which its abolition would reopen, is the kindness of relatives. One of the most palpable, and at the same time most grievous effects of this artificial system, is the dissipation which it has made of the ties and feelings of relationship. It is this which gives rise to the melancholy list of runaway parents, wherewith whole columns of the provincial newspapers of England are oftentimes filled. And then, as if in retaliation, there is the cruel abandonment of parents, by their own offspring, to the cold and reluctant hand of public charity. In some cases, there may not be the requisite ability; but the actual expense on the part of labourers, for luxuries that might be dispensed with, demonstrates that, in most cases, there is that ability. But it is altogether the effect of pauperism to deaden the inclination. It has poisoned the strongest affections of nature, and turned inwardly, towards the indulgences of an absorbent selfishness, that stream which else would have flowed out on the needy of our own blood and our own kindred. It has shut those many avenues of domestic kindliness by which, but for its deadening and disturbing influence, a far better and more copious circulation of needful supplies would have been kept up throughout the mass of society. We believe, that were the first fountain restored to its natural play, there would be discharged, from it alone, in the greatest number of instances, a competency for the closing years of the labourer;—and did this resource fail, that the second fountain would come in aid, and send forth, on the decaying parentage of every grown up and working generation, more than would replace the dispensations of pauperism.

A third fountain, on which pauperism has set one of its strongest seals, and which would instantly be unlocked on the abolition of the system, is the sympathy of the wealthier for the poorer classes of society. It has transformed the whole character of charity, by turning a matter of love into a matter of litigation: and so, has seared and shut many a heart, out of which the spontaneous emanations of good will would have gone plentifully forth among the abodes of the destitute. We know not how a more freezing arrest can be laid on the current of benevolence, than when it is met in the tone of a rightful, and perhaps, indignant demand for that, wherewith it was ready, on its own proper impulse, to pour refreshment and relief over the whole field of ascertained wretchedness. There is a mighty difference of effect between an imperative and an imploring application. The one calls out the jealousy of our nature, and puts us upon the attitude of surly and determined resistance. The other calls out the compassion of our nature, and inclines us to the free and willing movements of generosity. It is in the former attitude, that, under a system of overgrown pauperism, we now, generally speaking, behold the wealthy in reference to the working classes of England. They stand to each other in a grim array of hostility—the one thankless and dissatisfied, and stoutly challenging as its due, what the other reluctantly yields, and that as sparingly as possible. Had such been a right state of things, then pity would have been more a superfluous feeling in our constitution; as its functions would have been nearly superseded by the operation of law and justice. And the truth is, that this sweetener of the ills of life has been greatly stifled by legislation; while the amount of actual and unrelieved wretchedness among the peasantry of England, too plainly demonstrates, that the economy of pauperism has failed to provide an adequate substitute in its room. Were this economy simply broken up, and the fountain of human sympathy again left free to be operated upon by its wonted excitements, and to send out its wonted streams throughout those manifold subordinations by which the various classes of society are bound and amalgamated together —we doubt not that from this alone a more abundant, or, at least, a far more efficient and better spread tide of charity would be diffused throughout the habitations of indigence.

But there is still another fountain, that we hold to be greatly more productive even than the last, both in respect to the amount of relief that is yielded by it, and also in respect to the more fit and timely accommodation wherewith it suits itself to the ever varying accidents and misfortunes of our common humanity. There is a local distance between the wealthy and the poor, which is unfavourable to the operation of the last fountain, but this is amply compensated in the one we are about to specify;—and, some may be surprised, when we intimate, that of far superior importance to the sympathy of the rich for the poor, do we

hold to be the sympathy of the poor for one another. In the veriest depths of unmixed and extended plebeianism, and where, for many streets
together, not one house is to be seen which indi-
cates more than the rank of a common labourer,
are there feelings of mutual kindness, and capabilities of mutual aid, that greatly outstrip the
conceptions of a hurried and superficial observer:
And, but for pauperism, which has released immediate neighbours from the feeling they would
otherwise have had, that in truth the most important benefactors of the poor are the poor
themselves—there had been a busy internal operation of charity in these crowded lanes, and
densely peopled recesses, that would have proved
a more effectual guarantee against the starvation
of any individual, than ever can be reared by any
of the artifices of human policy. One who has
narrowly looked to some of these vicinities; and
witnessed the small but numerous contributions
that pour in upon a family whose distresses have
attracted observation; and seen how food, and
service, and fuel, are rendered in littles, from
neighbours that have been drawn, by a kind of
moral gravitation, to the spot where disease and
destitution hold out their most impressive aspect;
and has arithmetic withal for comparing the a-
mount of these unnoticed items with the whole
produce of that more visible beneficence which is
imported from abroad, and scattered, by the hand
of affluence, over the district,—we say that such

an observer will be sure to conclude, that, after all, the best safeguards against the horrors of extreme poverty have been planted by the hand of nature, in the very region of poverty itself—that the numerous, though scanty rivulets which have their rise within its confines, do more for the refreshment of its more desolate places, than would the broad streams that may be sent forth upon it, from the great reservoir of pauperism: And, if it be true, that it is just the stream which has dried up the streamlets, and caused them to disappear from the face of a territory, over which they would else have diffused a healthful and kindly irrigation —then should pauperism be abolished, let but humanity abide, in all the wonted attributes and sympathies which belong to her, and we may be sure, that for the supplies which issued from the storehouse of public charity, there would be ample compensation, in the breaking out of those manifold lesser charities, that never fail to be evolved, when human suffering is brought into contact with human observation.

We cannot, at present, expatiate, as perhaps we shall, on these compensatory processes, that would most surely be stimulated into greater power and activity by the abolition of pauperism; but the last of them is of such weight and importance in the argument, that ere we proceed to the main topic of this chapter, we may offer a few remarks in the way of illustration. Those sympathies, which lie deeply seated and diffusively spread among a population, form a mine of productiveness, that lies very much hidden from the eye of that philanthropy which moves on the elevated walk of city committees, and great national societies. Perhaps the most palpable argument that could be addressed to our institutional men, upon this subject, is the fact of the Bible Society drawing a larger revenue from the weekly pennies of the poor, than from the splendid donations, and yearly contributions, of the wealthy. It is a striking evidence of the power of accumulated littles, and proves how much the number compensates for the smallness of the individual offerings. Now, though this be a very palpable demonstration of the importance of the lower orders to the cause of charity, yet it is far from being an adequate demonstration. This fact, convincing as it is, does not sufficiently represent the might and the magnitude of those resources which lie deposited among the labouring classes, and would, in a natural state of things, emit a far more plentiful relief upon human indigence than is done by all the paraded charities of our land. It is delightful to perceive how readily the poor have been interested on the behalf of a great Christian society., But there is a still more forcible appeal made to their hearts, by the *spectacle* of human suffering, and in circumstances of life like their own. There is a more constantly plying address to their sympathies, in the disease or helplessness of a next-door neighbour, than even in the weekly recurrence of a visitor for their humble contribution. There is a common feeling among the men of the operative classes, inspired by the very condition which they in common occupy: for fellowship with one in his lot is felt as a sort of claim to fellowship with him in his love and liberality. In these, and in many other principles of our nature, there are daily and most powerful excitements to charity, which, if never interfered with by pauperism, would have yielded a far more abundant produce to the cause, than ever descended upon it, in golden showers, from all the rich, and mighty, and noble of the nation put together. It is the little, combined with the numerous and the often, which explains this mystery. Each offering is small—but there is an unknown multitude of offerers, and under incessant application too, from the near and the constant exhibition of suffering at their very doors. Had art not attempted to supersede nature, or the wisdom of man to improve upon that wisdom which poured into the human heart those sympathies that serve to oil and to uphold the mechanism of human society, there would have emerged out of this state of things, a far more plenteous dispensation of relief than the wealthy have ever given, or even, perhaps, than the wealthy could afford; whose occasional benefactions come far short, in the quantity of aid, of those kind offices which are rendered, and those humble meals which are served up, and those nameless little participations into which a poor householder is admitted with the contiguous families, and all that unrevealed good which circulates, unseen, throughout every neighbourhood where the native play of human feeling is not disturbed by the foreign and adventitious influences of a perverse human policy.

There is a statement, made by Mr. Buxton, in his valuable work upon Prisons, which is strongly illustrative of the force of human sympathy. In the Jail of Bristol, the allowance of bread to the criminals is beneath the fair rate of human subsistence; and, to the debtors, there is no allowance at all, leaving these last to be provided for by their own proper resources, or by the random charity of the town. It has occasionally happened that both these securities have failed them, and that some of their number would inevitably have perished of hunger, had not the criminals, rather than endure the spectacle of so much agony, given a part of their own scanty allowance, and so shared in the suffering along with them. It is delightful to remark, from this, that the sympathy of humble life, instead of the frail and imaginative child of poetry, is a plant of such sturdy endurance as to survive even the roughest of those processes by which a human being is conducted to the last stages of depravity. Now, if the working of this good principle may thus be detected among the veriest outcasts of human society, shall we confide nothing to its operation among the people and the families of ordinary life. If such an in-

tense and unbroken fellow feeling be still found
to exist, even after the career of profligacy is run,
are we to count upon none of its developments
before the career of profligacy is entered on? In
other words, if in prisons there be the guarantee
of natural sympathy against the starvation of the
destitute, is it too sanguine an affirmation of our
species, that there is the same and a stronger
guarantee in parishes? The truth is, such is the
recoil of one human being from the contemplation of extreme hunger in another, that the report
of a perishing household, in some deepest recess
of a city lane, would inflict a discomfort upon the
whole neighbourhood, and call out succour, in
frequent and timely forthgoings, from the contiguous families. We are aware that pauperism
lays an interdict upon this beautiful process.
Pauperism relaxes the mutual care and keepership which, but for it, would have been in more
strenuous operation; and has deadened that certain feeling of responsibility which would have
urged and guided to many acts of beneficence.
There can be little doubt, that the opening up of
this great artificial fountain has reduced that natural fountain, the waters of which are so deeply
seated, and so diffusively spread, throughout the
whole mass and interior of a population. But, in
countries where pauperism is unknown, and popular sympathy is allowed to have its course, it sends
forth supplies upon human want which are altogether incalculable; and still, in our own country,

is it ready to break forth in streams of rich and refreshing compensation, so soon as pauperism is done away.

It will be seen, then, that we do not hold a good Christian economy to be indispensable to the negation of pauperism. We think, that simply upon the absence of this system from any country, there will be in it less of unrelieved poverty than when the system is in full establishment and operation. We would confide this cause to the great fountains of relief which are provided by nature, and conceive that, when the people are left to themselves, they, in the first instance, by their own economy, would prevent the great majority of that indigence which now meets the dispensations of pauperism; that, in the second instance, the care of individuals, for the aged and the helpless of their own kindred, would, operating in each separate circle of relationship, work a mighty reduction on the territory of want; that, in the third instance, a still farther reduction would be effected, by the more copious descent of liberality from the wealthier to the poorer classes; and, to complete the wholesome process, that internal charity among the poor themselves would fill up the many countless vacuities which escape the eye of general observation. We cannot affirm, that never, in any instance, would there be a remainder of want unprovided for; but we are strongly persuaded, that it would fall infinitely short of the want which is now unreached and unrelieved by all the ministrations of legalized charity. And we reckon that this argument would hold, even apart from Christianity, on the mere play of those natural principles of self-preservation, and social and relative sympathy, which are inseparable from the human constitution. So that in Constantinople the condition of the people would be economically worse, were pauperism introduced among them; and, in London, the condition of the people would, at this moment, have been economically better, had pauperism never been instituted. In those great towns of continental Europe, where the compulsory relief of poverty is unknown, we read of no such distress as should urge the adoption of such an expedient. There may occur a very rare instance of positive starvation; but let it never be forgotten, that instances also occur in the British metropolis: and we do think it more likely to happen there, just because of pauperism, which has substituted the tardy and circuitous process of a court of administration, for the prompt and timely compassions of an immediate neighbourhood. So that, whatever the bearing may be of a good Christian economy, upon this question, we neither regard it as indispensable to the exemption of a country from pauperism, nor do we regard pauperism as conducive to the well-being of a country where Christianity is unknown.

But, though it were utterly misconceiving the truth and philosophy of the whole subject, to affirm that Christianity was indispensable, yet there is a way in which it acts as an element of mighty power and importance in this department of human affairs. It is most true, that nature, when simply left to the development of her own spontaneous and inborn principles, will render a better service to humanity than can be done by the legal charity of England; but it is also true, that Christianity urges this development still farther, and so gives an augmented and overpassing sufficiency to nature. It is true, that it is better to commit the cause of human want to the safeguards which nature has already instituted, than to a compulsory assessment; but it is also true, that Christianity strengthens these safeguards, and so creates a far more effective defence against those miseries that might be apprehended to ensue on the abolition of pauperism. It is true, that, in every assemblage of human beings, there are proper and primary fountains of relief, from the mere efflux of which there cometh the discharge of a more abundant blessing upon the poor than ever can be made to descend from the storehouse of public charity; but it is also true, that Christianity both quickens the play, and adds to the productiveness, of all these fountains. The man who is a Christian will be the most ready to labour with his own hands, rather than be burdensome; and, if he have dependent relatives, he will be the most ready to provide for those of his own house and of his own kindred; and, if he be rich, he will be the most willing to distribute and ready to communicate;

and, if he be poor, still, with his humble mite, will he aspire after the blessing that is promised to a giver, and shun, to the uttermost, the condition of a receiver. Christianity does not originate these principles in society, but Christianity adds prodigiously to the power and intenseness of their operation—so that without, perhaps, striking out any fountain diverse from those that we have already enumerated, does it, by simply stimulating these, call forth a mighty addition to those healing waters, that serve both to sustain the comfort and to assuage the sufferings of our species.

And let us not estimate the beneficial effect of Christianity, on this department of human life, merely by the number of people who have been so far influenced by its lessons, as to be spiritualised by them. This were, indeed, to reduce the worth and importance of the whole speculation. But there is, as we have already stated, an indirect power in Christianity to multiply, beyond the spread of its own essential principle through the hearts of men, those virtues which go to improve their social habits, and to rectify the many disorders which would otherwise agitate and disturb their social history. The sound Christian economy that regenerates the few for heaven, reforms the many into the frugality, and the industry, and the relative duty, and all the other moralities which stand allied with self-respect and decency of character upon earth. We should augur greatly more for a man of congregational habits, in regard to his providential management, and his unbroken independence, and his generous sympathy for neighbours and kinsfolk, than we should for the man who lived beyond the pale of all ecclesiastical cognizance, and spent his unhallowed Sabbath in shameful and sordid profanation. Now, what we affirm is, that a local, and, at the same time, a laborious clergyman, has the power of thus congregating his people, greatly beyond his power of converting them: and out of the civic virtues which he would be the instrument of diffusing through his parish, would there be a strong additional excitement given to all those various sources of distribution and supply, which were sure to be re-opened, and to re-issue, the moment that pauperism was withdrawn; and which, either by the prevention, or by the positive relief of indigence, would leave much less of human suffering unredressed, than we now witness under a full and long established operation of public charity.

But, beside the growth and multiplication of the civic virtues, we have, under a good parochial economy, other, and, perhaps, more powerful securities for an ample compensation being rendered to human want, should pauperism be done away. It would have the effect of enlisting the very pride and selfishness of our nature into the service. Out of the mingling and acquaintanceship that would ensue, among the various orders of society, there were a greatly more honourable feeling that would arise in the breasts of the poor, and uphold them

in their generous stand against the humiliations
of public charity. The homage rendered to the
dignity of each household, by the annual presence
of the minister, and the more frequent visitations
of his parochial agents, were not without its efficacy, in rearing a preventive barrier to stop the
descent and the degradation of many families.
When the rich go forth on a plebeian territory, in
the ostensible capacity of almoners, we are aware
what the character of that stout and clamorous
reaction is, which is sure to come back upon
them. But let them go forth on those topics of
our common nature, which tend to assimilate all
the ranks of life; let education, or piety, or friendship, be the occasions of those short, but frequent
interviews, where the inequalities of condition are,
for the time, forgotten; let Christian philanthropy, for which a right parochial apparatus would
give such ample scope and exercise, guide the
footsteps of our official men to the humblest of
our city habitations, and there suggest, in conversation, all that sense and sympathy can devise for
the immortal well-being of the inmates;—though
these applications should fail, in many thousand
instances, of their direct and primary design, yet
let them be repeated and kept up, and one result
will be sure to come out of them—a more erect,
and honourable, and high minded population, less
able than before to brook the exposure of their
necessities to the observation of another, and more
strenuous than before in sustaining their respecta-

bility, on that loftier platform to which they have been admitted, by the ennobling intercourse of their superiors in society.

There is one style of companionship with the poor, that is fitted to call forth a reciprocity, which all the ministrations of opulence cannot appease. There is another style of it, that is fitted to call forth delicacies of a far softer and more sensitive character than they often get credit for. The agent of a society for the relief of indigence, who carries a visible commission along with him, is sure to be assailed, in full and open cry, at every corner, with the importunities of alleged want. The bearer of a moral and spiritual dispensation will not, in the long run, be the less welcome of the two, nor will his kindness be less appreciated, nor will the courtesy of his oft repeated attentions fail of sending the charm of a still gladder sensation into the heart. The truth is, that it is in the absence of every temptation, either to cunning or sordidness, when the intercourse between the rich and the poor is in the end most gratifying, as well as most beneficial, to both; and these are the occasions upon which the unction of a finer influence is felt, with each of the parties, than ever can have place in the dispensations of common charity. When one goes ostensibly forth among the people as an almoner, the recoil that is felt by them, from the exposure of their necessities, is overborne, at the very first interview; and the barrier of delicacy is forced, and forced irrecoverably:

so as that deceit and selfishness shall henceforth become perpetual elements in every future act of fellowship between them. When one goes forth among them on a spiritual enterprise, and introduces himself on a topic that reduces to a general level the accidental distinctions of humanity, and addresses a poor man as a sharer in the common hopes and common interests of the species, he is relieved, for the time, from all sense of inferiority, nor will he be the first to revive it in his own breast, by descending to the language of complaint or supplication. It is thus that the acquaintanceship between the rich and the poor, which is sustained by converse with them on all other topics save that of their necessities, is sure to increase the reluctance of the poor to obtrude this last topic on the attentions of the wealthy. It is thus that a mere Sabbath teacher comes speedily into contact with such delicacies among the lower orders, as are not suspected even to exist by the administrators of a city hospital. And it is thus, that under a right Christian economy, there would arise, in the hearts, and among the habitations of the poor themselves, a most effectual barrier against all that importunate and insatiable urgency of demand, which has been so fostered among the people by debasing pauperism.

And the system of locality, when carried into effect, not only exposes the people to the view of their superiors, but it exposes them more fully and frequently to the view of each other. One sure result of this system is, that it supplies contiguous families with common places of resort, as the parish church and the parish schools; and furnishes them with objects of common interest and attention, as their minister, or the Sabbath teachers of their children; and groupes the inhabitants of small vicinities into occasional domestic assemblages, as when the minister performs his annual round of household ministrations, or under the fostering care of himself and his agents, the more religious of a district hold their weekly meetings for the exercises of piety. It is unavoidable, that with such processes as these, a closer and more manifold acquaintanceship shall grow up in every immediate neighbourhood; and that moral distance which now obtains, even among families in a state of juxtaposition, shall be greatly reduced; and the people will live more under the view, and within the observation of the little besetting public wherewith their ties of fellowship are now more strengthened and multiplied than before; and this, independently of all Christian and all civic virtue, will bring the natural pride of character into alliance with those various habits which go to counteract the vice and the misery of pauperism. The consciousness of a nearer and more impending regard than is now directed towards them, would make them all more resolute to shun the degradation of charity, and the obloquy they would incur by a shameful abandonment of their relatives, and even that certain stigma which would be affixed to them, were the liberality of some open-hearted neighbour eulogised in their hearing, and they felt themselves to suffer by the comparison. The local system, in short, would bring a sense of character into more quick and habitual play among the intimacies of a city population—and this were favourable to the growth among them of, at least, the more popular and respectable virtues—and, when they are a little raised, by education and intelligence, there is not a surer forfeiture of respect than that which is incurred by him who unworthily stoops to the attitude of a supplicant and a waiter on for public charity; nor is there a readier homage of popularity awarded, than that which is openly and cordially given, when a poor man shares of his humble means among the poorer who are around him.

And here let it be remarked, that though the direct power and principle of Christianity are limited to a few, yet that reflex influence which emanates from them upon the many, would tell with peculiar effect on the economic habits of the whole population. The one Christian of a city lane may fail to reach a spiritual lesson into the hearts of his acquaintances, and yet, by the very dress of his children, and the decent sufficiency of his whole establishment, hold forth another obvious lesson, that may be learned and copied by them all. And they may vie with him, at least, in decency of condition, if not in devoutness of character; and, though they decline to run the heavenly race along with him, yet will they far more readily enter with him into rivalship for the honour and the becoming air of independence upon earth. There is an utter inadvertency to the laws of our universal nature, on the part of those who think, that in the humblest circles of plebeianism, there is not the operation of the very same principles which may be witnessed in the higher circles of fashionable life. There is a style of manner and appearance that is admired among the poor, and which, when introduced by one of the families, constitutes it the leader of a fashion that is apt to be emulated by all the others. There is a certain *bon ton*, by which the average feeling of every district is represented; and nothing contributes more powerfully to raise it, than the residence of an individual, whose attention to the duties of his station has kept him nobly and manfully afloat above the degradations of charity. The infection of such an example spreads among the neighbours. What he shuns from principle they spurn at from pride; and thus the very envies and jealousies of the human heart go to augment our confidence, that should the economy of pauperism in our cities give place to a right Christian economy, there will, in the spirit and capabilities of the people themselves, be an ample compensation for all that is withdrawn from them.

We are most thoroughly aware of the incredulity wherewith all such statements are listened to, by men hacknied among the details of official business, and who hold every argument, that is couched in general language, and is drawn from the principles of human nature, to be abstract and theoretical. But they should be taught, that their institutional experience is not the experience which throws any light upon the real and original merits of this question—that though they have been working for years, with their fingers, among the accounts and the manipulations of city pauperism, their eyes may never, all the while, have been upon the only relevant field of observation—that practitioners though they be, it is not at all in the tract of their deliberations or their doings, where true practical wisdom is to be gotten—that the likeliest counsellor upon this subject, is not the man who has travelled, however long and laboriously, over the inner department of committee-ship, but the man who travels, and that on an errand distinct from common charity, over the outer department of the actual and living population. In one word, a local Sabbath teacher, with ordinary shrewdness of observation, and who meets the people free of all that disguise which is so readily assumed, on every occasion of mercenary intercourse between them and their superiors—from him would we expect a greatly sounder deliverance, than from the mere man of place or of penmanship, on the adequacy of the lower orders to their own comfort and their own independence. It is a sufficient reply to the charge of sanguine or visionary, which is so often advanced against our confident affirmations upon this topic, that we invite the testimonies of all those with whom a district of plebeianism is the scene of their daily, or, at least, their frequent visitations. And it is no small contribution which a good Christian economy will render towards the solution of this great political problem—that it so penetrates and opens up the interior of that mass which has hitherto been shrouded in the obscurity of its own denseness, from all previous inquirers—that it unseals this book of mystery, and offers a distinct leaf, which may be easily overtaken by each one of its labourers—that it can thus lay an immediate hand on the *ipsa corpora* of the question—and rear the true doctrine of pauperism on the same solid and inductive basis by which all truth and all philosophy are upholden.

We know not how great the artificial transformation is, which the pauperism of two centuries may have wrought on the individual habits, and the mutual sympathies, of a London population; or to what degree it may have overborne either the cares of self-preservation, or the kindnesses of neighbourly regard towards those children of misfortune and want, who chance to come within the range of their daily observation. We can well believe, that the sum which issues from legal charity, upon a given district of the metropolis, could not, all at once, be dispensed with: the native capabilities of the people being so much weakened and impaired, by the very system that now comes in aid of the deficiencies it has itself created. But of the very worst and most wretched vicinities of Glasgow, where pauperism is only yet in progress, and has not attained such a sanction and settlement as to have effaced the original habitudes of nature, we can aver that, under a right economy, and without the importation of any charity from abroad, each is sufficient in its own internal resources, for the subsistence of all its families. And were people only left to themselves, and made to feel that they were the alone rightful keepers of their own households and their own kinsfolk, and committed back again to those spontaneous charities, which the sight of suffering never fails to awaken—it would be found that the mechanism of human laws has, by thwarting and doing violence to the laws of the human constitution, superseded a previous and a better mechanism.

That district of the Saltmarket, which is referred to in the second chapter of this work, has now, for several years, been under the superintendence of the same teacher who originally assumed it. In respect of poverty, we should regard it as rather beneath the average state of our operative population; and, accordingly, it was proposed, at the outset, that all the expenses of the little institution which has been reared in it, including the rent of the room, with the cost of the fuel and candles, and a small library of books, should be defrayed by the subscriptions of the charitable.

But this had not been prosecuted with vigour enough to meet all the charges of this humble concern, and the teacher resolved to throw himself on the good-will and resources of the parents themselves. It is true, that by a small monthly payment, which is most cheerfully rendered on the part of his scholars, he has been enabled to overtake and to overpass all the expenses of his little seminary. The *materiel*, it may be thought, of this free-will offering is so insignificant as to prove nothing. But the alacrity wherewith it was rendered; the conscious ability that was indicated for the required sacrifice, and for a great deal more; the additional interest that was felt in the school, when each was thus led to regard it as a nursling and a dependant of his own; the unexcepted support that was given, not one family being deficient of its quota, though the very poorest of the territory had to share in it; the certain air and consequence of patronage wherewith this proposal invested all the contributors; the delight expressed by them at their own independence, not unmixed, perhaps, with somewhat of a generous disdain towards any obligation of the sort from their betters in society,—these were the tokens of a sufficiency and a spirit that still remain with the very humblest of our peasantry, and are enough to indicate such elements of moral greatness, as only need to be called back again from the dormancy into which they had been cradled by the hand of pauperism, when they shall rear anew, and in the bosom of our community, all those guarantees for the sustenance of our people that this cruel foster-mother has destroyed.

We are glad to understand that so good an example is now beginning to be copied, and that about ten of the Sabbath school districts, in that neighbourhood of the town, have been recently laid under the same system of management. There is a most willing concurrence, in them all, on the part of the population; and fitted as such an economy is, both to honour them, and to fasten, more tenaciously than before, the roots of each little association, among the families that are thus admitted to nourish and to uphold it, we would earnestly recommend the same practice to every other local teacher, who may have obtained a sufficient intimacy with the people, to have made sure of their confidence, and of the satisfaction which they feel in the kindness and usefulness of his labours.

We have already endeavoured abundantly to prove, that a good Christian economy is not indispensable to the negation of pauperism, in a country where it has never been established: seeing that the simple abolition of it would naturally, and of itself, work out a great improvement on the economic condition of the people. Still, however, Christianity would heighten and secure this improvement the more, by the re-enforcements it would bring, both to human sobriety and to human sympathy. And, in a country where pauperism is established, and where it is proposed, through the extinction of it, to commit the cause of human suffering back again to that individual care and kindness from which it has been so unwisely wrested by the hand of legislation—we think that nothing could more effectually speed and ensure this great retracing movement, than the parochial subdivisions, and the pure patronages, and the wholesome influences on the popular mind, which were attendant on the working of a right ecclesiastical apparatus, rightly administered. It were well that the existence of a good Christian economy, and the decline of pauperism, went gradually and contemporaneously together, so as that the complete establishment of the one, shall come, at length, to be the death and disappearance of the other; and, although the former be not absolutely essential to the latter, yet, we know of no other way, than through the attainment of the Christian desideratum, in which the economic desideratum would be arrived at with greater practical facility and smoothness, or with the hazard of less violence being rendered to the deeply rooted prejudices of the land.

It is on this account, that the merely secular philanthropist, reckless though he be of eternity, and all its concerns, should hail a good Christian economy, as he would the fittest and the likeliest instrument of a great civil and political reformation. And it is no less true, that the Christian philanthropist, though he sits comparatively loose to this world and all its evanescent interests, should desiderate the abolition of pauperism, as he would the removal of a deadly impediment in the way of that great spiritual reformation, to the hastening of which he consecrates his labours and his prayers. On the one hand, we fear not the contempt of the statesman, when we affirm, that the salvation of one soul is an achievement of surpassing worth and importance to the deliverance of our whole empire from the weight of its assessments for pauperism. And we fear not, on the other hand, the dislike of the theologian to our announcement, that the pauperism itself is a moral nuisance, which must be swept away from these realms, ere we can rationally hope for a very powerful or prevalent spirit of Christianity in the land. That which letteth must be taken out of the way. It is, indeed, a heavy incumbrance on the work of a clergyman, whose office it is to substitute among his people the graces of a new character, for the hardness, and the selfishness, and the depraved tendencies of nature, that, in addition to the primary and essential evils of the human constitution, he has to struggle, in his holy warfare, against a system so replete as pauperism is, with all that can minister to the worst, or that can wither up the best, affections of our species. With what success can he acquit himself as a minister of the New Testament, in the presence of this legalized and widely spread temptation, by which every peasant of our land is solicited to cast away from him the brightest of those virtues wherewith the morality of this sacred volume is adorned? By what charm shall he woo them from earth, and bear their hearts aspiringly to heaven, while such a bait and such a bribery are held forth to all the appetites of earthliness,—or, how can he find a footing for the religion of charity and peace, in a land broiling with litigation throughout all its parishes, and where charity, transformed out of its loveliness, has now become an angry firebrand, for lighting up the most vindictive passions and the fiercest jealousies of our nature?

It is a question deeply interesting to human morality, whether, when it lies within his choice, it is the more becoming part in man to face a temptation or to flee from it. The one, and consistent, and oft repeated deliverance of the gospel upon this subject, is, that in every case where it can be done, without the dereliction of what is incumbent in the given circumstances, the temptation ought to be shunned rather than resisted; and that we have no reason to calculate on the present success, or future moral prosperity, of any individual, who, uncalled, goes daringly and wantonly forth upon the arena of trial, however strenuous his purposes, and however firm his confidence of victory. " Enter not into temptation," is one of the recorded precepts of the New Testament; and " lead us not into temptation," is one of the prescribed prayers. It is our duty not merely to maintain a distance from evil, but as much as in us lies to maintain a distance from the excitements to evil. And it were well that this principle, one of the most important which relates to the discipline of character, and altogether suited as it is to the real mediocrity of the human powers, was not merely proceeded on in the walk and sanctification of private Christians, but was adverted to by those who, elevated to the guardianship of the public interests, ought not to overlook the most precious of them all, even the virtue of the commonwealth. What an Augean stable, for example, is the whole business of excise and custom house regulation!—nor were there a task more truly honourable to the legislature of Britain, that has been so busied of late with plans of economy for reducing the expenditure, than now to busy itself with the details of a still nobler reformation. It were a still higher walk of improvement, did the government, which now studies to bear as lightly as possible on the means of the people, study also to bear as lightly as possible on the morals of the people. To carry the abolition of pensions and places is reckoned a triumph in the contest between power and patriotism. But there is a yet more generous triumph in reserve, for a yet more unspotted patriotism—even the abolition of those many provocations which are now held out to fraud, and falsehood, and perjury, on the part of our regular traders, and to the more daring iniquities of contraband, on the part of a bolder and hardier population. It is, indeed, a melancholy lesson that we read of our nature, when we note of the practice of smuggling, how sure it is to flourish just up to the degree of encouragement that is enacted and provided by parliament—how, from the two elements of the risk and the profit, there may be computed a certain specific bounty upon this lawless adventure, that will specifically call out as much of crime and cupidity as shall seize upon every shilling of it—and how every addition made to the bounty, by some careless or unlucky clause, acts with all the certainty of physical attraction, in bringing on a consequent addition to the number of desperadoes, whom it lures from the pursuits and the peaceful habits of regular industry: Or, in other words, such is the fragility of principle among men, that accurately in proportion to the length and breadth of the temptation, will be the corresponding dimensions of an offence that has demoralised whole provinces of the empire—seducing the people from all the decencies and sobrieties of their former life, and utterly unsettling the domestic habit of their families.

We hold pauperism to be a still more deadly antagonist to the morality of our nation, though neither so sudden nor so ostensible in the mischief which it inflicts upon human principle; and, instead of striking out local and visible eruptions, in certain parts of the body politic, holding forth a cup of seeming bounty, but which is charged with a slow and insinuating poison, wherewith it

has tainted the whole frame of society. It effect-
eth its work of destruction, upon the character of
man, more by sap than by storm. The family
virtues have not been swept away by it with the
violence of an inundation; but they have drooped
and languished, and, at the end of a few generations, are now ready to expire. The mildew
which it has sprinkled over the face of the community, has fallen, in small and successive quan-
tities, from its hand; and it is only by an addition
made every year, to this deleterious blight, that
the evil at length is consummated. Like the
Malaire in Italy, it has now attained a progress
and a virulency, which begin to be contemplated
with the awe of some great approaching desola-
tion; and a sense of helplessness mingles with the
terror which is inspired by the forebodings of a
mighty disaster, that has been gathering along the
lapse of time, into more distinct shape and more
appalling magnitude. It is, indeed, a frightful
spectacle; and the heart of the Christian, as well
as of the civil philanthropist, ought to be solem-
nized by it. He, of all men, should not look on
with indifference, while the vapour of this teeming
exhalation so thickens and spreads itself throughout the whole moral atmosphere of our land: And,
when he witnesses the fell malignity of its operation, both on the graver and more amiable virtues
of our nature,—when he sees how diligence in the
callings, and economy in the habits, of individuals,
are alike extinguished by it, and both the tender-

nesses of relationship, and the wider charities of life, are chilled and overborne—we should expect of this friend to the higher interests of our species, that he, among all his fellows, would be most intent on the destruction of a system that so nips the best promises of spiritual cultivation, and, under the balefulness of whose shadow, are now withering into rapid decay, and sure annihilation, the very fairest of the fruits of righteousness.

CHAP. XI.

ON THE BEARING WHICH A RIGHT CIVIC ECONOMY HAS UPON PAUPERISM.

It will be seen, from the last chapter, that we hold the securities for the relief of indigence, which have been provided by nature, to be greatly better than those artificial securities for the same object, which have been provided by legislation; and that the latter have done mischief, because, instead of aiding, they have enfeebled the former. This matter should have been confided to the spontaneous operation of such sympathy and such principle as are to be found in society, among the individuals who compose it. And when the question is put to us, what is the best system of public management for alimenting the poor, we reply, that the question would come in a more intelligible form, were it asked, which of these systems is the least pernicious; or which of them is the least fitted to hinder or to disturb the operations of the natural system. We, in fact, hold every public management of this concern to have been deleterious; and think that pauperism, according to the definition we have already given of it, should not be regulated, but destroyed. Still, however, this cannot be done instantaneously; and one expedient may be better than another, for committing the cause of poverty back again to those charities of private life, from which it has been so unwisely wrested—and, by that same intermeddling spirit too, which has cramped the free energies and operations of commerce. The home trade of benevolence has been sorely thwarted and deranged by the impolitic bounties, and the artificial channels, and the unnatural encouragements, and all the other forcing and factitious processes, that a well-meaning government has devised for the management of a concern which should have been left to itself, and to those principles of its own, that would, if alike unhelped and undisturbed, have wrought out a far better result than we have now the misfortune to behold, and in a state of maturity almost big for immediate explosion. We should have deemed it better, that there had been no organ of administration, either in a town or parish, for the supplies of indigence; and that kindness and compassion had been left to work at will, or at random, among its families. Yet, one way may be assigned that is preferable to another, for retracing the deviation which has been made from the right state of matters,— and even although the movement should stop at a point short of the total abolition of public charity, yet, still if there be a conducting of this treatment from a more to a less pernicious system, an important gain shall have been effected to the interests of humanity.

The public charity of Scotland is less pernicious than that of England, only because less wide in its deviation from nature, and less hostile to the operation of those natural principles, that prompt both to the cares of self-preservation, and to the exercise of the social and relative humanities of life. It is not because positively more efficacious of good to the poor, that we give it the preference—but because negatively, it is more innocent of any violation to those sympathies and sobrieties of .conduct, which form the best guarantees for a population against the sufferings of extreme want. The philanthropists of England are looking to the wrong quarter; when, convinced of the superiority of our system, they try to discover it in the constitution of our courts of supply, or in the working and mechanism of that apparatus, which they regard as so skilfully adapted for the best, and fittest, and most satisfying distribution of relief among the destitute. When they read of the population of a Scottish parish upheld in all the expenses of their pauperism, for the sum of twenty pounds yearly, and that in many a parish of England the pauperism of an equal population costs fifteen hundred pounds, they naturally ask by what strenuousness of management it is, or by what sagacious accommodation of means to an end, that a thing so marvellous can be accomplished. The truth is, that the administrators for the poor in the Scottish parish, are not distinctly conscious of any great strenuousness or sagacity in the business. The achievement is not due to any management of theirs, but purely to the manageable nature of the subject, which is a population whose habits and whose hopes are accom-

modated to a state of matters where a compulsory
provision for the poor is unknown. The problem,
in fact, would have been resolved in a natural
way, had they not meddled with it; and, by the
slight deviation they have made from this way,
they have only given themselves a little work
in trying to bring about the adjustment again.
It is by the tremendous deviation of the English parish from the way of nature, that they
have so embarrassed the problem, and landed
themselves in difficulties which appear quite inextricable.

Between what is peculiarly the English, and
what is peculiarly the Scottish style of pauperism,
there is a number of parishes in the latter country,
in a sort of intermediate or transition state from
the one to the other. It is well known, that
throughout the majority of Scotland, the fund for
the relief of poverty is altogether gratuitous, being
chiefly upheld by weekly voluntary collections at
the church door, or by the interest of accumulated
stock, that has been formed out of the savings or
the bequests of former generations. This fund is
generally administered by the Kirk-Session, consisting of the minister of the parish and his elders;
and altogether the annual sum, thus expended, bears
a very moderate proportion, indeed, to the number of inhabitants in the parish. We are greatly
within the limits of safety when we say, that
throughout all the parishes where this mode of
supporting the poor is strictly adhered to, the av-

erage expense of pauperism does not exceed forty pounds a-year, for each thousand of the population. In some of the parishes, indeed, the relief is quite nominal—not amounting to five pounds a-year, for each thousand. And there is one very palpable and instructive exhibition, that is furnished out of the variety which thus obtains in different parts of Scotland—and that is, that where there is a similarity of habits and pursuits, and the same standard of enjoyment among the peasantry, there is not sensibly more of unalleviated wretchedness in those parishes where the relief is so very insignificant, than in those where a compulsory provision for the poor is now begun to be acted upon; and where they are making rapid approximations towards the ample distributions, and the profuse expenditure of England.

In England, it is well known, the money that is expended on their poor, is not given, but levied. It is raised by the authority of law; and the sum thus assessed upon each parish, admits of being increased with the growing exigencies of the people, from whatever cause these exigencies may have arisen. As the sure result of such an economy, the pauperism of England has swollen out to its present alarming dimensions; and, in many instances, the expenditure of its parishes bears the proportion of a hundred to one with the expenditure of those parishes in Scotland, which are equally populous, but which still remain under the system of gratuitous administration.

Now, in most of the border parishes of Scotland, as well as in many of its large towns, there is the conjunction of these two methods. There is a fund raised by voluntary contribution at the church doors; and, to help out the supposed deficiencies of this, there is, moreover, a fund raised by legal assessment. We can thus, in Great Britain, have the advantage of beholding pauperism in all its stages, from the embryo of its first rudiments in a northern parish, through the successive steps of its progress as we travel southward, till we arrive at parishes where the property is nearly overborne, by the weight of an imposition that is unknown in other countries; and where, in several instances, the property has been reduced to utter worthlessness, and so been abandoned. We can, at the same time, the better judge, from this varied exhibition, of the effect of pauperism on the comfort and character of those, for whose welfare it was primarily instituted.

We scruple not to affirm, that we feel it to be a desirable, and hold it to be altogether a practicable thing, to conduct a parish, of most heavy and inveterate pauperism, back again to that state in which pauperism is unknown, and under which it shall be found, that there is more of comfort, and less of complaining, than before, among all its families,—the gradual drying up of the artificial source, out of which relief at present flows, being followed up by such a gradual re-opening of those natural and original sources that we have already pointed to, as will more than repair all the apprehended evils that could ensue from the legal or compulsory provision for the poor being done away. But, instead of attempting to describe the whole of this transition at once, let us only at present point out the way in which a certain part of it may be easily accomplished. Instead of setting forth from the higher extreme, and traversing the entire scale of pauperism, down to the lower extreme thereof, let us take our departure from a point that is yet considerably short of the higher extreme, and travel downwards to a point that is yet also short of the lower extreme, or of the utter negation of all pauperism. We shall not be able to overtake any part of such a journey, without the guidance of such principles as belong essentially to the entire problem—nor can we make even but a partial retracing movement, without, perhaps, gathering such experience on the road, as may serve to light and prepare us for traversing the whole length of it. It is on this account, that the method of conducting a Scottish parish, which has admitted the compulsory principle into its administrations for the poor, back again to that purely gratuitous system, out of which it had emerged, should not be regarded with indifference by the philanthropists of England. It is, perhaps, better that the subject should first be presented in this more elementary and manageable form, and that a case of comparative simplicity should be offered for solution, before we look to a case of more appalling complexity and magnitude. It is like learning to creep before we walk, and submitting to a gradual process of scholarship, ere we shall venture to contend with the depths and intricacies of the subject. In describing part of a journey, we may meet with intimations and finger-posts, by which we shall be instructed and qualified for the whole of it. And, therefore, do we hold it better to explain the retracing movements which have been proposed for Scotland, or are now practising there, ere we proceed to discuss the specialities that obtain in the pauperism of England.

And it will be found to stamp a general importance on our present explanation, if it shall be made to appear, that the best civic economy which can be instituted, for the purpose of re-committing one of our transition parishes to that purely gratuitous system from which it has departed, is also the best for conducting an English parish to the same point, so soon as such a motion shall be made competent by the legislature; and even until that period shall arrive, that it is the best economy which can be devised for improving the administration, and mitigating the weight of an oppressive and long established pauperism.

Let us begin, then, with the alterations which appear indispensable in the civic economy of our great Scottish towns, in regard to their pauperism, in order that their present mixed or transition system be reduced to that voluntary system of contributions at the church doors, which obtains throughout the majority of our country parishes.

The great fault in the administration of city pauperism, is, that it is brought too much under one general superintendence. The whole sum that is raised by assessment for the whole town, is made to emanate through the organ of one general body of management. In some cases, the weekly collections, which still continue, in all the large towns of Scotland, to be received at the church door, are made to merge into the fund that is raised by the poor's rates, where it comes under the control and distribution of one and the same body of administrators. In other cases, the collections of the several parish churches are kept apart from the money that is raised by assessment, but still are thrown into one common fund, and placed at the disposal of another body, distinct from the former, but still having as wide a superintendence, in that they stand related as a whole to a whole—that is, in having cognizance over all the town, and in having to treat with applications from every part of it. We are aware that these bodies are variously constituted in different places—and that, just like the sets of our Scottish burghs, they have almost each of them its own speciality, and its own modifications. But in scarcely any of those towns which consist of more than one or two parishes, is there a pure independent parochial administration for each of them; but they all draw on a common fund, and stand subordinated to a common management. It is not necessary, save for the purposes of illustration, to advert to the peculiar constitution of the town pauperism in different places, when the object is to expose the mischief of one general property which attaches to each of them.

At the same time, it should be recollected, that every parish is shared into small manageable districts—each of which has an elder of the church attached to it. It is most frequently his office to verify and recommend the cases of application for relief; and often, though not always, it is through him, personally, that the relief is conveyed to the applicant. When the ecclesiastical and the legal funds are kept asunder, and assigned to distinct managements, he generally is the bearer of the application for relief to both, but more often the bearer of the relief back again from the former, than from the latter, of these funds. It sometimes also happens, that, instead of carrying up directly the case of an application from his district to the administrators of either of these funds, he carries it up to his own separate session, where it is considered, and if admitted, it goes through them to one or other of the fountain heads, along with all the cases that have been similarly approven, and is backed by the authority of the whole parochial session to which he belongs. The separate sessions thus obtain a general monthly sum for their poor from the higher body of management, to which they are subordinated—and this sum, parcelled out among the different members, brings them into contact with their respective paupers, who call on their elder for the relief that has been awarded to them.

Now, one evil consequence of thus uniting all the parishes of a town under the authority of one general board, is, that it brings out to greater ostensibility the whole economy of pauperism, and throws an air of greater magnificence and power over its administrations. This has a far more seducing effect on the popular imagination than is generally conceived. The business and expenditure of five thousand a-year for the whole town, have in them more of visible circumstance and parade, than would the separate expenditures of as many hundreds in each of its ten parishes. Pauperism would become less noxious, simply by throwing it into such a form as might make it less noticeable. For that relaxation of economy, and of the relative duties which follows in the train of pauperism, is not in the proportion of what pauperism yields, but of what it is expected to yield, and therefore is it of so much importance, that it be not set before the eye of the people in such characters of promise or of power, as might deceive them into large and visionary expectations. The humble doings of a Kirk-Session will not so mislead the families from dependence on their own natural and proper capabilities, as when the whole pauperism of the place is gathered into one reservoir, and made to blaze on the public view, from the lofty apex of a great and conspicuous institution. And it were well, not merely for the purpose of moderating and restraining the sanguine arithmetic of our native poor, that the before undivided pauperism should be parcelled out into smaller and less observable jurisdictions, but this would also have the happy effect of slackening the importation of poor from abroad. It is not by the actual produce of a public charity, but by the report and the semblance of it, that we are to estimate its effect, in drawing to its neighbourhood those expectant families, who are barely able to subsist during the period that is required to establish a legal residence and claim; thus, bringing the most injurious competition, not merely on the charity itself, but overstocking the market with labourers, and so causing a hurtful depression on the general comfort of our operative population.

But, secondly: the more wide the field of superintendence is, the greater must be the moral distance between the administrators of the charity and its recipients. A separate and independent agency for each parish, are in likelier circumstances for a frequent intercourse and acquaintanceship with the people of their own peculiar charge, than are the members and office-bearers of a great municipal institution for the poor of a whole city. In the proportion that such a management is generalised, do the opposite parties of it recede, and become more unknowing and more unknown, the one to the other. The dispensers of relief, oppressed by the weight and multiplicity of applications, and secretly conscious, at the same time, of their inability to discern aright into the merit and necessity of each of them, are apt to take refuge either in an indiscriminate facility, which will refuse nothing, or in an indiscriminate resistance which will suffer nothing but clamours and importunities to overbear it. And, on the other hand, the claimants for relief, whom the minute inquiries of a parochial agent could easily have repressed, or his mild representations, and, perhaps, friendly attentions, could easily have satisfied—they feel no such delicacies towards the members of a stately and elevated board, before whom they have preferred their stout demand, and, in safety from whose prying and patient inspection, they can make the hardy asseveration both of their necessities and of their rights. No power of scrutiny or of guardianship, can make compensation for this disadvantage. No multiplication whatever of agents and office-bearers, on the part of the great city establishment, can raise the barrier of such an effectual vigilance against unworthy applications, as is simply provided by the ecclesiastical police of a parish, whose *espionage* is the fruit of fair and frequent intercourse with the families, and can carry no jealousies or heart-burnings along with it. The sure consequence of those intimate and repeated minglings which take place between the people of a parish, and its deacons or elders, is, that a growing shame on the one side will prevent many applications which would else have been made, and that a growing command on the other, over all the details and diffi-

culties of humble life, will lead to the easy disposal of many more applications, which would else
have been acceded to. There may, in fact, be
such a close approximation to the poor, on the part
of local overseers, as will bring within their view
those natural and antecedent capabilities for their
relief and sustenance, that ought, we think, to have
superseded the ministrations of pauperism altogether. By urging the applicant to spirit and
strenuousness in his own cause, or by remon-
strating with those of his own kindred, or by the
statement of his case to neighbours, or, finally,
if he thought it worthy of such an exertion, by
interesting a wealthy visitor in his behalf—may
the Christian friend of his manageable district,
easily bring down a sufficiency for all its wants,
from those fountains of supply which were long
at work ere pauperism was invented, and will
again put forth their activity after pauperism is destroyed. But these fountains are too deep and internal for the observation of legal or general overseers, nor could they bring them to act, though they
would, on the chaos of interminable and widely
scattered applications that come before them. In
these circumstances, they have no other resource
than to meet them legally, which is tantamount, in
the vast majority of instances, to meeting them
combatively,—and then, other feelings come to ac-
tuate the parties than those which prompt, on the
one side, to a compassionate dispensation, and on the
other side, to a humble entreaty, or a grateful ac-

ceptance. It is thus, that a ministration, which ought to have been the sweetener and the cement of society, now threatens to explode it into fragments: And, sure result of every additional expenditure through the channels of an artificial pauperism, do we behold the rich more desperate of doing effectual good, and the poor more dissatisfied with all that is done than before.

But might not the full benefit of a parochial agency be combined, with the general superintendence and the ample revenue of a large city institution? In all our transition parishes, indeed, do not the dispensers of the public charity avail themselves of the information, and often act on the express certificates of the elders? Was not the Town Hospital of Glasgow, whence all the money raised by assessment is distributed, in the habit of being guided by the recommendations of those very men, to whom we ascribe such facilities for the right treatment of all the cases that might offer from among the families? Ere they found their way to the general body of management, they had to pass through the local, or ecclesiastical agents, of their respective parishes. And the same of the General Session in Glasgow, which was more an exchequer than any thing else, whence money was sent out for the supply of the separate sessions, which, meanwhile, were at liberty, both by their individual members and in their meetings, to treat with their applicants just as they would have done, had they been thoroughly independent of each other. Admitting the first objection to this complex economy to be valid, it is not in general seen how the second is equally so; as the examination and approval of the different cases may still lie with the different sessions, very much in the same way as if each session had been left to square its own expenditure with its own separate and peculiar resources.

It is of importance plainly and fully to meet these questions, for they apply to the actual state of pauperism in nearly all the large towns of Scotland. There is either a general fund made up of what is levied by assessment, and what is collected at the church doors, placed under one management; or these funds are kept distinct the one from the other, and placed under two separate managements, both of which are alike, however, in that they have the same range of superintendence over all the families of all the parishes. The Town Hospital of Glasgow is a reservoir for the whole produce of the assessment, and out of which the supplies were made to emanate, alike, on the cases of pauperism which they admitted to relief from the town at large. And the General Session, till lately, was the reservoir for all the weekly collections that were received throughout the different churches—which were thrown into one fund, and brought under the disposal of this body, and then distributed at their judgment, not among the individual poor, but among the separate sessions—and to these sessions belonged the immediate cognizance of all the cases that were relieved from this source in their respective parishes. Now the question is, what will be gained by the reduction of this general management into local and completely independent managements? The good of this change would be obvious enough, if the General Session had been charged with the examination of all the particular cases of pauperism, and now devolved this work on the separate Sessions of the separate parishes. But this, in fact, was the very business of the parochial Sessions under the old system. And the General Session was little more than a depository where the collections were all lodged, and out of which they were again issued to the parochial Sessions, after due regard being had to the comparative necessities of each of them. By the change in question, each Session is permitted to retain its own collections, and to make its own uncontrolled disbursements out of them. How does this, it may be asked, improve the administration? It vests no new facilities of examination over the cases of particular applicants—for this is what each Session and each elder of that Session could have carried to as great a degree of strictness, and could have conducted as advantageously under the full influence of all their previous acquaintanceship among their people, before the change, as it is in their power to do after it.

This brings us to the third objection against the system of a general superintendence over the pauperism of all the parishes, and of a general fund, out of which each shall draw for its own expenditure. We have already, in our first objection, spoken to the mischievous effect which an economy so big and so imposing had upon the expectants of charity; and we have now to state its mischievous effect on the administrators of charity. The imagination of a mighty and inexhaustible fund is not more sure to excite the appetite, and so to relax the frugal and providential habits of its receivers, than it is sure to relax the vigilance of its dispensers. To leave to each Session the right of sitting in judgment over the cases of its own parochial applicants, after having wrested from it its own peculiar revenue, and then to deal forth upon it from a joint stock, such supplies of money as it may require for its expenditure, is the most likely arrangement that could have been devised for establishing in each parish a most lax, and careless, and improvident administration. For first, it slackens the interest which each Session would otherwise have taken in the amount of its own income. It will care far less for the prosperity of an income which is sent upwards to a General Session, and there merges into a common fund for behoof of the whole city, than it would have cared had the income remained its own, and been appropriated to the exclusive behoof of its own peculiar territory. There will be no such pains to stimulate the weekly collection of any one parish, on the part of its minister and elders, when the good of it is in a great measure unfelt or lost sight of, by its being buried in the common fund of ten parishes, and reflected back upon themselves only in a small fraction of income, which they partake along with the rest at the monthly distribution—as when the whole is lodged in their own depository, and entered upon their own books, and applied to their own distinct and independent purposes.—But secondly, and what is of more importance still, the complex and general system complained of, slackens the interest which each Session would otherwise have taken in the strenuousness of its own management, and the strict economy of its own expenditure. If we wish to see, in the business of a Kirk-Session, somewhat of the same alertness and quicksightedness, and patient attention, wherewith an individual in private life looks after the business of his private affairs, we must throw it upon its own resources, and so leave it to square its own outgoings by its own incomings. It is not in human nature that any one corporation can be so tender of the funds of another, as it would be of its own— nor is there a more effectual method of encouraging, in one set of administrators, a facility in the admission of new cases, than to place with another set of administrators the fund for supplying them. Under the local and independent system of pauperism in a great town, the competition among the parishes would be, which shall best square its own separate expenditure by its own separate resources. Under the general system the competition is in the opposite way—which shall draw most from the common stock, for enabling it smoothly to get over the expenses of its own smooth and indolent management. The effect is unavoidable. A Kirk-Session will be at no pains to augment that local revenue which it is not permitted to appropriate—and it will be at as little pains to husband that general revenue in which it has only a small fractional concern, and out of which, also, its allowances are drawn. It is thus that languor, and listlessness, and easy indifference, will characterise all those separate managements, under which the new cases that are admitted in the first instance, will pour every month, with most pernicious facility, into the domain of pauperism; and against this the scrutinies of every year that take place under the general management, will be found to raise a most vain and impotent barrier.

Such a constitution for ten parishes, has the like pernicious influence on the affairs of their pauperism, as it would have, if adopted by ten individuals for the conduct of their ordinary business. It is conceivable, that each might be left all the year round, to the details both of his own separate counting-house, and of his own family expenditure —only, that he had to throw all his profits into a common stock, and to draw therefrom such sums as he required, for the maintenance of his establishment. It must be quite obvious, how much an arrangement of this sort, would slacken both the labours of the counting-house, and the economics of the family—and that no yearly review by a com-

mittee of the whole number, could prevent such
an effect. Not one of them, it is to be feared,
would be so careful and industrious in trade, when,
instead of realizing his own individual gains, he
was only to share them with others, over whose
operations in the meantime, he had little or no
control. And neither could we feel so secure of
his frugality at home, when, instead of drawing
from his own peculiar repositories, he drew from
the treasury of a general concern. The competition between individuals so unwisely assorted together, would be, who should labour least in the
duties, and who should spend most of the produce
of this ill-devised scheme of partnership. But ill-
devised as it would be, it just exemplifies the system of a General Session for the whole town, with
the Sessions of the various parishes subordinated
to its control. It is by the resolution of this complex mechanism into its separate parts—it is by
isolating and individualising each of the parishes—
it is by vesting it with a sovereignty over its own
income, and leaving it to the burden of its own
expenditure—that you give an impulse to each
Kirk-Session similar to that which presides over
the economy of private life, where each man ap-
propriates his own gains, and pays his own charges;
and where, in consequence of so doing, he is both
far more diligent in his professional calling, and
far more frugal in his household and personal expenses, than he would have been under such an

artificial combination, as we are now attempting to expose.

Our desire, that the general system of management for the poor, shall be superseded by the independent local system, is not so much founded on the impulse it would give towards the augmentation of the revenue in each parish, as on the vigilance and care that it would be sure to introduce into the administration of that revenue. It would work both of these effects; but we would be disguising our own views of the truth and philosophy of this whole subject, did we rate the former of these effects as of any importance at all, when compared with the latter of them. We affirm, that a great revenue for public charity is not called for in any parish; but if public charity in some shape or other, is to be perpetuated amongst us, all we hold necessary is, that it be placed under the guardianship of men, who shall feel themselves under the necessity of being prudent, and considerate, and wary, in the dispensation of it. It is because the general system releases them from this feeling, and the local or parochial system brings it forth again into practical operation, that we are so anxious for the abolition of the one, and the substitution of the other in its place: And let the income be what it may, we have no fear, under this improved management, of each distinct population being upheld on their own capabilities, in greater comfort and independence than before, and that too in the very poorest of the parishes.

And, it is not by leaving the poor to a greater weight of endurance, that such an effect is anticipated. By shutting up the modern avenue to relief, they are simply conducted to those good old ways, from which, for a season, they have been allured, but which, so long as the nature of humanity remains unaltered, they will still find, in every way, as open, and as abundant of kindly and refreshing pasture as before. The closing of that artificial source, out of which the supplies of indigence have emanated for years, would be sensibly felt in any parish, were it not instantaneously followed up by a re-action on the natural sources; and did not the withdrawment of what wont to flow upon them from one quarter, find an immediate compensation from other quarters, which were in danger of becoming obsolete, by the unnatural direction that has long been imprest on the ministrations of charity. The truth is, however, that there is not a parish in Scotland so far gone in pauperism, but that all which it yet yields could be safely withheld from the population; and a slight addition to their industry, and thrift, and relative duty, and neighbourly kindness, would greatly more than overbalance any imaginary loss, which, it might be feared, would be sustained by the cause of humanity. To all sense there would be as little, and in positive reality, there would be less of unrelieved want under the reformed order of things, than before it,—and the whole amount of the change, were a population somewhat more exempted from distress, and somewhat more prosperous in its general economics, with the mighty advantage of a more healthful moral regimen, from the impulse and free play that had been restored to the sobrieties and the sympathies of our nature.

But this need not remain a mere theoretical anticipation—nor will it be enough to satisfy the public, that it is announced in the oracular phraseology of one, who may be rendering to the picture of his own sanguine imagination, that homage which is only due to truth, in one of her living fulfilments, or, in one of her actual exhibitions. This matter admits of being brought to the test of experiment; and the demand of all practical men is for facts, rather than for principles. And yet, in affirming principles, one may be only affirming such truths as are strictly experimental. The urgency of the law of self-preservation, is an experimental truth; and the certainty wherewith this law will operate to the revival of a certain measure of economy, on the removal of those temptations which had served to relax it, is another; and the great strength of relative attachments, is another; and the dread of all that disgrace which would be incurred by the unnatural abandonment of those parents or kindred, to whom pauperism no longer holds out an asylum, is another; and the force of mutual sympathy among neighbours, is another; and the greater alacrity of that spontaneous kindness which is felt by the rich towards the poor, when the irritation of legal claims, and legal exactions, does not extinguish it, is another: And, on the strength of all these known and oft ascertained principles of our nature, may it be not rashly conjectured, but most rationally inferred, that when pauperism is swept away, there will be a breaking forth of relief upon the destitute, from certain other outlets which pauperism had stopt, or, at least, the effusion of which, pauperism had stinted. Still, however, it were far more satisfactory that the thing be tried, than that the thing be argued; and of vastly greater authority than any speculation however ingenious, upon universal principles of our nature however sound, would we hold the specific result of any experiment that may have been made on a specific territory.

It is on this account that we feel disposed to estimate at so high a value the experience of Glasgow; nor are we aware of any given space on the whole domain at least of Scottish pauperism, where a touchstone so delicate and decisive of the question could possibly be applied—and we are most confidently persuaded, that if the progress of this city towards the English system could possibly be arrested, then it may also be arrested with equal or greater facility in any parish of Scotland—judging that to be indeed an *experimentum crucis,* which is made with such materials as an exclusively manufacturing population, and at such a time too as that of the greatest adversity which the trade of the place had ever to sustain in the history of its many fluctuations. But it will be necessary to premise a short general account of the method in which its pauperism wont to be administered.

Each parish is divided into districts called proportions, over which an elder is appointed; whose business it is to receive from the people belonging to it, and who are induced to become paupers, their first applications for public relief. The fund which principally arises from the free-will offerings that are collected weekly at the church doors of the different parishes, is kept distinct from the fund that arises out of the legal assessments; so that when any application was made to the elder from his district, he had to judge whether the case was of so light a nature, as that it could be met and provided for out of the first and smallest of these funds; or whether it was a case of such magnitude as justified the immediate transmission of it to the administration of the second fund. It so happens, that excepting on rare occasions, the primary applications for relief, are brought upon the fund raised by collections, and therefore comes in the first instance, under the cognizance and control of the Kirk-Session of that parish, out of which the applications have arisen. So that generally at the first stage in the history of a pauper, he stands connected with the Kirk-Session to which he belongs, and is enrolled as one of their paupers, at the monthly allowance of from two to five shillings.

It is here, however, proper to remark, that the different Kirk-Sessions did not retain their own proper collections, for a fund out of which they might issue their own proper disbursements; but that all the collections were thrown into one mass, subject to the control of a body of administrators, named the GENERAL SESSION, and made up of all the members of all the separate Sessions of the city. From this reservoir, thus fed by weekly parochial contributions, there issued back again such monthly supplies upon each subordinate Session, as the General Session judged to be requisite, on such regard being had, as they were disposed to give to the number and necessities of those poor that were actually on the roll of each parish. So, that in as far as the administration of the voluntary fund for charity was concerned, it was conducted according to a system that had all the vices which we have already tried to enumerate, and the mischief of which was scarcely alleviated, by the occasional scrutinies that were made under the authority of the General Session, for the purpose of purifying and reducing the rolls of all that pauperism, which lay within the scope of their jurisdiction.

But we have already stated, that even in the first instance, some cases occurred of more aggravated necessity and distress, than a Kirk-Session felt itself able for, or would venture to undertake. These were transmitted direct to the TOWN HOSPITAL, a body vested with the administration of the compulsory fund, raised by legal assessment, throughout the city, for the purpose of supplementing that revenue which is gathered at the ·church door, and which, with a few trifling additions from other sources, constitutes the sole public aliment of the poor, in the great majority of our Scottish parishes. There were only, however, a small number who found their way to the Town Hospital, without taking their middle passage to it by the Kirk-Session; so that the main host of that pauperism which made good its entry on the compulsory fund, came not directly and at once from the population, but through those parochial bodies of administration for the voluntary fund, whose cases, as they either multiplied in number, or became more aggravated in kind, were transferred from their own rolls to those of this other institution. This transference took place when the largest sum awarded by the Session was deemed not sufficient for the pauper, who, as he became older, and more necessitous, was recommended for admittance on their ampler fund, to the weekly committee of the Town Hospital. So that each Session might have been regarded as having two doors—one of them a door of admittance from the population who stand at the margin of pauperism; and another of them, a door of egress to the Town Hospital, through which the occupiers of the outer court made their way to the inner temple. The Sessions, in fact, were the feeders or conductors by which the Town Hospital received its pauperism, that after lingering a while on this path of conveyance, was impelled onward to the farther extremity, and was at length thrust into the bosom of the wealthier institution, by the pressure that constantly accumulated behind it.

It will be seen at once, how much this economy of things tended to relax still more all the Sessional administrations of the city; and with what facility the stream of pauperism would be admitted at the one end, where so ready and abundant a discharge was provided for it at the other. We know not how it was possible to devise a more likely arrangement for lulling the vigilance of those who stood at the outposts of pauperism—and that, too, at a point where their firm and strenuous guardianship was of greatest importance; even at the point where the first demonstrations towards public charity were made on the part of the people, and when their incipient tendencies to this new state, if judiciously, while tenderly dealt with, might have been so easily repressed. To station one body of men at the entrance of pauperism, and burden them only with the lighter expenses of its outset, from which they have the sure prospect of being relieved by another body of men, who stand charged both with the trouble and expense of its full and finished maturity—there could scarcely have been set a-going a more mischievous process of acceleration towards all the miseries and corruptions which are attendant on the overgrown charity of England. In some recent years, the pauperism of Glasgow has about trebled the amount of what it stood at in 1803.

The great thing wanted, in these circumstances, was to make full restitution to a Kirk-Session of those elements which are indispensable to the prosperity of every other management, and both to

the spirit and success wherewith it is conducted—
to assign to it an undivided task, and furnish it
with independent means for its thorough accomplishment—to throw upon it the whole responsibility of acquitting itself of its own proper business,
on the strength of its own proper resources—and,
for this purpose, to cut it off by a conclusive act
of separation, from all those bodies, a connection
with which had made it alike indifferent either to
the matter of its own revenue, which it felt no interest to augment, or to the matter of its own expenditure, which it felt no interest to economise.
To disjoin it from the Town Hospital, all that
seemed necessary was to shut the door of egress,
by which its pauperism had been in the habit of
finding vent to that institution, and to make the
door of ingress from the general population, the
only place of public repair, not merely for the
lighter, but for the more urgent and aggravated
cases of distress that occurred among its families.
To disjoin it from the General Session, all that
seemed necessary, was a permission to it from that
body, to retain its own proper collections, and to
have one unmixed and unfettered control over the
distribution of them. It appeared likely that in
this way a healthful impulse might be given both
to the congregation who furnished the Sessional
revenue, and to the agency who expended it—that
the latter more particularly thrown upon their own
means, and their own management, would have
the greatest possible excitement for suiting the one

to the other—that in this way the initial movements towards pauperism would meet with the requisite vigilance, and have to undergo the most strict and attentive examinations. And, though this might seem to lay a great additional burden of superintendence on each Session; yet, was there reason to believe, that under such a system the labour of management would eventually be reduced with them all; for, in proportion to the pains bestowed on each new application, was it hoped, that the number of them would be greatly diminished, by the very knowledge, on the part of the population, of the now more searching ordeal through which they had to pass. There would besides, be a mighty alleviation to the fatigues of office, by the very simplification of its attentions, and duties, and by the release that would ensue from the attendance which was required of each elder, on those more general bodies wherewith his own parochial Session was joined and complicated, into a most unwieldy system of operations. It had really all the feeling of emancipation, to break loose from the control, and the controversy, and the inextricable confusion, which attached to such a piece of ponderous and overgrown mechanism, to retire from it into one's own snug and separate corner, whereon he could draw near to the subjects of his own petty administration, and bestow upon them an attention and a care, from which he was no longer distracted by those generalities that had before bewildered him—to have the degradation incurred by the abridgment of that territory on which the minister and his elders shared in authority and importance with the great city corporation, most amply made up by the charm of that newly felt liberty, wherewith they might now preside over all the details of their own little concern, and wield an unfettered sovereignty within the bounds of their own limited but now thoroughly independent jurisdiction.

But we ought not to animadvert on the errors of an old system, without remarking how very little the fault of them, or the absurdity of them, are chargeable on any living individuals. The General Session of Glasgow, like the similar bodies of management for the poor, in other great towns, was originally the parochial Session of its one parish, and was simply continued in the existence of its authority after the division and multiplication of parishes. It did not originate in any scheme of combination, and is more the vestige of a former state of things, than a recent economy that has been framed and adapted to our actual circumstances. Its utter unsuitableness to another state of things than that which obtained at the time of its institution, bears in it no reflection upon the sagacity either of our present or any former race of public administrators. The mal-adjustment that there is between an old institution and a new state, is the fruit not of mismanagement, but of history, the events of which no wisdom could have foreseen, and no authority could or ought to have counteracted. That should not be branded as an ill-devised scheme, which may at the first have been founded in wisdom ; and has been perpetuated down to the present times, not by the folly, but merely by the *vis inertiæ* of succeeding generations. In the conduct of the public men of Glasgow, respecting its pauperism, there is no room for criticism, but much for admiration and gratitude. The mighty obstacle in the way of every civic reformation, is the adhesiveness of our civic rulers to that trodden walk of officiality, on which, as if by the force and certainty of mechanism, they feel a most obstinate tendency to persevere—and there is no disturbance more painful, no dread more sore and sensitive, than that which is excited in their bosoms, by schemes and systems of innovation. And therefore was it the more fortunate, that, with a management full of incoherence, and ready to sink under the load of its own unwieldiness, there should, at the same time, have been such an unexampled largeness and liberality of spirit among its administrators, and an openness to the lights of generalization, that is rarely to be met, associated with the detail and the tenacious habit of practitioners.

We should not have dwelt at such length on the old constitution of pauperism in Glasgow, had it not exemplified the most essential vices which still attach to almost all the great towns of Scotland. We are not aware of any such town, consisting of more than one parish, where there is an independent fund, and an independent management, for

each of the parishes. They are generally implicated, though in various ways, the one with the
other; and there are even instances, where, instead
of being landed unawares into such an arrangement,
by the increase and multiplication of parishes, the
merging of the separate and local jurisdictions into
one comprehensive of them all, has been deliber-
ately entered upon, for the purpose of giving greater
weight and efficiency to the administration. It has
been thought that the wisdom, and the vigilance,
and the strenuousness, would have been augmented,
by this extension and complication of the mechanism. But this, at least, is one department of human experience, where the maxim has been found
not to apply, that in the multitude of counsellors
there is safety. We have already, however, sufficiently expounded our reasons for thinking, that,
in every instance, this process of generalization
ought to be retraced; that both an independent
revenue, and an independent control should be restored to each of the parishes: And, we are
most thoroughly persuaded, that with no other revenue, than that which is obtained by weekly
collections at the church doors, and no other superintendence than that which may be severally
and distinctly exercised by each of the Kirk-Sessions, it were a most practicable achievement to
bring the whole pauperism of our large towns under a most strictly parochial economy, in the course
of a few years; and thus to re-establish, even in
those places which are most deeply and virulently

affected by the example of our sister country, the old gratuitous system of public charity, which obtained at one time universally in Scotland.

And, for this purpose, it is not necessary to withdraw, or in any way to meddle with the allowance of any existing pauper. He may be upheld in his present aliment; and that, too, under the present economy, which may be allowed to subsist in all its wonted relationships to the pauperism that is already framed, until that pauperism shall be swept away by death. Should, for example, so many of the poor have been admitted on the fund raised by assessment, and placed under a peculiar administration of its own, as in Glasgow—these poor may be left untouched, and suffered to receive of that fund just as before. It is only necessary that no new cases be henceforth admitted upon it, in order, by the dying away of the old cases, to operate a sure, though gradual, relief on this compulsory provision, which thus, in a few years, might be done away with altogether. Meanwhile, each parish should be left to its own treatment of its own new applicants, and that, on its own proper resources. Or, if instead of a fund by assessment, vested in a separate body of management, this and other charitable funds are united into one, and brought under the control and cognizance of one court, as a General Session, or a body made up of representatives from the various corporations of the place, there were still a way of meeting, by a temporary arrangement, all who are already taken on as

paupers, so as that they shall be alimented as formerly; while each parish, released from all foreign
jurisdiction, could give its unfettered care and attention to the new applications. Thus, the united
fund that is distributed over the whole city, will,
of course, send forth its largest proportions to the
poorest parishes. And the sum presently expended
on the pauperism of such a parish, may very greatly
exceed the sum collected at its church doors.
Now, the way to accommodate this matter, were
for the managers of the united fund to allocate to
that parish as many of its poor as were equivalent
to its collections—and after they had resigned these
poor, and the collections along with them, they
would find themselves just as able as before, with
their remaining fund, for the remaining poor that
were still left upon their hands, of whom, however,
by the operation of death, they would speedily be
relieved altogether. Again, it is conceivable of
one of the richer parishes, that the expense of its
poor may fall short of its collections, in which case,
the managers of the united fund might retain as
much of the surplus as would enable them to aliment that excess of poor which had been devolved
upon them from the poorer parishes. As these
poor die, however, there will always less of this
surplus be required, which, when disengaged, ought
to remain with the richer parish from which it had
emanated. We are quite aware of a tendency and
a temptation here to connect the rich parish permanently with the poor one—to keep up a stream of

communication between the wealth that is in the
one, and the necessities which are conceived to be
in the other. And for this purpose, there must be
kept up an organ of transmission, or court, to direct and sit in judgment over this generalizing and
equalizing process; or, in other words, a superintendence still, over the pauperism of the whole city.
There is no obstacle in the way of reformation,
which we more dread, than the imagination that
there is, of a justice and an expediency in taxing
the wealthier departments of the town for the pauperism of the whole—or, which is tantamount to
this, in drawing the excess of the larger collections to those parishes, where the demand for relief is more urgent, and the collections smaller.
This may be necessary till the whole of that
existing pauperism, which has been accumulated
under the present system, shall be seen to its termination. But, most assuredly, it is not necessary
that it shall be perpetuated after this. There is not
a district of the town, however poor, the economy
of which will not be more prosperous in all the
branches of it, by having all its public charity
placed under an internal management of its own,
and thrown upon the resources which are inherent
to itself, than by having its sessional revenue fed
and amplified from a foreign quarter. This is a
system which ought to expire with the expiration
of all the cases that have been admitted under it;
for, if upheld or revived in any shape whatever, it
will re-land the parishes in all the evils of a lax

administration, on the part of the managers, and a rapacious expectancy on the part of the people. This is a matter which can easily be brought to the test of experience. Let the poorest city parish in Scotland be taken up as it at present stands—let its present collection be compared with the present expense of its pauperism—let it be relieved of the whole excess of its poor by the existing management, and be thrown on its own resources, with just such a number of paupers as can be maintained in their present allowances, on the proper and peculiar revenue of the Kirk-Session to which they belong, —let the elders go forth upon their tasks with this simple change in their feeling, that they have now an expenditure to preside over which they must suit to that free and separate income that has been left in their hands,—and, though a little more of strenuousness may be required at the outset, than they had wont to bestow on the duties of their office, yet will they be sure to find, that pauperism is a bugbear, which shrinks and vanishes almost into nothing, before the touch of a stricter inquiry, and a closer personal intercourse with the families. They will find, that by every new approach which they make to the subjects of their care and guardianship, the capabilities of the people themselves rise upon their observation; and that every utterance which has been made about the stimulating and the re-opening of the natural sources for the relief of indigence, in proportion to the closing of the artificial source, is the effusion not of fancy, but of experience. The task may look a little formidable to them at its commencement. But they may be assured of the facility and the pleasure in which it will at length terminate—and that clamour, and urgency, and discontent, will subside among the poor, just according as they are less allured from the expedients of Nature and Providence for their relief, by the glare and the magnitude of city institutions. Along with the humbleness, there will also soon be the felt kindliness of a parochial economy, after the heartless generalities of the present system have been all broken up and dissipated—and, baiting a few outcries of turbulence or menace, which would have been far more frequent and more acrimonious under the old economy than the new, will every Kirk-Session, that enters fearlessly upon the undertaking, speedily make its way to the result of a parish better served, and better satisfied than ever.

And, the more to encourage and to open the way for such an enterprise as this, it were well, at the outset, to hold out more favourable terms to the poorer of our city parishes. It were no great addition to the burden of the general management, if, in the case of a parish where the collection is small, and which is at the same time among the most heavily laden of any with its existing pauperism, the whole of this pauperism was lifted away from the parochial management, and the collection were freely and altogether given up to it. This were only the surrender or the loss of the collection on the part of the general body of management, which might be made up for the first year by a small addition to the assessment; and which, at all events, would most amply be atoned for in a very short time, by the dying away of old cases, without the substitution of any new cases whatever in their place. Meanwhile, the Kirk-Session left to an unfettered control over its small but independent revenue, and having no other pauperism to meet with, but that which shall be formed and admitted by itself, would feel themselves incited to the uttermost patience and industry, and diligent plying of all their expedients in the treatment of the new applications. To begin with, in fact, they would have a revenue without an expenditure, and their weekly collections would, for a time, outstrip the gradual monthly additions which they made to their new pauperism. The extent to which that time might be prolonged, would depend on the stimulus which they gave to the liberality of the congregation, and still more on the stimulus they would receive themselves, to a careful and considerate administration. There is not a Session so poor of income, as not, under such an economy, to accumulate a little stock, in the first instance,— but, let it ever be recollected, that the final success, in all cases, would be mainly due, not to the means, but to the management. With both together, there is not a parish so sunk in helplessness, that might not be upheld in public charity on the strength of its own proper and inherent capabilities. And this, without harshness; without a tithe of those asperities and heart-burnings among the people, which are the sure attendants on a profuse dispensation; without the aspect at all of that repulsive disdain which frowns on the city multitude, from the great city institution. This is one of the precious fruits of locality, and of a local administration. Its nearer and more frequent mingling with the families, would both reveal the natural sources which exist in every community, for the relief of indigence; and would further act upon those sources so powerfully, though silently, as to admit, without violence, of the great artificial source being nearly dried up altogether. The sure result, at all events, would be a far blander and more pacific society; and with greatly less of public and apparent distribution among the poor, would there, at the same time, be greatly less of complaining on our streets than before.

It will be perceived, that nothing can be more smooth, and more successive, than the retracing process, which is here recommended. There is no violence done to any existing pauper. There is no sudden overthrow of any old general institution, which simply dies its natural death with the dying out of the old cases. There is no oppressive or overwhelming load placed upon any of the local institutions, which, however humble be its means, is left to treat with the new cases alone, and will, therefore, have a very humble expenditure to begin with. The pauperism that has been accumulated under

a corrupt system, surely but silently melts away
under the operation of mortality. And all that we
have said of pauperism being an unnecessary and
artificial excrescence upon the body politic, obtains
its experimental fulfilment in the fact, that every
city parish, disengaged from the former economy
of matters, and thrown on its own proper resources, however scanty, will weather the whole demand that is made for public charity, up to the
full weight and maximum of the new applications.

And, yet though the process be a very sure, it
will be found that it is a very short one. In Scotland, we should think, that the average for a generation of pauperism, will not exceed five years.
In that period, the old generation will have well
nigh disappeared, and have been replaced in the
full magnitude which need ever be attained by the
new generation. The bulky and overgrown parent,
that wont to scare and burden the whole city—
and that, both from its size and its expensive habits
of indulgence, will be succeeded by a few small,
docile, and manageable children. The old general institution, relieved altogether of its charge,
will cease its heavy assessments for a maintenance
that ever craved, and was never satisfied : And,
each member of the subdivided management into
which it has been rendered, will have its own separate task, and with means inconceivably less than
its wonted proportion, will be at no loss for its own
separate achievement. And we again affirm, that
under the new *regime*, moderate of income as it

is, its administrators will see far less of penury, and feel far less of pressure, than they ever did under the old one.

It is thus, that in a very few years, all the transition parishes of Scotland, may be conducted back again to that purely gratuitous system from which some of them have been receding and widening their distance, for several generations. It is well, that the method of collection on the Sundays, has not been totally abandoned in any of these parishes: for this furnishes a distinct object to which the retracing operation may be made to point, and whither, with no great strenuousness of attention, on the part of the parochial administrators, it may be made very shortly to arrive. It is true, that since the introduction of assessments into the country parishes, there has been a very natural decline of the collection at the church doors. But small as it is from this cause, it would revive again under any arrangement that pointed to the abolition of a poor's rate. But we again repeat, that the success of such an experiment depends not on the sufficiency of the positive means, but on the certainty wherewith the people may be made to accommodate their habits of demand and expectation, to any new system of pauperism that may be instituted, provided that it is introduced gradually, and without violence. In the transition parishes of the country, the collection is generally thrown into a common fund, with the money raised by assessment; and the whole is placed under the joint management of the Heritors and Kirk-Session. The retracing process, in such a case, is very obvious. Let the Kirk-Session be vested with the sole management of the gratuitous fund, in which it will be the wisdom of the Heritors not to interfere with them. Let all the existing cases of pauperism, at the outset of the proposed reformation, be laid upon the compulsory fund, and seen out without any difference in their relation, or in the rate of their allowance, from what would have obtained under the old system. Let the Session undertake the new cases alone, with the money raised from the freewill offerings at the church doors, which offerings they may stimulate or not as they shall see cause. Let them give their heart and their energy to the enterprise, and a very few years will find the parish totally relieved of assessments, by the dying away of the old pauperism; and the revenue of the Session, as drawn from purely Scottish sources, will be quite competent to the expenses of the new pauperism.

Even though the experiment should at length fail—though in two or three years it should be found, that the collection is overtaken and outstript by the new applications—it has one very strong recommendation which many other experiments have no claim to. There will have been no loss incurred by it. Matters will not be in a worse, but to a moral certainty, will be in a better situation than they were at the commencement of the undertaking. There can be no doubt, that, as the effect of the proposed arrangement, more care and caution will be expended on the new admissions than before ; and that thus the influx of all the recent pauperism will be more restrained than it would otherwise have been. The old pauperism, in the hands of the old administrators, will melt away at a faster rate than the new pauperism in the hands of the Kirk-Session will be accumulated ; and even though the Kirk-Session should at length be overpowered by this accumulation, and have to give in as before, to the necessity of recurring again upon the fund by assessment, they will meet that fund lightened upon the whole by the period of their separation, and refreshed by the breathing time which it has gotten for the new draughts and demands that may be made upon it. We have no apprehension ourselves of any such necessity ; but it ought certainly to encourage the trial of what has been suggested, that even, on the worst supposition, and though the trial should ultimately misgive, the result will, at all events, be perfectly innocent, and, on the whole, be in some degree advantageous.

But we have no hesitation as to the final success of the experiment; and it is thus that we meet the imputations of wild and theoretical, which have been so clamorously lifted up against the enemies of pauperism. We know not how a more close, and pertinent, and altogether satisfactory proof can be attained of the truth of any principles whatever, than that which is so patently and directly accessi-

ble on the question before us. The affirmation
is, that if the people of a parish are not lured
away from their own proper and original expedients for the relief of human suffering, by
the pomp, and parade, and pretension, of a great
public charity—there will be less of complaint,
and less, too, of distress in that parish, than
when such a charity is flashed upon their notice,
and so the eye and disposition of the people are
turned towards it. We know not how a way more
effectual can possibly be devised for reaching the
evidence by which to try the soundness of this affirmation, than simply to dissociate a city parish
from all those magnificent generalities of the place
wherewith it stood related formerly, and thus to
cause its administration for the relief of the poor
shrink into the dimensions of a humble and separate parochial economy. Let it not be burdened with the liquidation of the old pauperism, but
let it be tasked with the management of the new.
When a Kirk-Session has thus had the spring and
the stimulus of its own independence restored to
it, let it be abandoned to its own specific treatment of all the specific applications. We do not
ask it to blink or to evade, but openly to face all
the complaints, and all the claims, which are preferred against it,—not to go forth upon this new
charge steeled against the looks and the language
of supplication, but giving a courteous reception
to every proposal, patiently to inquire, and kindly
and Christianly to dispose of it. There is only

one expedient, the use of which, on every principle of equity and fair self-defence, must be conceded to them. They should be protected against
the influx of poor from other parishes; and, if
there be no law of residence mutually applicable
to the various districts of the same city, then it is
quite imperative on the Session that is disengaged
from the rest, not to outstrip, in liberality of allowance, the practice which obtains under that prior
and general management from which it has separated: else there would be an overwhelming importation of paupers from the contiguous places.
It is enough surely for the vindication of its treatment, if it can make out, in every specific instance,
that the applicant has been as generously dealt
with, as any other in like circumstances, and *whose
case has been as well sifted and ascertained*, would
have been in any other department of the town.
With this single proviso, let a detached and emancipated Kirk-Session go forth upon its task—and let
it spare no labour on the requisite investigations,
and let it ply all the right expedients of prevention, the application of which is more for the interest of the claimant than for the interest of the
charitable fund—let it examine not merely into his
own proper and personal capabilities, but let it
urge, and remonstrate, and negotiate with his relatives and friends, and lay down upon himself the
lessons of economy and good conduct,—in a word,
let it knock at the gate of all those natural fountains of supply which we have so often insisted on,

as being far more kindly and productive than is the artificial fountain of pauperism, which it were well for the population could it be conclusively sealed and shut up altogether,—let every attempt, by moral suasion, and the influence of a growing acquaintanceship with the families, be made on the better and more effective sources for the relief of want, ere the Session shall open its own door, and send forth supplies from its own store-house, on the cases that have been submitted to it; and it will be found, as the result of all this management, prosecuted in the mere style of nature and common sense, that the people will at once become both more moderate in their demands, and, on the whole, more satisfied with the new administration under which they have been placed. We are really not aware how this question can be brought more closely and decisively to the test of experiment, than by a body of men thus laying their immediate hand upon it; and, surely, it were only equitable to wait the trial and the failure of such an experiment, ere the adversaries of pauperism shall be denounced either as unpractised or as unfeeling spectators.

CHAP. XII.

ON THE PRESENT STATE AND FUTURE PROSPECTS OF PAUPERISM IN GLASGOW.

It will be seen, from the exposition that has been already given of the state of pauperism in Glasgow, that, previous to the breaking up of its old economy, each distinct parish had its sessional poor, who were maintained out of the share that was adjudged for their support by the General Session; and it had its more advanced or hospital poor, who had, either in the shape of inmates or of out-pensioners, been transferred to the fund raised by assessment. The expense of the hospital poor greatly exceeded that of the sessional, in as much as the revenue of the former institution greatly exceeded that of the latter,—the sum raised by assessment being once so high as twelve thousand pounds a-year, whereas the annual collections at the church doors, seldom or never reached two thousand pounds. When the parish of St. John's was founded in September, 1819, the cost of the sessional poor within its limits, was only two hundred and twenty-five pounds, yearly, though its population amounted then to upwards of ten thousand; and, after the deduction which has been made from it by the still more recent parish of St. James', amounts now to upwards of eight thousand, which is something more than a tenth

part of the population of the whole city. In respect of wealth, too, we should hold it to be considerably beneath the general average of the inhabitants of Glasgow; consisting, as it does, almost
exclusively, of an operative population. So that
had it remained under the general system for the
other parishes, its Session could not have been
charged with glaring mismanagement, should it
have been found, at the end of a period of years,
that the expense of the whole poor of St. John's
amounted to a tenth part of the sessional and hospital revenue for the whole city—adding, of course,
to the money that went directly for the personal
subsistence of the paupers, the money that was
necessarily expended in the service and various offices of the two general institutions. In other
words, under the average and ordinary style of
management for one tenth of the population of
Glasgow, in the average circumstances of that
population, the whole expense of its pauperism
should be from twelve to fourteen hundred pounds,
yearly.

The experience of a few former years in another
parish of Glasgow, warranted the anticipation of an
annual collection at the church door of St. John's,
of about four hundred pounds. By detaching this
parish, then, from the General Session, there was a
surrender made on the part of that body, of the
whole difference between the sessional revenue of
St. John's, and its sessional expense, which a-
mounted, at the commencement, to only two hun-

dred and twenty-five pounds, yearly. It is true, that this surrender would ultimately be felt by the Town Hospital, on which institution the burden of all the deficiencies, of all the parishes, was laid. But, then, the compensation held out for this surrender, to the Town Hospital, was, that it should be relieved from the burden of all the future pauperism, which else would have flowed into it from the parish of St. John's. The door of egress from the Session of that parish to the Town Hospital, was forthwith and conclusively to be shut—while the door of ingress to the Session from the parochial population, was to be opened more widely than before, by its being made the only place of admittance both for the lighter and the more aggravated cases of necessity that might occur. Still it was a generous compliance on the part both of the General Session, and of the Town Hospital, thus to forego the immediate good of a hundred and seventy-five pounds, and this for the distant, eventual, and, as yet, precarious good, of one-tenth of the territory of Glasgow being finally reclaimed from the dominion of its general pauperism. It was true, that this surplus of £175, was all that the Kirk-Session of St. John's had to count upon, for extending the allowance of its paupers, at that state of their advancing necessity, when they wont, under the old system, to be transferred to the Town Hospital; and it may be thought to have been a little adventurous, perhaps, on the side of one of the parties in this negotiation, to have undertaken, on a revenue of four hundred pounds, to meet all the expenses of a concern, which, under another system of administration, might easily have absorbed, at least, three times that sum, yearly. But, on the other hand, there was still an uncertainty that hung over the issue of this untried speculation ; and, therefore, the utmost credit is due to the other parties in this negotiation, for the facility wherewith they acceded to the parish of St. John's, a favourite and much desired arrangement.

In the following brief statement of the operations which took place under this arrangement, it were of importance, that the reader should separate what properly and essentially belongs to the matter of pauperism, from that which, though connected with the details of its management, was in no way indispensable to the success that has attended them,—else he might be led to regard it as a far more ponderous and impracticable business than it really is, and, therefore, not so readily imitable in other parishes.

Of this collateral description, we hold to be the institution of Deacons. This was adopted in the parish of St. John's, not so much for a civil as for an ecclesiastical purpose—more for the sake of disjoining the elders from pauperism, than for the right administration of pauperism itself. The truth is, that it could not be distinctly foreseen, at the commencement, what would be the requisite degree of vigilance and examination under the new system; and, therefore, was it deemed of importance, that the elders, whose office was more of a spiritual character, should be relieved from the labour and the invidiousness that might have attached to the strict treatment of all the new applications for public charity. As the matter has turned out, however, it is now decisively ascertained, that pauperism, under an independent parochial regime, is a thing so easily managed, and so easily reducible, that an order of deacons, however to be desired on other grounds, is not indispensable to the specific object for which they are appointed. We certainly prefer that elders should be protected from any violation, however slight, on the strictly ecclesiastical character which belongs to them; and one of the sorest mischiefs that attached to the old system in Glasgow, was the grievous mutilation inflicted upon this character, by this body of men being so implicated with the concerns of an overgrown and rapidly accelerating pauperism. On the setting up of a separate parochial system, it will be found, that this evil is greatly mitigated. For our own parts, we hold the utter extirpation of what is evil, to be a better thing than its mitigation—and, therefore, while pauperism, in its very humblest degrees, is to be perpetuated, we count it desirable, that in each parish there should be an order of deacons. Others, however, may not attach the same value to this consideration; and, therefore, for the purpose of distinguishing things which are really distinct, do

we affirm, that for the one design of conducting a
transition parish back again to the pure and gratuitous system of Scottish pauperism, an order of
deacons is not indispensable.

There was another circumstance connected with
the pauperism of St. John's, that had also more of
an accessory or fortuitous character, than any essential relationship with the success of its administration. This was the institution of an evening
church service, on the Sabbaths, for the accommodation of parishioners. Neither is this of essential imitation by other parishes—the purpose of
such an arrangement being purely ecclesiastical.
But the reason why it is here introduced, is, that
it enables us more distinctly to mark the operation
of the new system, in the two great branches into
which it is resolvable. The first branch consists of
the sessional paupers, that had already been admitted, anterior to the commencement of our proceedings, and whose annual expense, as already stated,
amounted to two hundred and twenty-five pounds.
These the elders retained under their management,
and to meet the charges of which, they had the
produce of the weekly offerings of the day or
general congregation, assigned to them. The
second branch consists of the new applicants for
parochial relief, the consideration and treatment
of whose cases, were devolved upon the deacons,
and who, meanwhile, were put in trust and keeping
of the evening collections, or the free-will offerings of the parochial congregation. This arrange-

ment does not materially affect the process, but it serves to throw a clearer and more discriminative light upon it; and leads us to ascertain, first, in how far a Town Hospital, or a compulsory fund, is called for, to provide for the advancing necessity of those who have previously been admitted on the lists of pauperism—and, secondly, in how far a very large collection at the church doors, or the accumulation of a sessional capital from this source, is called for, to provide for the eventual demands that may, for aught that was previously known, have been thickened and multiplied to a degree that was quite overwhelming, in consequence of the number and urgency of new applications.

The charge upon the elders' fund, it will be seen, was liable to an increase from one source, and to a diminution from another. The expense of the pauperism laid upon this fund at the outset, was two hundred and twenty-five pounds, yearly. But, on the one hand, the state of many of the paupers would become more necessitous, as they grew older and more infirm, and, but for the new arrangement, they would have been transferred to the larger allowances of the Town Hospital,—and as that communication was now shut, the extension of the allowances devolved upon the Session. On the other hand, there was a relief upon the fund from the death of paupers; and the uncertainty, at the commencement of their proceedings, was, whether the extended allowances by the Session, in lieu of the Town Hospital allowances, would be more or less than compensated by the gradual disappearance of the existing cases from death. The anticipation was, that, at the first, the increase of expense from the one quarter, would prevail over the diminution of expense from the other; but, that, after a short temporary rise of demand upon their revenue, there behooved to be a very rapid subsidency by death. Meanwhile, it was thought, that could the evening collection be found to meet, for a time, the new applications, the day collection might, at length, be relieved, even of all the pressure which originally lay upon it,—in which case, it might either be accumulated for the purpose of meeting the burden of the new cases, when they became too heavy for the deacons' fund; or be applied to any other legitimate purpose that stood connected with the good of the parish. It is remarkable, that the charge on the elders' fund, did experience the slight increase of a few pounds, sterling, during the first year of their separate and independent administration; but, that, now, as was to be expected, the cause of diminution by death, largely and rapidly prevails over the cause of increase by extended allowances. This was soon to be looked for in the course of nature—as, generally speaking, in Scotland pauperism implies considerable age—so that a generation of pauperism passes rapidly away. The expense of the Session, for the maintenance of those original cases that were devolved upon them, in September, 1819,—an expense that is defrayed from the offerings of the day congregation, is now considerably less than it was at the commencement, and is in a course of rapid diminution.

But the far most interesting branch of this whole process, and that on which the success of the attempt most essentially hinged, was the treatment of the new cases to be admitted on the evening collection, after they had undergone the requisite examination by its distinct administrators. The fund placed at their disposal, was not one-fifth of the fund assigned to the elders for their operations, —being contributed by a much poorer congregation. But, then, at the outset, at least, of their proceedings, they had little, or more properly, nothing to do. They had no previous stock of already formed pauperism to begin with—their only business being to meet, with the means intrusted to them, all the future applications. It will, therefore, be seen, how gradually and successively the burden of their management and expenditure, behooved to grow upon them—and that, even scanty as the evening collection was, a little capital might accumulate in their hands during the earlier period of their administration : And the uncertainty, that time alone could resolve, was, how long it might take ere the expense of the new cases equalised the humble revenue that was confided to them, and ere the capital was consumed, and ere the necessity arrived of calling in the aid of the day collection, to make head against the accumulation of new applicants. The question could only be decided by experience, and the result has, indeed, been most satisfactory. At the end of two years and a-half, the evening collection is still more than equal to the maintenance of the new cases; and the small capital that has been formed from this source alone, is still upon the increase; and, judging by the rate of application from the commencement, during a season, too, of singular adversity, there is a most warrantable confidence, that the deacons' fund will be found equal to the full weight of cases, the maximum of which will be attained when the period of an average generation of pauperism is completed. And, should the evening or parochial collection be actually found to weather the lapse of the old, and the coming on of the new generation, then will the Session, relieved, in a few years, by death, of all the existing pauperism of 1819, have the fund, constituted by the general or day congregation, transferrable to any other philanthropic purpose, that might be deemed most conducive to the good of the labouring classes in the parish; and the gratifying spectacle will be exhibited, of all the parochial pauperism upheld by the parochial offerings on the Sabbath evening,— Or, in other words, a large and, almost, entirely plebeian district of the town, defraying all the expenses of its own pauperism, on the strength of its own unaided capabilities.

A result so gratifying has certainly exceeded our own anticipations. We have never thought, that public charity, for the relief of indigence, was at all called for by the state and economy of social life—or, that, the artificial mechanism of a legal and compulsory provision for the poor, had ever any other effect than that of deranging the better mechanism of nature. But we did not think, that a population would have conformed so speedily to the right system, after that the poison and perversion of the wrong system had been so long diffused among them—or, that, when the great external reservoir was shut, out of which the main stream of pauperism wont to emanate, they would have found such an immediate compensation, by their immediate recourse to those fountains of supply, which exist within themselves, and lie embosomed among their own families, and their own neighbourhood. But so it is,—and that, without any other peculiarity of management on our part, than a careful, and considerate, and, we trust, humane examination of every new claim that is preferred upon us. The success of this enterprise, in fact, is not so much the doing of the agency, as it is of the people themselves—and it hinges not so much on the number of applications repressed by the one party, as on the greatly superior number of applications that are forborne or withheld by the other party. We do not drive back the people; but the people keep back themselves—and that, simply because there is none of the glare or magnificence of a great city management to deceive their imaginations, and allure them from their own natural shifts and resources; and because they are further aware, that should they step forward, they will be met by men, who can give them an intelligent as well as a civil reception; who are thoroughly prepared for appreciating the merits of every application, and, at the same time, firmly determined to try every right expedient of prevention, ere the humiliating descent to pauperism shall be taken by any family within the limits of their superintendence. The very frankness with which this is announced, is liked by the people; and let there be but an easy and a frequent mingling between the managers and the subjects of their administration, and there will be no difficulty in establishing a community of sentiment between them; the very tone of hostility towards pauperism that is manifested by the former, being positively caught and sympathized with by the latter, who, though of humblest rank in society, can, when rightly treated, display a nobility of heart, that makes them the best coadjutors in this undertaking. The parochial agency, in fact, have had little more to do than to hold out a face of intelligence to the people, on the subject of their necessities; and this has been followed up by an instantaneous slackening of the parochial demand. There is not one of them, who will not attest, that, the trouble and management of his assigned district, fall marvellously short of his first anticipations. The truth is, that there is not one application for five, that there wont to be under the old system. It is unfair to deceive a population,—and a population are vastly too generous to like one the worse for coming to an open and decisive understanding with them. Our object is not to devise for the people new expedients of relief, but as much as in us lies, to keep them closely at their own expedients—not to perform more than in other parishes, but to promise less—not to strike out any additional sources, from which to send forth an abundant administration upon human necessity; but, wherever it is possible, to commit it back again to those pre-existent sources, from which it ought never to have been tempted away, in quest of a remedy that lay more nearly and comfortably within its reach. We have no new way, by which to maintain the poor. We have only abandoned that old way, which so grievously misled them. And when the people are not misled, they do not move. If they are not previously set agog, they give little or no disturbance. If they are not seduced from their own capabilities, they silently abide by them—and every act of friendly intercourse on the part of any observant philanthropist, with the lower orders, will serve to satisfy him the more, how much our distance from the people has kept us in entire delusion regarding them; and led us, more particularly, to underrate both their own sufficiency for their own subsistence, and the noble spirit by which they are already actuated, or, which, under a right system of attentions, can most speedily be infused into them. This has been the whole drift of our experience. To make it universal, the principle of locality has only to be connected with pauperism, and to be carried downwards by a minute enough process of subdivision, and to be freed of all those obstructions, which lie in the way of its close and unfettered application. The problem of pauperism is resolved simply on the removal of certain disturbing forces, which ought never to have been put into operation. To arrive at it, we have not to do what is undone, but to undo what is done. To break up the general management of a great city, and substitute small and separate managements in its place, is an important step of this process. And, we repeat it, that it operates not so much by a positive good influence emanating from the new machinery that is thus formed, as by the withdrawment of the positive bad influence, which emanated from the old machinery. The credit of a prosperous result, is not so due to the manner in which the agents of the new system conduct themselves under it, as to the manner in which the people, of their own accord, conduct themselves under it. And let it always be understood, that the efficacy of a near, and vigilant, and local superintendence, operating independently, and within itself, and left to its own means, and its own management, does not lie so much in the resistance which it actually puts forth against advances which are actually made, as in the powerful, and almost immediate tendency of such an arrangement, to beget a general quiescence among the families of that territory over which it operates.

And, to prove that there is nought whatever of peculiar might or mystery, in our transactions, beyond the reach of most ordinary imitation, it may be right to state the very plain steps and inquiries, which take place, when any applicants come forward. This, perhaps, will be most effectually done, by simply transcribing the method of proceeding that was adopted, and has been persevered in from the commencement of our operations.

" When one applies for admittance, through his deacon, upon our funds, the first thing to be inquired into is, if there be any kind of work that he can yet do, so as either to keep him altogether off, or, as to make a partial allowance serve for his necessities. The second, what his relations and friends are willing to do for them. The third, whether he is a hearer in any dissenting place of worship, and whether its Session will contribute to his relief. And, if, after these previous inquiries, it be found, that further relief is necessary, then there must be a strict ascertainment of his term of residence in Glasgow, and whether he be yet on the funds of the Town Hospital, or is obtaining relief from any other parish.

" If, upon all these points being ascertained, the deacon of the proportion where he resides, still conceives him an object for our assistance, he will inquire whether a small temporary aid will meet the occasion, and states this to the first ordinary meeting. But, if instead of this, he conceives him a fit subject for a regular allowance, he will receive the assistance of another deacon to complete and confirm his inquiries, by the next ordinary meeting thereafter,—at which time, the applicant, if they still think him a fit object, is brought before us, and received upon the fund at such a rate of allowance as, upon all the circumstances of the case, the meeting of deacons shall judge proper."

Of course, pending these examinations, the deacon is empowered to grant the same sort of discretionary aid, that is customary in the other parishes.

On the strength of these simple regulations, and in virtue, too, of our separate and independent constitution—such is the stimulus that has been given, on the one hand, to our parochial management, and such are the wholesome restraints, on the other hand, that have been laid on the parochial demand, as have enabled us to economise our recent pauperism, at least, ten-fold beyond what we either could or would have done under the general and complex system, from which we count it our privilege to have been so totally disengaged. With our small but separate revenue, we have more of the feeling of sufficiency, than when the door was open for us to all the wider and wealthier charities of the place: And if the principle be admitted, that as much good is done by a provision for human want, through the stimulated economy of individuals, or the stimulated kindness of those whose duty it is to relieve it—then are we persuaded, that, small as our dispensations are, we have as well served and as well satisfied a parish, as any other that can be referred to in the city.

The thing of greatest importance in this statement is, that the success of the enterprise does not at all hang by the magnitude of the collection. It is not upon the strength of the means, but upon the strength of the management, that the expense of one of the poorest of our city parishes has been transferred, from the fund raised by assessment, to the fund raised by the free-will offerings at the church-door. There is nothing, it must at once be perceived by the attentive reader, that ought to deter the imitation of other parishes, in the oft-alleged superiority of that revenue which lies at the disposal of the Kirk-Session of St. John's. It is not, let it be well remarked, by that revenue, that the most essential step of this much contested problem has been overcome. The only alimentary use to which the day collection has been put, is in upholding the Sessional pauperism that had been previously formed, and was actually found, at the commencement of this operation; and this it has done so effectually, that a great yearly surplus over the yearly expenditure, and a surplus too which must rapidly increase, is left in the hands of the Kirk-Session. But the whole amount of any existing pauperism soon passes away; and by far the most interesting question relates to the present management, and the future probable amount of the new pauperism wherewith it shall be replaced. Now it ought, most demonstrably, to prove how little essential a great revenue is to the object of meeting and of managing this pauperism, when it is made known that all the new applications have been satisfactorily disposed of for two years and a half, under the administration of the Deacons, whose alone ordinary fund consists of the evening collection, the annual amount of which does not exceed eighty pounds sterling. We have no doubt, that on this humble revenue alone, the new applications will continue to be met, till the whole pauperism accumulated under the old system, shall have died away. Then will the parish of St. John's be simply and purely in the condition of a Scottish country parish, with the whole expense of its pauperism defrayed, not by the offerings of wealthy day-hearers from all parts of the city, but by the humble offerings of an evening congregation that consists chiefly of parishioners, and of those in the labouring classes of society.

We fondly hope then, that one great difficulty which is often conjured up in opposition to this undertaking will, henceforth, be conclusively done away—*viz.* that the means of the parish of St. John's are so exceedingly ample as to place its process, for the extinction of pauperism, beyond the reach of imitation by the other parishes. Another, which has been frequently alleged, is that the management must be so very strenuous, as that the labour of it will only be submitted to by men

who act under the impulse of novelty, or who feel
their responsibility and honour involved in the success of what many have stigmatized as a wild and
irrational speculation. We are quite sure that
there is not a Deacon belonging to the parish who
could not depone, from his own experience, to the
utter futility of this imagination. They all, without exception, find to be true what we have already affirmed, that the problem for the extermi-
nation of pauperism, is not resolved by any forth-
going of unexampled wisdom or activity on their
part, but by a ready accommodation, on the part
of the people, to a new system of things, in which
they have willingly, and almost without a murmur,
acquiesced. The task may look insuperable in the
gross, but its obstacles all vanish in the detail.
When the territory is once split into its several
portions, and assigned to the several agents, each
of them is sure to find, that the whole time and
trouble of the requisite inquiries fall marvellously
short of his first anticipations. We deny not that
upon each particular application, more of care may
be expended than under the lax and complicated
administration of other days; but this is amply
compensated by a great and immediate reduction
in the number of these applications—so, in fact,
as almost to reduce into a sinecure that office,
which when regarded from a distance, had been
magnified into one of mighty and almost insurmountable labour. We are the more solicitous to
do away this objection, for we too should decry

every plan to the uttermost, as bearing upon it the character of Utopianism, that could not be accomplished by every-day instruments, operating on every-day materials. Any exemplification, however imposing, if gotten up by such extraordinary means, and such extraordinary management, as to distance all imitation, were but a useless and unsubstantial parade—the treacherous glare and splendour of a meteoric flash that soon passed away; instead of radiance from such calm and enduring light as might diffuse itself throughout all the abodes, and be mingled with all the doings of humanity.

And, as we are now engaged in treating with the scepticism of our many antagonists, let us here recur to another evasion, by which they have tried to dispose of the undoubted success of the parochial experiment in St. John's. This success has been repeatedly ascribed to the efflux of the poor from the parish of St. John's, on the other parishes of Glasgow; as if they were glad to escape from the parsimonious administration that had been established there, to those quarters of the city, where the stream of public charity flowed as kindly and as abundantly as before. But neither is this a true solution of the phenomenon in question. There is nought of which the whole agency in St. John's are more desirous, than the establishment of the same barrier of mutual protection, among the parishes within the royalty, that is raised by the law of residence between the parishes of Scotland in general. They are quite sure that they would be gainers by such an internal arrangement among the parishes of Glasgow, and would be most willingly responsible for the maintenance of all who had gotten a legal residence within their own territory, could they be alike defended from the inroads of the poor, or of the paupers that belong to other parts of the city. The truth is, that on the first year of the reformed pauperism in St. John's, the importation of paupers from the city into that parish, just doubled the exportation of paupers from the parish into the city; and ever since, the balance has been greatly to our disadvantage. It is further understood, that when part of the parish was sliced off and incorporated with the new parish of St. James', several of the poorer families left the district that had been thus alienated, and retired within the present limits of the parish of St. John's. Such are the facts, whatever difficulty may be conceived to attend the explanation of them. And it may, perhaps, help our comprehension of it, if we reflect that judgment and firmness need only to be tempered with civility, in order to make them virtues of great and popular estimation—that the connivance which yields to the unfair or extravagant demands of the poor, has really not the same charm to their feelings as the courtesy which does them honour—that the lower orders of society can bear to be dealt with rationally, if they be, at the same time, dealt with frankly, and ingenuously, and openly—that, when the cause of human indigence is thrown on the co-operation of their own efforts, and their own sympathies in its behalf, it is then placed in the very best hands for the mitigation of all its sufferings—and that a very slight impulse, given to the general heart of any assembled population, will greatly more than compensate for the deprivations which ensue, when the pomp and the circumstance of all visible charity have, at length, been done away.

But the thought will recur again, that the people cannot be served under such an arrangement, and therefore cannot be satisfied—that suffering and starvation must be the necessary accompaniments of an abridged pauperism—that one must bring a cold heart, as well as a cold understanding, to this sort of administration—that a certain unrelenting hardness of temperament, on the part of those who preside over it, is altogether indispensable to its success—and that, when the success is at length obtained, it must have been at the expense of pained, and aggrieved, and neglected humanity.

Coldness, and cruelty, and hardihood, are the inseparable associates of legal charity, and it is under the weight of its oppressive influences that all the opposite characteristics of our nature—its tenderness, and gentleness, and compassion, have been so grievously overborne. These, however, are ready to burst forth again in all their old and native efflorescence, on the moment that this heavy incumbrance is cleared away from the soil of humanity. It is indeed strange, that the advocates of pauperism should have so reproached its enemies for all those stern qualities of the heart, wherewith it is the direct tendency of their own system to steel the bosoms of its hard and hacknied administrators; or, because the latter have affirmed that the cause of indigence may safely be confided to those spontaneous sympathies which nature has implanted, and which Christianity fosters in the bosom of man, they should therefore have been charged by the former with a conspiracy to damp and to disparage these sympathies—with an attempt to eradicate those very principles on which they repose so much of their dependence, and to the power of which, and the importance of which, they have rendered the award of a most high and honourable testimony.

The difference between the administration of a great public revenue for indigence, and the administration of a small one, seems to be this. The dispensers of the former are not naturally or necessarily led to bethink themselves of any other way by which a case of poverty can be disposed of, than simply by the application of the means wherewith they are entrusted. And as these means, under a system of assessment, admit of being augmented indefinitely, they are apt to conceive that there is an adequacy in them to all the demands of all the want that can be ascertained. At any rate, they seldom reckon on any other way of providing for human need, than by the positive discharge of legal aliment thereupon. So that their only, or, at least, their chief business in the intercourse they have with the applicants, is simply to rectify or to dismiss their claim, on the investigation they have made into their palpable resources, upon the one hand, compared with their palpable exigencies, upon the other. In the whole of this process, there is much of the coldness and formality of a court of law; and the very magnitude of the concern, along with the unavoidable distance at which the members of such an elevated board stand from those who venture to approach it, serves to infuse still more of this character into all the large and general managements of pauperism. All is precise, and rigorous, and stately; or, if any human feeling be admitted, it is not the warmth of kindness, but the heat of irritation. The repeated experience of imposition; and the consciousness of inability thoroughly to protect themselves from the recurrence of it; and the sensation of a growing pressure, against which no other counteractive is known, or even put into operation, than that of a stern, or a suspicious treatment, which only calls forth a more resolute assertion, on the part of the aggressors upon public charity—these are what have instilled a certain acerbity into all its ministrations. So that, with the thousands that are scattered over that multitude which the great city institution hath drawn around it, there is not one softening moral influence which is thereby carried abroad amongst them—no exhibition of tenderness upon the one hand, and no gratitude, that can only be awakened by the perception of such tenderness, upon the other—no heart-felt obligation among those whose plea hath been sustained; while among those who are non-suited, may be heard the curses of disappointment, the half-suppressed murmurs of deep and sullen indignation.

It is least of all from a quarter like this, that the administrators of a small parish revenue ought to be charged, with any defect of sensibility in the work that they have undertaken. The very circumstance of having adventured themselves upon it with a revenue that is small, proves a confidence in the other resources that nature has provided for the alleviation of human want; and it is in the act of stimulating these resources, or of pointing the way to them, that they get into close and kindly approximation with the humblest of the families. There is not a more cheering experience that has met us on our way, than the perfect rationality of the lower orders, when rationally and respectfully dealt with; and the pliancy wherewith they defer to a remonstrance that is urged with civility, and, at the same time, has the force and the weight of its own moral justness to recommend it. It is the more minute, and free, and familiar intercourse which takes place between a population and their parochial office-bearers—it is this which throws a sort of domestic atmosphere around the doings of a Sessional administration. The scantiness of its means, it may be alleged, will necessarily reduce

the elder or the deacon to his shifts, in the management of his district. And so it does. But they
are the very shifts by which the business of human
charity is transferred to its right principles; and,
after this is accomplished, there is both more of
genuine satisfaction among the poor, and more of
genuine sympathy among all those whose duty it
is to succour or to uphold them. The whole of
our delightful experience on this matter has gone
to assure us, of the cheapness and the facility
wherewith the substitution may be completed of a
natural for an artificial charity. And, let it never
be forgotten, that the main springs of this natural
charity are all to be found among the population
themselves; and, that by dint of persuasion and of
friendly intercourse, they are easily led to re-open
them. That all who are able, should charge themselves with the maintenance of their aged relatives—that to the uttermost, a man's own hands
should minister to his own necessities, and those
who are with him—that every exorbitant demand
on the liberality of others, is an injurious encroach-
ment on the fund that is destined for the relief of
real and unquestionable misery—that the poor who
are moderate in their applications, or who forbear
them altogether, are the best friends of all those who
are poorer than themselves—that no inferiority of
station, therefore, exempts from the virtue of beneficence; and that the humble contributions of
time, and service, and such little as they can spare,
by the lower orders, form by far the most impor-

tant offerings that can be rendered to the cause of charity—that pauperism is the last and the worst expedient to which they can betake themselves, and which ought never to be tried but in cases of extreme urgency, and when all the previous resources have been exhausted*—Let any philanthropist go forth among the people, and having earned their confidence, let him fill his mouth with such arguments as these; and he will never find them to be an unwilling or an impracticable auditory. To charge such a regimen as this with coldness and hardihood, and remoteness from all sympathy with human feeling, is a gross paralogism on all truth and all nature. It is true, that under its influence, the expenses of public charity may lessen every year—yet so far from this being any indication of extinct tenderness, or frozen sensibilities in the midst of us, it may serve most authentically to mark the growth of all those better habits, and of all those neighbourly regards, which ensure to every parochial family the greatest comfort and the greatest contentment, that in the present state of humanity, are attainable.

We have now breathed in both these elements— that of a parish, whose supplies for the poor were enforced by stout legality; and that of a parish

---

* If those previous resources were brought rightly to bear on every case of human suffering, they would anticipate the operations of pauperism altogether.

where this way of it has been totally superseded by the gratuitous system: and, certainly, our feeling is, that the air in which we now move, is of a softer and more benignant quality than before. Nor is it difficult to comprehend why, in this new state of things, many asperities ought to have subsided. When a people are more thrown upon themselves, they soon find, that as it were by *expression*, they draw additionally more out of their own proper resources, than they ever drew from public charity—so as to be positively in circumstances of greater comfort and sufficiency than ever. But more important still: Whatever of intercourse there is between the rich and the poor under this reformed economy, is purified of all that soreness and bitterness which attach to the ministrations of charity, so long as the imagination of a right is made to adhere to it. There no longer remaineth this freezing ingredient, either to chill the sympathies of the one party, or the gratitude of the other. And, on the whole, there is nothing more certain, than that when compulsory pauperism is abolished in any parish, and the interest it would provide for is left to the operation of spontaneous charity, then does the tone of this little commonwealth become less harsh and less refractory than it was—a kindlier spirit is felt throughout; and it soon becomes palpable as day, under which of the two systems it is that we have the more humanized, and under which of them it

is, that we have the more hard-favoured population.*

---

* It was by an unlooked-for coincidence, that while engaged in the preparation of this Chapter, the Author had to make his appearance at the
bar of the General Assembly, which is the supreme Ecclesiastical Court in
Scotland; and had there to advocate his measures for the reformation of the
pauperism of St. John's. He has since published the Speech which was
delivered on that occasion; and by a long appendix to it, has relieved himself of much of that matter, which, perhaps, would have been of too local and
ephemeral a character for a more general work. There, in p. 59—64, the
reader will find a few of those more minute and specific instances of parochial management, which may serve, perhaps, to appease the humanity that
had been before offended, by the imagination of a certain cold-blooded severi-
ty in the system, that went to explode all public charity: To that list of
instances, we shall just subjoin one more, for the purpose of correcting
another imagination that lies in the opposite extreme from the one adverted to in the text.

We have heard it insinuated, then, by another and distinct class of sceptics
from the former, that we have hitherto succeeded in our experiment not
by the harshness of our treatment, but by its excessive kindness and liberality. The suspicion is, that there may be a sort of secret or underhand
juggle on the part of our agents—as if we appeased by stealth the clamours of our else dissatisfied population, and bribed their acquiescence in an
economy, to the success and establishment of which, we have so strongly
committed ourselves. Here, too, our antagonists are just as wide of the
truth, as in all their other attempts to explain away the undoubted prosperity of this much questioned and much resisted enterprise. There can be no
doubt, that the abolition of legal charity would be instantly followed up by
the growth and the more busily extended operation of private and personal
charity; and this so far from being an argument against the abolition, is one
of the best and most effective considerations in its favour. But most assuredly, the far promptest and most productive sympathy that were then
called into action, would be the mutual sympathy of neighbours and residenters among the population themselves; and, we should deem this of
tenfold greater importance to the poor, than the whole amount of bene-
faction or of aid that can be rendered to them, either by the kindness of
their parochial office-bearers, or by the influx of liberality from without.

With regard to our own agents, in particular, it so happens, that there
is a very great variety in the stations of life which they themselves occupy.

The parish of St. John's is no longer solitary in regard of its pauperism. The Outer-Kirk parish

Some of them, we are proud to say, have nought but personal worth and wisdom to qualify them for the charge which they have kindly undertaken. We do not hold the wealth of our office-bearers, to be at all indispensable to the prosperous management even of the poorest districts in the parish; and, if we are sensible of any difference between those proportions where relief might be conveyed to the indigent in this way, and those other proportions where there can be none, we would say, that upon the whole, the latter are in the more quiescent and satisfied state of the two; and that whatever outbreakings of rapacity, or of undue expectation have occurred, come chiefly, as was to be anticipated, from the former.

Yet we cannot, therefore, say, that it is the part of an elder or deacon, if he have of this world's goods, to shut his bowels of compassion against any actual case of necessity that comes before him. This were his duty as a Christian man in any condition of life; and there is nought surely in his assumption of a Christian office, nor is there ought in his peculiar relationship with those who have their geographical position upon his assigned territory, that should reverse his obligations, or lay an arrest on the spontaneous flow of his liberalities towards them. It is his part, precisely as it is that of others, to do good unto all as he has opportunity—and should the opportunity be more patent and of more frequent reiteration within the district of his superintendence than beyond it, this, of course, decides the question for him, as to the place and the people, to whom his private beneficence will take its most abundant and natural direction. Let human sympathy come as oft as it may into contact with human suffering, and let what will come out of it. To qualify a man for this peculiar charge, it is surely not necessary to put violence upon his faculties or his feelings; to lay his heart under some process of artificial coagulation; or to bear down the workings of his own free inclination towards any act of kindness or liberality among the families of his population, that with the same converse, and the same observation, he would have been prompted to among other families. But if not necessary to thwart his benevolent propensities by laying an interdict upon them, neither is it necessary to urge them onward by any artificial stimulant whatever. Let a philanthropist but assume several hundreds of a contiguous population, and let him move amongst them daily, if he will, not however in the ostensible character of an almoner, but of a friend—and he will not, in the prosecution of his labours, meet with more of solicitation, because of their temporal wants, than he will know clearly and

of Glasgow has also made its conclusive separation
from the Town Hospital; and it did so, on more

Christianly how to dispose of. And should he be of circumstances to do
good and to communicate, in his own person, still he will not find that he
stands either in an unmanageable or in a ruinously expensive relationship
towards them. He may have to describe an initial period of simplicity and
alarm upon his own part, and, perhaps, of occasional exaggeration upon
theirs. But after that he has been fairly disciplined into a sound experience
upon the subject, and the matter has been reduced under his hands to its just
and rational dimensions, then will he find how true is the exclamation of
Hannah More, " O how cheap is charity, O how expensive is vanity!"

Now, if an individual could thus stay the importunities of a whole district, this of itself were argument enough of such capabilities among the
people themselves, as marked pauperism to be a thing uncalled for. All
that he could ever do on the uttermost stretch of his liberality, were so mere
a bagatelle to the subsistence of his many families, as to form in itself no
substitute at all for the provisions of a legal charity; and if, therefore, he
without inconvenience, or even so much as the feeling of a sacrifice, could
succeed in maintaining the quiescence of a population amounting to several
hundreds; this of itself were the most strong and palpable evidence of all
such provision being superfluous. The truth is, that any personal contribution of his to the necessities of his district, bears so insignificant a pro
portion to its extent, that in as far as the *materiel* of his benevolence is concerned, it makes no sensible difference whether it shall be rendered or withheld. And the only thing that stamps an importance on his benefactions,
is the moral influence that attends them—the demonstration it holds forth
of his good-will to the people among whom he expatiates—and, more particularly, the excitement that it gives to the play and the fermentation of
their own sympathies. The anecdote that follows, we give merely as a plain
example of this, and as proving how readily the people themselves may become the most effectual instruments of their own mutual comfort, and of
their own independence.

A young man who had lodged several years with a family of the parish,
took ill of consumption. His means were speedily exhausted; and the people with whom he lived, who had been kind and liberal to their uttermost,
could not be expected to charge themselves with the whole burden of his
maintenance. The Town Hospital, in virtue of our subsisting arrangement,
was not open to receive him; but he had himself expressed a longing preference to be with his relatives in the country, who were at the distance of

generous terms, and at a bolder adventure, than characterized the outset of the enterprise in St. John's. For there was no excess of its Sessional

---

more than 100 miles, and were not able to transport him in that careful and sheltered way, which the state of his health had made so requisite. In these circumstances, the deacon certainly did give his best attention to the peculiar exigencies of the case; and, among other things, made interest with the proprietor of a stage-coach, to allow him an inside birth for the fare of an outside passenger. Such easy services in behalf of a sufferer as these, are never lost on that little neighbourhood of sympathy and observation by which he is surrounded: And, accordingly, in the present instance, neighbours did lend their most willing co-operation to this labour of love: and a subscription had only to be headed, and set a-going amongst themselves; and, while the sum that was thus raised formed by far the most precious contribution to the necessities of the case, it also carried the gratifying evidence along with it, of the power that lies in a little leaven of well-timed charity—how leavening the entire mass, and working its own quality throughout all the members of it, it can thus enlist upon its side the alacrity and the spare means of a whole population. It was not by the importation of money from without, but by the healthful operation of motives and principles within that the difficulty was provided for. A parochial agent may be in humble circumstances: but there are other tokens by which good-will is manifested than the giving of silver and gold. Such as he has he may give— his advice—the aid of his time and trouble—and on the strength of these, he will earn such a moral ascendency as shall stimulate like processes for like emergencies, and call forth those powerful and harmonized efforts which form an equivalent defence against all the extremities to which our species are liable. It is thus, that a man of sense and of character may fearlessly take upon himself the superintendence of a lot of population; and that, without a farthing to bestow upon their necessities, but on the strength of their inward capabilities alone, either rightly directed, or even left to their undisturbed operation. Unless, by a blight on the face of nature, or some peculiar and extraordinary visitation, not one instance of starvation will ever occur amongst them. The thing in the even and ordinary course of human life is morally impossible. And while this ought not to set aside among the rich, that ancient law of sympathy, which is coeval with nature, and re-echoed by the gospel of Jesus Christ, throughout all its pages, it ought certainly to set aside the provisions of a modern and artificial pauperism.

revenue over its Sessional expenditure. The expense of poor that were upon it at the time of its disruption from the old system, was about equal to its collections; and yet, without any surplus, did it simply withdraw itself from the wealthier institution, and undertake both to send no more paupers there, and to meet, upon its own resources, all the new cases that offered from their own population. In defect of all present pecuniary means for such an achievement, it first instituted a scrutiny of the existing poor upon its roll; and then stimulated the weekly collection by the announcement of their new system from the pulpit; and, last of all, resolved on a most strict and careful inquiry into the claims and circumstances of all future applicants. Its experience was in striking harmony with that of the Kirk-Session of St. John's in one particular. There took place a sudden diminution in the number of applications. We should not like to be too minute, or too prying of inspection into the concerns of others': But it is not too much to say in the general, that, by our latest information, they were going on most prosperously, and most hopefully; and we feel confident, that by the dying away of the old cases belonging to that parish, which are on the funds of the Town Hospital, and by the arrest that has been laid on the influx of all new cases to that institution, there will another large department of Glasgow be speedily cleared of all its compulsory pauperism.

The General Session has now ceased altogether from its charge of the weekly collections at the church-doors of any of the parishes in Glasgow. Each Kirk-Session retains its own—and those of them that need to have the expenses of their pauperism supplemented by foreign aid, stand connected simply and exclusively with the Town Hospital. The complexity of the old mechanism is in so far reduced, as that the combination of the parishes, one with another, in all the matters of ordinary administration for the poor, is now broken up. And things are certainly more manageable than before, for the work of ulterior reformation—in that each parish may, without thwarting, or opposition from its neighbours, negotiate its own separate and peculiar arrangement with the Town Hospital.

There are ten parishes in Glasgow. Two of them, St. John's and the Outer Kirk, have reached, or are in certain progress, toward the ultimate condition of parishes that are under a strict gratuitous economy. To be delivered of the assessment, it is necessary that the remaining eight parishes should be reduced to this condition also. It so happened of three of these, viz. the North West, St. George's, and St. James', that the expense of their Sessional poor was beneath the amount of their weekly collections—so that, on the dissolution of the General Session, they found themselves all at once in fair circumstances for separating from the Town Hospital, and each attempting its own pauperism single-handed. And, accordingly, they have partially, or rather almost totally, begun their own independent expenditure on their own independent resources. There is still, we understand, a remainder of occasional aid, that more by the force of habit than of necessity, they still continue to receive from the Town Hospital. But, with this exception, and an exception that could well be dispensed with, they take the whole of their new pauperism upon their own funds : And having now ceased the transmission of their cases to the fund by assessment, they have only to wait the disappearance of their Hospital pauperism by death, when they too shall arrive at the desired landing-place.

And here would we urge it on the Kirk-Sessions of these three parishes, how desirable it were, that they acted on the principles of a total and conclusive separation from the Town Hospital; that they ceased from every sort of intromission with it; and swept away even the last vestiges of dependence, by which the need or importance of such an institution could at all be recognized. It were greatly better, if in as far as their poor too are concerned, the faintest shadow of argument for a compulsory provision were utterly done away. Pity it were, that for the sake of a few rare and trifling extraordinaries, the whole burden of which they could most easily take upon themselves, they should forfeit that place of entire and absolute independence, which they are so well entitled to occupy, and so abundantly able to maintain. In the present style of their operations, they are laying no material burden on the fund by assessment; and why keep up even so much as a nominal obligation to it, or offer any sort of quit-rent acknowledgment at all, to a superiority that ought now to be cast off, and suffered to fall into utter and irrecoverable desuetude. Were it a mere question of complimentary deference to the Town Hospital, this might willingly be rendered. But it ought never to be forgotten, that any accession, however trivial, to the need of its services, bears along with it an accession to the need of its existence. It is because of this, that the acceptance even of the slightest boon from that institution is greatly to be deprecated. The homage may be insignificant—but it is not innocent—because it will be magnified into an arrangement for the continuance of a system that ought to be razed from the foundation. Pauperism will never be brought under a right economy, till all that is legal and compulsory in its ministrations, shall be not regulated, but destroyed. At all events, with these three parishes, there do exist, in their present means, and with but one step more, in their recent change of management, the capabilities of their own entire independence—in which, should they persevere for a very few years, then, by the operation of death

on their present hospital cases, shall we behold
half the domain of Glasgow altogether cleared of
its compulsory pauperism.

But there still remain five parishes, which though
not now connected with each other by the inter-
medium of a General Session, are still connected
each by its own separate tie of dependence and
obligation with the Town Hospital. The expenses of their Sessional poor, at the resolution of the
old system into its separate parts, went beyond
their receipts by collection; and each of the Sessions has this difference made good to it by distinct
supplies of money from that institution. And besides this, the transference of paupers goes on, as
formerly, from the Sessional to the Hospital lists;
so that there still remain five open ducts of conveyance from about one half of Glasgow to the fund by
assessment. The truth is, that without some such
initial arrangement as we have all along recommended, the present state of matters was quite
unavoidable. None of these Sessions had the means
to defray the allowances, even of the existing paupers upon their roll—and far less was it to be expected, that they would undertake each the burden of its whole new pauperism, without the
conveyance of its future excesses to the Town
Hospital. They were already labouring under the
weight of a present excess; and without a special
act of accommodation on the part of the Town
Hospital, towards each of the parishes so circum-

stanced, their emancipation from compulsory pauperism appears to be impracticable.

Were these parishes barely relieved by the Town
Hospital of the overplus of their Sessional poor—
were so many made to pass into the state of its
out-pensioners, and so many left on each Session,
as should just, with their present allowances, ab-
sorb the whole of its own proper revenue, we think
that even on this arrangement, there is not one of
them which could not, with the buoyancy of their
new felt and conscious independence, so stimulate
its means upon the one hand, and its management
upon the other, as to weather the demands of its
new pauperism, aye and until its old pauperism, by
the operation of mortality, had all been swept away.
But we should be inclined to grant a more favourable outset—to pass still more of their Sessional
paupers into the lists of the Town Hospital, and
perhaps, in some instances, to relieve them of the
whole weight of their existing pauperism.   At all
events, we should rather, for the sake of their
encouragement, that they started with an excess
of revenue above their present expenditure—but
with the full understanding, that to their treatment of all the future applications, we looked for
the conclusive deliverance of the Town Hospital
from the influx of all new pauperism.   We again
affirm our unqualified confidence in their success;
and that nothing is wanting but the consent of the
proper parties to these arrangements, for the extir-

pation of compulsory pauperism from the whole of Glasgow.

The vices of such a system as that under which they are now acting, we have already endeavoured to expose. Nothing can be worse, than to place the management of pauperism with one set of administrators, and the finding of ways and means for the expense of it with another. They, more especially, who stand at that place where the first movement is made by the population towards public charity, should be under every possible excitement to a close investigation; and, above all, to a diligent use of those various expedients of prevention, by which the application may either be stayed or be postponed. Now this is the very place that is occupied by the members of Kirk-Sessions in Glasgow—and a more effectual method could not be devised of opening the widest possible door for the influx of new cases, than to charge a Kirk-Session with the primary examinations of pauperism, and to lay the ultimate expense of it on another institution. In these circumstances, it is not only a most conceivable, but a most likely thing, that disunited though the Town Hospital should be from the charge of five of the city parishes, there will no sensible relief be felt, because of an almost instantaneous compensation in the augmented expense of the remaining five that adhere to them. The disease which had been cleared away from one half of the domain, might, and from the pure operation of the faulty economy alone, gather to such increased virulence in the remaining half, as to perpetuate an unalleviated and, perhaps, growing burden upon the community—and cause the ignorant and unthinking to wonder, why pauperism should be at once so reduced in its geographical dimensions, and so unreduced in its demands on the still assessed and heavy laden citizens.

Even, though one-half of Glasgow should, by the adoption of the parochial system, free itself of all dependence on the Town Hospital, yet let the other half remain on its present footing with that institution, and nothing more likely than that the assessment over the whole city, shall not only maintain its present amount, but shall press forward as urgently to its own increase as ever. All will depend on the practical administration of it. Should those who are in the management feel the impulse of a rival spirit with the emancipated parishes, they may certainly, by dint of strenuousness, and of determined endeavour, keep down, and even reduce their expenditure. But, on the other hand, it is equally possible, that by a very slight relaxation of care and vigilance on their part, the demand may be just as overbearing from that fragment of the population wherewith they shall then have to do, as formerly from the whole mass. In affirming this, we do not charge the office-bearers of a compulsory pauperism, either with incapacity, or with any defect of conscientious regard to the public interest. The charge that we prefer is not against them, but against the arrangements of that economy, wherewith it is their misfortune, and not their fault, that they are implicated. They must, in fact, have more of care and of principle, than are to be looked for in average humanity, should they be able to make head against the disadvantages of their most awkward and ill-assorted system. The falling away of two or more parishes from their superintendence, will, doubtless, be a relief to them in the mean time. But nothing is more natural, than that the very feeling of relief should induce a certain, though almost insensible remissness of practice, and a consequent facility in the admittance of new cases from that part of the territory which is still attached to them. The very men who would make a stand and an effort to prevent any addition to the burden of the community, might not feel just so intense a desirousness for the purpose of lightening the burden beneath that degree to which the community are already habituated. And from the moment, that they let down, though by ever so little, the defences of caution, and watchfulness, and strict investigation, from that moment they will let in additional pauperism. They may soon draw around them, from their remaining parishes, such a force and vehemency of new applications, as shall keep up, in its former magnitude, the whole business of their administration ; and then the wonted pressure of demand from without, shall be in its old state of equilibrium, with the wonted re-action of prompt and vigorous resistance from within.

Should this be the actual result of the late changes that have taken place in Glasgow—should a few of it parishes have wrought back their way to the gratuitous system, and the rest be still found as burdensome as formerly were all the parishes put together, we cannot think of a more impressive exhibition of the truth of our whole argument. To every considerate beholder, it must carry a demonstration along with it of the efficiency of the parochial administration on the one hand, and of the ruinous, and irrepressible, and altogether indefinite mischief that lies in a general and compulsory system, upon the other. It will prove, that wherever the principle of legal charity is acted upon, there is in it a creative power of evil, which can be kept under by no device of management, and be restrained by no limitation of territory—a virus that will scarcely admit of being mitigated, and from which society can never be delivered, but by its total extirpation.

Yet such is the blind impetuosity wherewith every suggestion for the reformation of existing abuses is liable to be opposed—such is the sensitive, instead of the rational style of that hostility, through which the course of improvement has frequently to force its way—so resolute often are the prejudice and the pre-determination that urge on the unreflecting cry of its adversaries, that it were no astonishment to us, though a phenomenon so palpably decisive of the tendency of assessments, as that of their continued increase on a curtailed territory, should have an altogether contrary interpretation given to it ; and it be even appealed to as an argument for recurrence to the old system, that in spite of all the abridgments which have been made upon it, the public burden is still unlightened, and no relief hath come out of the boasted innovations.

It is not he who is most versant in the detail, and drudgery, and penmanship of an old system—it is not he who is most qualified to pronounce on the merits or demerits of a new. All familiar though he be with the records, and the documentary informations of office, he may still be an utter stranger to the alone competent arena for the determination of this controversy. The experience of a mere practitioner in some of the inner departments of a poor's house, is totally dissimilar from the experience of a diligent observer on the hearts, and habits, and household economy of the poor—and it were well if this distinction was more adverted to by those who are loudest in their demand for practical wisdom, and in their outcry against the rash and confident anticipations of theory. It is not the man who has wildered all his days among the bye-tracts of error, it is not of him that you would most readily inquire the highway to truth ; and his very familiarity with the windings and ambiguity of that labyrinth in which

he long has been involved, forms in our mind
a presumption against any deliverance of his on the
question at issue. It is on this account, however,
that a ten-fold homage is due to him, who, though
nurtured from the infancy of his public life among
institutions that are wrong, has nevertheless, by
the pure force of a vigorous homebred sagacity,
seized upon and readily apprehended that which
is right. This is not wisdom aided by the lights
of a local or personal experience—but, much higher exhibition, it is wisdom forcing her way through
the besetting obstacles wherewith she was encompassed; and evolving herself into the clear region
of day, through all the intricacies of a mechanism,
that only serves to cloud and to confuse the apprehensions of ordinary men. This has been fine-
ly exemplified by the civil and municipal functionaries of Glasgow—and, on closing our narrative
of the present state and future prospects of pauperism in that city, we gladly offer the meed of
our acknowledgments to men, without whose
prompt and intelligent concurrence, there might
never have been opened the only practicable avenue to reformation.

The Barony of Glasgow is one of its suburb
parishes, and has now a population of more than
fifty thousand. There is something very instructive in the history of its pauperism. The assessment was first resorted to in 1810—much against
the advice and opinion of those who were most

versant in the details of the administration for the poor, antecedently to that period. We know not on the one hand, how to quote a more decisive experience against the wisdom of a compulsory provision, even for a large and wholly manufacturing population, than by appealing to the fact, that till 1810, the expenditure of this parish, the most populous in Scotland, seldom exceeded £600 annually—proving, that for the legal system of relief, there exists no natural and permanent necessity, in any circumstances whatever—though, after it is once adopted, there will arise, in all circumstances, an artificial necessity of its own creating, which will furnish the advocates of pauperism with a ready argument for its continuance. And we know not, on the other hand, a more striking evidence of the effect of an enlarged public charity, to multiply its cases, and enlarge the boundaries of its own operation, than that after 1810, the expenditure became about five times greater than before, in the short space of seven years. We would put the question to those among the heritors of the Barony, who were most in earnest for the establishment of a poor's rate, if they are sensible of having made the slightest progress towards the fulfilment of their benevolent anticipations— Can they say, that the poor are at all better off, under the present regime, than before?—or, that they have landed their parish in a better economy than that from which they have so recently departed? It is still time for them to retrace their movement—and not, most assuredly, for the sake of their property, but for the sake of what is far more valuable, the comfort and character of a numerous population, would we like to see their promptitude and vigour embarked on what some might denounce as a cause of selfishness, but which, in the most emphatic sense of the term, is indeed a cause of true philanthropy and patriotism.

The following occurs to us as the proper steps for the retracing movement that we now have suggested. Let the church, and each of the three chapels of ease, be permitted to retain their own collections; and let each have a defined locality annexed to it, within which it shall be the business of the respective office-bearers to meet all the demands of the new pauperism. There behooved to be, at first, a slight extension of the assessment, for the old pauperism, in order to make up for this surrender of the church and chapel collections. But for this there would be a speedy compensation in the death of the existing paupers—for, meanwhile, from the districts that had been assigned to the new managements, there would be no additional cases transmitted to the compulsory fund. And we repeat, that it will be due not to the want of means, but to the want of management, if the collections, at these various places of worship, be not found adequate to all the fair demands of their respective territories.

But even after the present system is broken up thus far, the separate managements would still

be too unwieldy.* These could gradually be relieved by the erection of additional chapels, a

---

* Some years ago, Dr. Mitchell of Anderston, a most estimable and
highly respectable minister of the United Secession, offered to undertake
the pauperism of a locality in the Barony parish, with the collections at
his Chapel, on an equitable condition of relief, from the assessment, to the
members of his congregation. If this offer were repeated, and followed up
by similar offers, in other quarters of the parish, it might be the germ of a
very important reformation. Should the dissenting ministers in large towns,
consent to assume a locality, they would find, most assuredly, nothing oppressive in the management of its new pauperism. For the small part of
their collections, that they should find it necessary to expend, they would
soon obtain compensation, in the relief of their wealthier hearers, from the
assessment that is now levied upon them. And we should look, in time,
for a compensation still more gratifying. The office-bearers of each dissenting chapel, would, under this arrangement, be exposed to frequent calls of
intercourse with the population of their assigned districts—and their right
of entrance and inquiry, would soon come to be recognised throughout all
the families—and many are the expedients and facilities that might thus occur, for carrying the lessons of Christianity amongst them—and the ministers
of our Secession would instantly be translated into the full benefit and influence of locality—and they might earn in consequence a rich moral and
spiritual harvest, wherewith to uphold and recruit their various congregations. And so little jealousy do we entertain of this progress, that we
should rejoice in it as a precursor to those liberal and enlightened views,
which have been promulgated by the venerable pastor of the Barony. The
day is perhaps coming, when localities primarily assumed by Presbyterian
ministers of the Dissent, for the reduction of pauperism, may, at length, be
transformed into parishes ; and, they retaining their own style of patronage,
and tolerating us in ours, may, at length, with the only important difference
betwixt us thus compromised, consent to sit down beside us, under the
canopy of our national establishment.

But, if such be the repulsion between the zealots of the establishment on
the one hand, and the zealots of dissenterism on the other, that any entire
co-alition of the parties is nauseous to both, and even the first step of the
approximation that we have now recommended, is not likely to be entered
upon—then, as the latter are so insensible to the charm and power of locality,
it is peculiarly incumbent on the former, who remain in sole possession of
this mighty instrument, to turn it to all the advantages of which it is suscep-

measure that might be advocated on higher grounds than the advantage of a reduced and rectified pauperism. Yet we should rejoice, if on this latter impulse only, men of wealth and influence could be prevailed upon to lend their aid to a cause, that has better considerations to recommend it, than even its subserviency to the best of all civic reformations.

---

tible. The extinction of pauperism is only one of those advantages and blessings, to the achievement of which the present apparatus of our church establishment is very nearly commensurate, but which would be prodigiously accelerated by the multiplication of chapels, or the subdivision of parishes.

CHAP. XIII.

ON THE DIFFICULTIES AND EVILS WHICH ADHERE EVEN TO THE BEST CONDITION OF SCOTTISH PAUPERISM.

THE Gorbals of Glasgow forms the other of its suburb parishes. Its inhabitants amount to upwards of twenty-two thousand, whose occupations are wholly of a mercantile and manufacturing character. Unlike to the Barony, it has no landed wealth whence it might derive those supplies for the relief of indigence, which many deem to be indispensable among families that are subject to all the vicissitudes attendant upon trade. This, then, in the eyes of many, were the likeliest of parishes for a compulsory pauperism, and a rapidly growing assessment—and did there really exist any natural necessity for such a provision, one should think that of all other places, it was here where the necessity would be most urgently and imperiously felt, and where a poor's rate would be most unavoidable. But if, instead of this, the Gorbals shall be found to have kept the simple parochial economy that was bequeathed to us from our ancestors, and to have flourished under it—this might well lead us to suspect, whether after all, a system of public and legalised charity, be essential to the wellbeing of any population.

This parish never has admitted an assessment—
and the whole of its sessional expenditure for the
poor, is defrayed from a revenue of about £400 annually. So little, in fact, has the circumstance of
its being an exclusively manufacturing parish,
brought along with it the necessity for a poor's
rate, that its expenditure is fully as limited as in
many of the most retired and wholly agricultural
parishes of the north. It does not amount to £25
a-year for each thousand of the population—and
yet, on the general blush and aspect of this industrious community, may it be confidently affirmed,
that it not only offers to our notice an aggregate
of families, in every way as well-conditioned, and
as exempt from the rigours of extreme wretchedness, as are those of the assessed city to which it
is contiguous; but that it will bear, in this respect,
a comparison with the most heavily assessed towns,
in any of the great manufacturing districts of England. There must be a mockery in the magnificence of those public charities, which have not
to all appearance bettered the circumstances, or
advanced the comforts of the people among whom
they are instituted, beyond those of a people
where they are utterly unknown. And, when we
look to such a parish as the Gorbals, still an unimpaired monument of the olden time, though in
full exposure to all those failures and fluctuations
of commerce, which form the chief argument on
the side of modern pauperism—the conclusion is
irresistible, that had there been enough of wisdom

in the other towns and parishes of Scotland for withstanding the first introduction of a poor's rate among them, there would have been as little of unreached and unrelieved poverty in each as there is at this moment; and the charity of good will, unaided by the charity of compulsion, would have sufficed, at least as well as now both do together, for all the wants and sufferings of our land.

It may be thought by some a little gratuitous to affirm, at a glance, that the lower orders of unassessed Gorbals are in circumstances of as great comfort and sufficiency, as are those of the assessed Barony, and of the still more heavily assessed Glasgow. But on this subject there was a very interesting numerical exhibition afforded in the year 1817, a year of such low trade and miserable wages, that it was deemed necessary to raise an extraordinary subscription, of more than £10,000, for the relief of our operative population, both in the city and suburb parishes. The population of Gorbals is greatly inferior to either that of Barony or of Glasgow—being somewhat beneath one-half of the former, and one-third of the latter. But the whole relief awarded to it, by the committee, did not come to one-third of the relief granted to the Barony, nor to one-seventh of that granted to Glasgow. So that, in the judgment of practical men, sitting in examination over the number and urgency of all the applications that actually came before them, the distress of the Gorbals, in the season of a great common calamity, was far short of that of the other two portions of the manufacturing community that were alike involved in it. And, if we are to estimate the relative degrees of sufficiency in ordinary times, by the inverse degrees of suffering in a time of extraordinary depression, there is room to believe, that the establishment of a compulsory provision has not only not advanced the condition of the labouring classes, but has positively aggravated the hardships to which they are liable. It has, in fact, unsettled their habits of economy and foresight; and, cruellest of all impositions, has misled them, by lying promises, from the only true source of a people's comfort and independence.

But before we leave the instance of Gorbals, we must advert to one observable peculiarity in the administration of its pauperism. It is well known, that in Glasgow, the elders, generally speaking, live at a considerable distance from their respective proportions—so as to have but a very slight acquaintance, and but very rare and occasional intercourse with the families. In Gorbals it is not so. It has been the practice there, when a vacancy occurs in the eldership, to seek for a successor among the inhabitants of the local district that falls to be provided. It is true, that this arrangement is liable to be disturbed to a certain extent, by changes of residence. But still upon the whole, the sessional affairs of the parish have the benefit of being conducted by a residing agency, where many of the members have their own dwelling-places within the territory of their own special superintendence. Now, were there any urgent and indispensable call for a large charitable revenue to a large population, or any glaring maladjustment between so small a public expenditure, on the one hand, and so vast a multitude of artizans and labourers on the other, as we find in the parish of Gorbals—then the best thing for its sessional administrators would be to live at the greatest possible distance from their respective territories— that so they might evade the force and vehemence of the many applications with which they might be otherwise encompassed. It must be a puzzling phenomenon to all who strenuously advocate the cause of pauperism, that in the Gorbals we should behold a parish with upwards of twenty thousand people served, and, on the whole, satisfied, by a public expenditure of about £400 a-year. Now, were a result so marvellous in their eyes brought about by any dexterous or unfair juggle, surely the right policy for the operators thereof would be to retreat as far as they could from all converse, and observation, and criticism on the part of the common people—and we should behold the elders of this parish, each skulking in distance and concealment from the clamour of unappeased families, and the remonstrance and outcry of their sympathizing neighbourhood. Instead of which, they place themselves fearlessly down in the very midst of all these possibilities; and on their slender means do they brave an encounter with all the real or imagined poverty that is around them; and surely if there were an outrageous shortcoming, on their part, from the fair and honest claims of the vicinity in which they dwelt, they could not have the toleration, and much less the esteem that we doubt not they enjoy. It is a truly instructive exhibition, to witness the solicitude of the able and experienced minister of that parish, for elders who shall have their personal occupancy each within the limits of that district which is assigned to him as the field of his labours. Did he feel burdened by the inadequacy of his parochial means to his parochial necessities, it would be his policy to have elders as much beyond the reach of his population as possible, rather than to have them placed at the distance of a walk of five minutes from one and all of the families. It would be his interest, that the administrators of this humble revenue never could be found, rather than be found, as they now are, at all times; because they generally live upon the domain of their own jurisdiction, and mingle hourly and familiarly with the people of their own charge. So to station these parochial office-bearers, each within his own portion of the mass of parochial pauperism, is one of the closest and most satisfying applications that can well be made of the touch-stone of experience to this question. There can be no blinking of the question with such a treatment of it. And the thing that has been proved, or rather the thing that has been found in consequence, is, that the way of bringing pauperism down to its right dimensions, is to face, and not to flee from it—that, instead of starving it by unmanfully running away, the better method of reducing it is by proximity and thorough investigation, to probe it to the uttermost—that the nearer you come to it, it dwindles the more into insignificance before you—that it grows into real magnitude by the distance of its administrators, as well as grows into a still greater apparent magnitude, when seen through the medium of distance by beholders—but, that from thence it may, by personal approximation and intercourse, be followed back again into the nonentity from which it never would have sprung, had it not been conjured up by the wand of legislation.

Wherever there is jugglery between two parties, there is disguise with the one or the other of them —and disguise is certainly favoured by the mutual distance at which they stand. When the parochial office-bearers and the poor, mingle so intimately together, as in Gorbals, and a cheap administration is the result of it, we infer that this is all which is genuinely required by the real state and exigencies of the population. But when they stand more widely apart the one from the other, as in Glasgow, and a profuse or expensive administration comes out of it, we should say of this, that it was partly owing to a delusion between the parties, because of their intervening distance. So that, instead of inferring from the moderate expenditure of Gorbals, that any juggle has been practised there on those who apply for public charity, we should rather infer, from the profuse expenditure of Glasgow, that a juggle is in daily practice and operation there, on those who dispense it.

Now we think that by the retracing process, which in our former chapters we have so often explained,* there is not an assessed parish in Scotland which does not admit of being conducted back again to that state from which the Gorbals never has departed. And yet, it ought not to be concealed that there are evils and difficulties even in the very best condition of Scottish pauperism. It has done less mischief than the pauperism of England, only because less outrageous in its deviation from the system of a free charity, prompted by nature, and stimulated as much as it may by the spirit of Christianity. But there is still a taint and a mischief belonging to it, which it would be well to expose—and that, both in justice to the real truth and philosophy of the subject, and also for the sake of our southern neighbours, many of whom have been misled into an unqualified veneration for the economy of our Scottish parishes. We do conceive that the overgrown pauperism of England is reducible; but we think that a still better landing-place might be provided for it, than even our own

---

See Vol. II. Chap. XI. p. 131.

parochial administration. It is good in every reformation to point well from the very outset: And if such a movement of reformation, on the part of England, shall ever be attempted, it were certainly right that the best of possible directions should be given to it; and, instead of a change from the more to the less imperfect, it were desirable that the line of regress from its present system should be so drawn, as to terminate in that system which is most accordant with the universal and abiding principles of our nature. We are aware of many in England, who would rejoice in a translation from their own corrupt and oppressive method of public charity, to the comparatively light expenditure of the North. But if any translation is to be adventured on, and the hazards of a great revolution in our domestic policy are to be encountered, at any rate, then the purely rectilinear path of sound principle had rather be chosen, than another path, however slightly divergent it may be from the former one.*   It is on this account that we should like to estimate the precise amount of our own error, and our own divergency. It may both serve as a land-mark by which to guide our future suggestions on the pauperism of England; and, by its tendency to expose, and perhaps to remedy the evils of our own peculiar sys-

---

* That we do not vindicate Scottish pauperism as being in itself a good, but merely indulge it as being the less of two evils, must be apparent from the whole of Chapter X. and the introduction to Chapter XI. of this work.

tem, may form an appropriate close to our observations upon Scottish pauperism.

We hold it then to be an evil, attendant even on
the very humblest of our sessional administrations,
that still their efficiency, for the relief of indigence,
is so apt to be overrated. There is a great defect
of arithmetic in the popular mind. It is the creature of imagination and habit; and easily imposed
upon by the glare of publicity, does it often award
a delusive power and importance to the objects of
its contemplation. It is thus, that even a Kirk-
Session, stands in loftier guise to the eye of parishioners, than is at all warranted by the might or
the magnitude of its operations. There is about it
an air of promise and of pretension, that is greatly
beyond its power—nor is it easy to unmask this
imposture, or, exposing the actual dimensions of
our public charity, to convince our population of
the real insignificance which belongs to it.

Now, this of itself is a serious mischief. The
disturbance which an artificial process of charity
gives to the natural processes, is not in proportion
to the quantity of relief that is administered thereby, but in proportion to the quantity of relief that
is counted upon. The relaxation of economy, on
the part of an expectant upon public charity, is
in the accurate ratio of the hope that is felt, and
not of the hope that is realised. It is enough for
the purpose of a vitiating influence among a population, to set up a visible appearance of distribution
in the midst of them, with even an undefined

chance of its being made, on given emergencies, to bear upon one or other of the families. It is no satisfying answer to this, that the produce of our parochial charity is but small—for the anticipation, in almost all cases, greatly outstrips the experience —and thus, to a certain degree, are the people lured away from self-dependence—the only solid basis on which their prosperity can be reared. And more than this—the delusion to which we now advert, is not confined to the poor. They, whose duty it is to succour them, fully participate therein—and the existence of a court of supply has often appeased those personal sensibilities, which would have been ten times more available to the cause of charity. Neighbours feel, to a certain extent, disburdened of their obligation, because of the perceived calls and inquiries that have been instituted by a Kirk-Session upon a distressed household—and of the periodical allowance, however meagre, which they understand to be rendered to it. Both the hand of industry, and the hand of private benevolence, are slackened by the presence of this meddling intruder, on the natural habits and sympathies of men : and if we think that the lower classes of society in England are worse conditioned than they else would have been because of their poor rates—we do truly and conscientiously think, that the collections of Scotland might, though in but a fractional degree, work a degradation both on the comfort and character of the peasantry of our land.

It is cruel first to raise a hope, and then to disappoint it—and there are two expedients by which this cruelty might be done away. The first and most obvious expedient, were to meet the hope by a liberality more adequate to the high pitch at which it is entertained. This has been attempted in England—and we venture to affirm, as the consequence of it, a tenfold amount of unappeased rapacity, and of rancorous dissatisfaction, and of all that distress which arises where the expectation has greatly overshot the fulfilment. The second expedient were utterly to extinguish the hope, by the total abolition of public charity for the relief of indigence. This has not been attempted in Scotland—and there are reasons, both of a prudential and of an absolute character, why we should deem the attempt to be not advisable. But, meanwhile, if the sessional charity of Scotland is to be kept up, it is but honesty to proclaim its utter insignificance in the hearing of all the people. They should be taught that in trusting to it, they only trust to a lying mockery. The way to neutralise the mischief of our parochial dispensations, is by a frank and open exposure of their utter worthlessness—for we know not how a more grievous injury can be done to the poor, than by holding out such a semblance of aid to them as might either reduce, by ever so little, their own economy, or deaden, by ever so little, the sympathy of their fellows. A full feeling of responsibility to the demands of human want and human suffering should be kept

alive among the families of every neighbourhood—
and for this purpose ought it to be a matter of
broad understanding and notoriety, that there is
positively nothing done by any of our Kirk-Sessions
which should supersede the care of individuals for
themselves or their keepership one for another.
The elder who effectually teaches this lesson in his
district, does more for the substantial relief of its
needy, than by any multiplication whatever of public allowances—and even without one farthing to
bestow, may thus be the instrument of a great
alleviation to the ills and hardships of poverty.
It is a downright fraud upon our population, to
keep up the forms of a great public distribution,
without letting them know that the fruits of it
are so rare and scanty, as to be wholly undeserving
of all notice or regard from them. The understanding should go abroad over a whole parish,
that none are relieved from their duties. Each
Kirk-Session ought to make full demonstration of
its own impotency—and better far, that its functions as a public almoner were forthwith to cease,
than that in the slightest degree, it should either
lull the vigilance of self-preservation, or seduce
kinsfolk and neighbours from that post of benevolent guardianship which they else would occupy.

It may startle some of our countrymen to be
told, that the sessional charity of Scotland may be
deleterious, and certainly is not indispensable to
the well-being, or to the right economy of any of
its parishes. The English reader has much greater

reason to be startled by the affirmation, that his parish, of a thousand people, with its expenditure for the year of fifteen hundred pounds, might have its public charity reduced to twenty pounds a year, and with infinitely less of clamour and disaffection among its families than there is at this moment. Now, if a parish could survive the shock of a revolution so marvellous, what is the mighty explosion or overthrow that would ensue, if the last remaining fragments of the system were made to disappear? If an English parish could be reduced to the condition of a Scotch one, in respect of its pauperism, then it were but adding one little step more to a wide and gigantic transition, should the Scottish pauperism be altogether swept away. And, when we wonder at the prejudice and incredulity of the South, as to the competency of the former achievement, let it not be forgotten, that this is fully overmatched by the incredulity of our own countrymen, when they protest against the latter achievement as wholly impracticable.

We are unable to comprehend on what principle a charitable expenditure of less than £500 a year, can be deemed essential to the good economy of a parish, with more than 20,000 people—or how the abolition of such an expenditure, would inflict a great and permanent derangement on the state of such a community. A very slight impulse indeed, on the popular feeling and popular habits, would fully balance the loss of so paltry a ministration. And the change in question, would, of it-

self, create such an impulse. We believe that a
most wholesome reaction would ensue on the cessation of all public charity; and that private charity,
then emancipated from delusion, would come
forth with a tenfold blessing upon the poor of our
land.

In the great majority of our Scottish parishes, all
which the administrators of the public charity profess to do, is to " give in aid." They do not hold
themselves responsible for the entire subsistence of
any of their paupers; they presume in the general,
on other resources, without inquiring specifically
either into the nature or the amount of them. It
says much for the truth of our whole speculation,
that in this presumption they are almost never dis-
appointed; and that whether in the kindness of
relatives, or the sympathy of neighbours, or the
many undefinable shifts and capabilities of the pauper himself, there do cast up to him the items of a
maintenance. It is instructive to perceive how
small a proportion the monthly allowance of a
Kirk-Session must often bear to the whole support
of an individual, who yet has no other visible means
that can be specified: and the only inference to be
made from this is, that the public charity of Scotland has not yet superseded those better operations
of care and kindness among families, on which we
think that the whole of human indigence might be
fearlessly devolved. All that a Kirk-Session generally does is to come forth with a minute and insignificant fraction, as its offering to the cause:

and still the question remains, Whether in so doing it does not abridge the supply that cometh from other quarters, more than it supplements them. We feel no doubt in our minds, that upon the whole, it does so—that there is a state, and a circumstance, and a form about the proceedings of this body, calculated to magnify the hope of its expectants, and of their friends, greatly beyond its power to meet or to gratify the appetite which it may have kindled—that, had it not been for its own little contribution, the whole present aliment of almost all its pensioners, would have been overpassed by the free and undeluded benevolence of nature, more powerfully aided, as it then must have been, by that economy which even the humble pauperism of Scotland has somewhat relaxed, and by that duteous attention among friends and kinsfolk, which it has somewhat superseded. We do not believe that the whole sessional charity of Scotland, in those parishes where assessments are unknown, renders more than a fifth part to the maintenance of all its enrolled paupers. The remaining four-fifths are yielded from other sources, which, if not disturbed, and somewhat enfeebled by the sight of an imposing apparatus of relief, would have more than made good the deficiency which now is not permitted to be thus overtaken. And therefore do we think, that without that show of charity which is held forth by the parochial system of Scotland, but which is not substantiated, the peasantry of our land would, on the strength of their own unseduced habits, have exhibited an aspect of greater comfort, and been in a still higher condition than they now occupy.

But, save for a great purpose, an innovating hand should not be stretched forth against the institutions and the established practices of a country—and, therefore, would we not plead for the abolition of our Scottish pauperism. We think that its comparatively harmless character entitles it to this toleration; nay, that it is susceptible of such improvements, in the administration of it, as to make it altogether innocent, if not salutary. There is even a way, that we shall explain presently, by which it might be made the organ of unquestionable benefit to the population, and especially in great towns, might be turned to the direct object of elevating both the morality and the scholarship of our land. Yet, however adapted to the good of a country where it has long been established, this is no reason why it should be introduced, with all its peculiarities, into a country where it is still unknown: nor does it follow, that because unwise to put down the existing economy of our Scottish parishes, it should therefore be held forth as a faultless model, or proposed as the best substitute for the present pauperism of England.

We have already said that the first evil of Scottish pauperism was that which attached to all public charity,—its liableness to be over-rated. It is not enough to say that experience will correct this evil. There is a want of arithmetic among the poor, in virtue of which a monthly half-crown, or a quarterly half-guinea sounds far more magnificently in their hearing than either a penny, or three halfpence a day. The daily meal that is sent by a kind neighbour dwindles into a thing of nought when compared with the wholesale allowance which issues either from the city Board or the parochial vestry; and the neighbour himself feels relieved of the obligation that lies upon him, by a spectacle which deceives him as much as it does the object of his sympathy. Rather than this, it were well that the cause of human want should be thrown, an unprotected orphan, on the random charities by which it is every-where encompassed. But if this may not be, let all such public charity as ours be preceded by the herald of its insignificance. Let each elder make open demonstration of its nullity to the people under his charge; and that, both to keep alive, as far as may be, the self-dependence of the poor, and to keep alive, among all who have aught to give, an unabated sympathy with the needs and the sufferings of our species.

When accompanied by such a corrective as this, the parochial charity of Scotland may be disarmed of all its mischief, and even be transformed into an instrument for raising and purifying still more the economic habits of her people. It brings the lowest of them into frequent and familiar converse with men, so far elevated above the common mass of society, as to have been intrusted with the duties of an office, that is both sacred in its nature, and

implies a certain superintendence over the concerns and the character of families. Let him who
fills this office be at once both worthy and enlightened; and by every act of intercourse may he
bring a distinct good even upon the secondary
habits of the population. Even an application for
sessional relief might be so improved, and so turned
by him. He might evince to their satisfaction the
arithmetic of its worthlessness. He might remonstrate with them on the folly of making so great
and humiliating a descent, for so paltry a compensation. He might go round with this argument
among all the relatives, and draw from them a liberality and an aid that would put parish charity
to shame, and bring it down to its right place in
the popular estimation. Such an elder as this may
at once heighten the delicacies of the poor, and
quicken the sympathies of the beneficent in his district; and the blessing that he might thus confer
upon the families, can only be equalled by the mischief that would ensue, were he to share with them
in the delusion, that the charity of a Kirk-Session
was the grand specific for human want, and make
use of it accordingly. If the blind lead the blind,
there will be unavoidable degradation. But when,
instead of this, the whole truth and principle of
the matter are completely unfolded; and the fair
and friendly conference is often entered upon; and
the duty is fearlessly pointed out, both that the
poor man ought to economise, and that friends and
relatives ought to feel for him,—then it is wonderful

how soon a kind and common understanding may come to be established between the elder who so expatiates over his territory, and the people who occupy it. Every thing can be made of them when they are dealt with frankly and rationally. No truth needs to be kept up from them, and there is nothing to fear from the announcement, in their hearing, of whatever has its own sense, and its own moral justness to recommend it. And, more particularly, let the revenue of the Session be only made to take a sound direction—let it be appropriated to some object that is at once popular and salutary—let it be allocated to the endowment of schools, or to a full provision for the unforeseen impotency, whether of body or of mind, wherewith Nature marks off a given number of unfortunates, in every neighbourhood, for the unqualified tenderness of all their fellows—let it be made palpable as day, that every one whom the hand of Providence hath smitten with blindness, or derangement, or some such special infirmity as hath made him through life the child of helplessness, is cherished and upheld to the uttermost—and let the elder be enabled to go forth among his people with the argument, that by the forbearance of their demands, they allow a more copious descent of liberality on families more abject than their own; and we despair not, at length, of a full concurrence, on their part, in that system by which indigence is left to the compassions of private benevolence, and unforeknown impotency alone is left to the care of benevolent institutions.

But there is another evil of more recent origin
in Scottish pauperism, and which is a serious obstacle in the way of a good practical understanding between the managers of a parish and its population—and that is, the imagination of a legal right
which a poor man has to subsistence from the
hands of the Kirk-Session. This is a new spirit
among our countrymen; but it is growing apace in
all those districts where assessments have been introduced, and the effect is just what may have
been anticipated. There is not one of those principles in our nature, which if left to their own unfettered operation, would have wrought the best
and the kindliest distribution of relief, that this
hard and heterogeneous legality does not counteract. For it gives a tenfold edge to the rapacity of
expectants—and it arms, with a kind of defensive
jealousy and rigour, the hearts of the administrators against them—and it displaces from what
would else have been a business of charity, all the
feelings, and all the characteristics of charity—and
it associates the complacency of justice, and of a
conscious right, with that neglect, on the part of
relatives and neighbours, of which they would have
otherwise been ashamed—and so, the elder who
goes forth upon his territory, the conceived object
of responsibility and of prosecution for all the distress that may be found in it, is not in such circumstances for a pleasing and a prosperous management, as if, delivered from the obligations of
Law, he went forth on the footing of spontaneous

philanthropy. In the one way of it, friends are apt to do little, that they may leave the largest possible space for the attentions of the elder. In the other way of it, a very small attention from the elder would be so seconded by the charity of popular benevolence, that however large the space he might leave to be filled up, it were sure to be overtaken. An elder with the legal means of a Kirk-Session in his hand, but at the same time, under the weight of its legal obligations, is not in so fit a condition for being the benefactor of his district, as if, without either the means or the obligations that now attach to his office, he went with nought but the visits, and the inquiries, and the recommendations of Christian kindness among its families. The people make common cause against the man on whom they fancy that the needy have a claim; and they make common cause with the man from whom the needy obtain a sympathy and an aid that are altogether gratuitous. The pauperism of Scotland has done somewhat to thwart the operation of this principle; and we think that it has locked up more of private benevolence through the land, than it has replaced by its own distributions.

It is on this account that we have often looked both with admiration and envy to the method of public charity that obtains among many of our Scottish dissenters. The produce of their weekly collections, or at least part of it, is often distributed among the poor of their own congregations, and who, at the same time, sustain a character that makes them admissible to Christian ordinances. There is nought of legality whatever in this administration, and much, we are persuaded, of the precious feeling both of sympathy and gratitude still adheres to it. We should deem it a mighty improvement in our pauperism, were this practice tolerated by our Courts of Law in the congregations of the establishment; and were a Kirk-Session held to acquit itself of all its obligations to the poor, by simply alimenting those poor who were the members of its own church. We should have no fear, under this arrangement of things, for the outfield population, who, in many of our country parishes, bear no sensible proportion to the whole, though, in great towns, they form the vast majority of our lower orders. Yet such is our confidence in those native forces of sympathy and of self-preservation, that we have so oft insisted on, as to believe of our general poor that a surer comfort and sufficiency would accrue to them, were they dissevered from sessional relief altogether. Not that we recommend the abolition of our present territorial superintendence by elders, whose office it is to render the attentions, and to exemplify the virtues of Christianity among the people of their assigned charge. But sure we are, that even as the benefactors of the poor, they would be translated into tenfold efficiency did they cease to be the objects of any legal demand or legal expectation; and they would speedily demonstrate, both by the more quiescent state of their districts, and the actually better economy which obtained among their families, that neither a public fund by assessment, nor a public fund by collections for the relief of indigence, was indispensable, or even added to the well-being of any population.

It is conceivable of some one parochial domain in Scotland, that within its limits the law of pauperism had ceased to be in force—that the people there had been thrown beyond the pale, or the fancied protection of this law—that, unlike to the consecrated ground on which no debtor could be legally apprehended, it was a kind of outcast or proscribed territory on which no poor man could legally demand one morsel of aliment to keep him from famishing. Let it comprise some thousands of our operative and city population, and be without more of recognition from the upper classes of society, than the ordinary apparatus of a church, and a minister, and an eldership would naturally attach to it. We affirm, from all that we have seen or learned of the internal structure of every such community, that its ecclesiastical office-bearers are in better circumstances for upholding a well-served, and a well-satisfied parish, without the law of pauperism, than with that law. Every movement of benevolence that was made by them to a poor family, would call out a tenfold power of co-operation from the surrounding observers. The effect of such an arrangement on the hopes, and habits, and sympathies of the people, would just be less

of actual necessity among them; and that necessity, when it did occur, more promptly and abundantly met by a busier operation of internal charity than before. It would thus become clear as
day, that Law had acted as a drag on the laborali-
ties of our nature; and that, on the removal of
this drag, these liberalities had found their own
surer and speedier way among the families of the
destitute. Law has wrought a twofold mischief.
It has both whetted the appetency for relief, and
stinted the supplies of it. The abolition of the
law of pauperism would curtail this misery at both
ends. That the starvation of a single individual
would ever arise from such a state of things, we
affirm to be a moral impossibility; but, as a certain
result of it, would we at length be landed in a
more peaceful and prosperous community than before.

Were such an experiment tried, and did such a
result come out of it, it would be held by many as
decisive of the truth of our speculation. But, on
a little reflection, they will perceive, that the experiments which have actually been made, though
not so striking, are still more decisive. In truth,
the state of every unassessed parish in Scotland
may be regarded as a distinct evidence against the
need of any public charity for indigence. The
whole expenditure, in many of them, does not
amount to twenty pounds sterling, in the year, for
each thousand of the population—a mere show of
relief, that might well have been dispensed with,

as more fitted to impede the charity of nature than to supplement it; and that a parish should be upheld under such an economy, is proof in itself, that it could have been as well, if not better upholden, without any artificial economy at all. The result of a well-satisfied parish is not in consequence of the sessional revenue, but in spite of it; and this holds eminently true both of Gorbals, and of the retracing parishes in Glasgow, where the management is conducted under the heavy disadvantage of a population tinctured, in some degree, with the legal imaginations of England. It were an easier management far, to have both the revenue of the one party, and the right of the other, utterly swept away; and sure we are, that with such an arrangement, there would be less than now of actual and unrelieved want in our parishes. In a word, our sessional apparatus, with all the hopes and desires that it carries in its train, is to be regarded, not in the light of a facility, but of an obstruction; and that we have succeeded therewith, in warding off a compulsory provision, is a more impressive demonstration still of the native capability which there is among a people to supersede pauperism, than if, without one farthing of public expenditure, we had arrived at the same result with a people that urged no claim, and felt no expectation.

We are quite aware, at the same time, of the strength of our Scottish predilections on the side of a Sabbath offering. The removal of the plates from the church-doors would be felt as a sore de-

secration, both by many of our priests, and by
many of our people. And, deeming as we do,
that it is in the power of a good administration,
very much to neutralise the mischief that is inherent in this as in all other public charity; and that,
even with certain precautions which we are to enter upon, is convertible into an instrument of great
positive benefit to all our parishes, we, among
others, should regret the abolition of it. What
has been found so innocent in practice might well
be tolerated in a country where it has been long
established, even notwithstanding its unsoundness
in principle. So that were it the only question,
What is best to be done with pauperism in Scotland?—we should incline to its remaining as it is,
in all those parishes where assessments are unknown: and only setting up an impassable barrier
between the gratuitous and the compulsory systems
of public charity, we should restrain its perpetual
tendency to merge, as it has done throughout our
border counties, into English pauperism. And we
should be further satisfied that in those latter parishes, by the methods which we have already explained, the minister and elders were to take their
direction back again to the good old way of their
forefathers. But though it were wrong to offer
pain or disturbance to the old and confirmed associations of one country, that is no reason why, in
another country, free from these associations, there
should be the blind unvarying adoption of a system that is at all exceptionable; or that, on the

question, What is best to be done with the pauperism of England? any deliverance should be given that is not conformable, at all points, to the sound and universal principles of our nature.

But ere we pass on to this momentous and interesting part of our argument, let us advert to a few of those leading principles, on which, we hold it a practicable thing, to perfect the administration of our Scottish pauperism.

And, first, we think that a great moral good would ensue, and without violence done to humanity, were the Kirk-Session forthwith to put a negative on all those demands that have their direct and visible origin in profligacy of character. We allude more particularly to the cases of illegitimate children, and of runaway parents. It should ever rank among those decent proprieties of an ecclesiastical court, which can, on no account, be infringed, that it shall do nothing which might extend a countenance, or give a security to wickedness. In the case of exposed infants, a necessity may be laid upon it. But sure we are, that generally, and without outrage to any of our sympathies, the criminal parties may be safely left to the whole weight of a visitation that is at once the consequence and the corrective of their own transgression. We know not a more pitiable condition than that of a female who is at once degraded and deserted; but many are the reasons why it should be altogether devolved on the secret and unobserved pity which it is so well fitted to inspire.

And we know not a more striking exhibition of the power of those sympathies, that we have so often quoted as being adequate, in themselves, to all the emergencies of human suffering, than the unfailing aid, and service, and supply, wherewith even the child-bed of guilt is sure to be surrounded. It is a better state of things when, instead of the loud and impudent demand that is sometimes lifted upon such occasions, the sufferer is left to a dependence upon her own kinsfolk, and neighbours, and to the strong moral corrective that lies in their very kindness towards her. We think, that if every instance of a necessity which has been thus created, were understood to lie without the pale of the sessional administration, and to be solely a draught on the liberalities of the benevolent, we both think that these liberalities would guarantee a subsistence to all who were concerned, and that, at the same time, in a more intense popular odium, there would arise a defensive barrier against that licentiousness which the institutions of our sister country have done so much to foster and to patronise. It must shed a grievous blight over the delicacies of a land, when the shameless prostitute is invested with a right, because of the very misdeeds which ought to have humbled and abashed her—when she can plead her own disgrace as the argument for being listened to, and, on the strength of it, compel the jurisdictions of the country to do homage to her claim—when crime is thus made the passport to legal privileges, and the native unloveliness of vice is somewhat glossed and overborne, by the public recognition which has been thus so unwisely extended to it.

In the case of a family that has been abandoned by its regardless and unnatural father, and where there is no suspected collusion between the parents, there is pity unmingled with reproach to the helpless sufferers. And our whole experience assures us, that this pity would be available to a far larger, and more important aid, than is rendered, on such occasions, by any of the public charities in Scotland. The interference of the Kirk-Session has the effect of contracting the supplies within the limits of its own rigid allowance; and better even for the members of the deserted household, that they had been suffered, each to merge into such an asylum of protection and kindness as the neighbourhood would have spontaneously afforded. But better still—there would, under such a regimen as this, be fewer instances of abandonment. The man who, without remorse, could leave his offspring to the charge of a public body, and a burden on a public fund, would need to have still more of the desperado in his heart, ere he could leave them at random to the care of his old familiars in society. To the honour of our nature, there is a moral certainty in this latter case, that there will be no starvation; but the sympathy of individuals will not be so often put to the trial of such a runaway experiment, as would the care and responsibility of a Kirk-Session. And better, surely, that such an occurrence as this should be placed in the list of those casualties for which no legal provision has been made, than that any thing in the institutions of our country should tend to slacken or to supersede the ties of relationship. In a community that had not been thrown into derangement by pauperism, the desertion of a family would be as rare and appalling a visitation, as the destruction of their all by fire; and, like it too, would call forth as prompt and productive a sympathy from neighbours, while the indignation felt by all at the calamitous event, in which all had been made to take an interest, would strengthen the popular habit the more on the side of all the relative and family obligations.

It might appear to many a harsh and unfeeling suggestion, thus to withdraw the hand of public charity either from illegitimate or deserted children. We are satisfied that both human crime and human suffering would be greatly abridged by it—that, in the first instance, a much smaller number of these unfortunates would fall to be provided for—and that, in the second instance, there would come forth, from some quarter or other, an actual sustenance to all. Such is the result which we would most confidently anticipate, and it would most strikingly demonstrate the alertness of individual benevolence, when no artifical economy stood in its way.

But, secondly, if that indigence which is the effect of crime might be confined to the charities of private life, we may be very sure that the indigence which is not associated with crime will be largely and liberally met by these charities. In the absence of all legal provision there would be greatly less of this indigence, and greatly more of this liberality; but as there does exist a legal provision, then is it the part of him who is intrusted with the dispensation of it, so to manage, as that the one shall be prevented, and the other shall be promoted to the uttermost. For this purpose he should ever ply the lesson among his people, that the charity of a Kirk-Session is the last resort which should come in the train of every other lawful expedient—that it is the duty of all to ward off the necessity of this humiliation from the poor brother who is just standing upon the verge of it—that, in this cause, it is the duty of the applicant himself to put forth all his powers of economy and labour, and the duty of his relatives to minister to his need, and the duty of his neighbours to interpose, and, if possible, to save him from the parish : and lest the minister or the elder who so expatiates should appear to be one of those who would lay burdens on the shoulders of other men, which he himself will not touch with one of his fingers, it is his duty to exemplify all that he thus strenuously recommends. It is not known at how cheap a rate the demand from whole thousands of a city population could thus be disposed of, or how soon, by this culture of honesty and frankness, their families could be weaned from all desire, and all dependence upon public charity.

And we have only to add, on this part of the subject, that while such a state of things would naturally, and of itself, bring on a far closer interchange of kindness between the higher and lower classes, this, however desirable for its own sake, is not indispensable for the sake of filling up the vacancies that might be created by the withdrawment of public charity. It is the unquestionable duty, and ought, at all times, to be the delight of the rich, fairly to meet with poverty, and to investigate and to bestow. One of our chief arguments for re-committing the business of alms to a natural economy, is, that the wealthy and the poor would thereby come more frequently into contact, and that would be made to issue upon the destitute, from the play of human feelings, which is now extorted without good-will on the one side, or gratitude on the other, by the authority of human law. It were an incalculable good, if, in this way, the breath of a milder and happier spirit could be infused into society: But, arithmetically, it is not true, that the free-will offerings of the rich are essential as a succedaneum to the allowances of pauperism—or, that, unless the former to some given extent, can surely be reckoned upon, the latter must, to a certain extent, continue to be upholden. The practical result that would come out from the cessation of all public charity, were, in the first instance, a very great abridgment of expectation or demand on the part of the applicants—and, secondly, while the personal attentions and liberalities of the rich would be multiplied in consequence, on those poor, who shall be with us always ; yet, confident we are, that even in the most plebeian of our city parishes, these poor would, in the stimulated kindness of relatives and neighbours, meet with far their most effectual redress, and by far their fittest and readiest compensation.

But, thirdly, there is a class of necessities in the relief of which public charity is not at all deleterious, and which she might safely be left to single out and to support, both as liberally and as ostensibly as she may. We allude to all those varieties, whether of mental or of bodily disease, for which it is a wise and salutary thing to rear a public institution. We hold it neither wise nor salutary to have any such asylum for the impotency that springeth from age ; for this is not an unforeseen exigency, but one, that, in the vast majority of instances, could have been provided for by the care of the individual. And neither is it an exigency that is destitute of all resource in the claims and obligations of nature, for what more express, or more clearly imperative, than the duty of children ? A systematic provision for age in any land, is tantamount to a systematic hostility against its virtues, both of prudence and of natural piety. But there are other infirmities and other visitations, to which our nature is liable, and a provision for which stands clearly apart from all that is exceptionable. We refer not to those current household diseases, which are incidental, on the average, to every family, but to those more special inflictions of distress, by which in one or more of its members, a family is sometimes set apart and signalized. A child who is blind, or speechless, or sunk in helpless idiotism, puts into this condition, the family to which it belongs. No mischief whatever can accrue from every such case being fully met and provided for—and it were the best vindication of a Kirk-Session, for the spareness of its allowances, on all those occasions where the idle might work, or kinsfolk might interpose, that it gives succour to the uttermost of its means, in all those fatalities of nature, which no prudence could avert, and which being not chargeable as a fault, ought neither to be chargeable as an expense, on any poor and struggling family.

It may be at once seen, wherein lies the distinction between the necessities of signal and irremediable disease, and those merely of general indigence. A provision, however conspicuous, for the former, will not add one instance of distress more to the already existing catalogue. A provision for the latter, if regular and proclaimed, will furthermore be counted on—and so be sure to multiply its own objects, to create, in fact, more of general want than it supplies. To qualify for the first kind of relief, one must be blind, or deaf, or lunatic, or maimed, which no man is wilfully—so that this walk of charity can be overtaken, and without any corrupt influence on those who are sustained by it. To qualify for the second kind of relief, one has only to be poor, which many become wilfully, and always too in numbers which exceed the promise and the power of public charity to uphold them—so that this walk can not only never be overtaken, but, by every step of advancement upon it, it stretches forth to a more hopeless distance than before, and is also more crowded with the thriftless, and the beggarly, and the immoral. The former cases are put into our hand by nature, in a certain definite amount—and she has farther, established in the human constitution such a recoil from pain, or from the extinction of any of the senses, as to form a sure guarantee against the multiplication of them. The latter cases are put into our hands by man, and his native love of indolence or dissipation becomes a spontaneous and most productive fountain of poverty, in every land where public charity has interposed to disarm it of its terrors. It is thus, that while pauperism has most egregiously failed to provide an asylum, in which to harbour all the indigence of a country, there is no such impossibility in the attempt to harbour derangement, or special impotency and disease. The one enterprise must ever fall short of its design, and, at the same time, carry a moral deterioration in its train. The other may fulfil its design to the uttermost, and without the alloy of a single evil that either patriot or economist can fear.

The doings of our Saviour in the world, after he entered on his career as a minister, had in them

much of the eclat of public charity. Had he put
his miraculous power of feeding into full operation, it would have thrown the people loose from
all regular habits, and spread riot and disorder
over the face of the land. But there was no such
drawback to his miraculous power of healing. And
we think it both marks the profoundness of his
wisdom, and might serve to guide the institutions
and the schemes of philanthropy, that while we
read of but two occasions on which he multiplied
loaves for a people who had been overtaken with
hunger, and one on which he refused the miracle
to a people who crowded about him for the purpose
of being fed, he laid no limitation whatever on his
supernatural faculties, when they followed him for
the purpose of being cured. But it is recorded of
him again and again, that when the halt, and the
withered, and the blind, and the impotent, and
those afflicted with divers diseases, were brought
unto him, he looked to them, and he had compassion on them, and he healed them all.

This then is one safe and salutary absorbent for
the revenue of a Kirk-Session. The dumb and the
blind, and the insane of a parish, may be freely alimented therewith, to the great relief of those few
families who have thus been specially afflicted.
Such a destination of the fund could excite no beggarly spirit in other families, which, wanting the
peculiar claim, would feel that they had no part
or interest in the peculiar compassion. There is
vast comfort in every walk of philanthropy, where

a distinct and definite good is to be accomplished, and whereof, at a certain given expense, we are sure to reach the consummation. Now, this is a comfort attendant on that separate direction of the poor's money which we have now recommended— but the main advantage that we should count upon, is its wholesome effect on the general administration and state of pauperism. The more systematically and ostensibly that the parochial managers proceeded on the distinction between special impotency and general indigence, the more, at length, would the applicants on the latter plea, give way to the applicants on the former. The manifest superiority of the first claim to the second, would go at once to the hearts of the people; and mere indigence would be taught, that in the moderation of her demands, there was a high service of humanity rendered to still more abject helplessness than her own. The Sabbath offering might gradually come to be regarded as a sort of consecrated treasure, set apart for those whom Providence had set apart from the rest of the species. Nor would indigence suffer from this rejection of her claims by public charity. She would only be thrown back on the better resources that await her in the amenities and kindnesses of private life. And it is thus that a great positive good might be rendered out of the parochial administration, to one class of sufferers, while both the delicacies of the general poor, and the sympathies of that individual benevolence on which all their wants might safely be devolved, would be fully upholden.

We are quite confident that such a direction of
the sessional means, if steadily persevered in, would
at length carry the acquiescence both of the popular habits and the popular approbation. And if
followed out, it might lead, and more especially
in city parishes, to a most beneficial economy.
There would be no harm in stimulating the liberality of a congregation for the support of a parish
surgeon, who might be at the free command of the
families. There would be no harm in thus supporting a dispensary for good medicines, or in purchas-
ing an indefinite right of admittance to an hospital
for disease. We specify these objects chiefly in
order to demonstrate, how, without taking down
the apparatus of Scottish pauperism, it might still
be made subservient to blessings of a very high and
unquestionable character, and without any of that
injurious taint which ordinary pauperism is seen to
bring along with it, on the spirit and independence
of a population.

There are many other absorbents which might
be devised for the surplus of the sessional income,
that would be salutary as well as safe—and thus
all public charity might in time be diverted
away from the relief of mere indigence. We should
count, as the effect of this, on a great abatement
of all the sufferings of poverty, because, instead
of being thereby abandoned, it would only be
transferred to the guardianship of a far better and
more effective humanity. And we should have
pleasure in stimulating the liberality of a congre-

gation, when turned to a purpose that did not hazard the moral deterioration of the people. There is something ticklish and questionable in every dispensation under which a public distribution of alms is held out to the necessitous—and the perpetual tendency of our Scottish to pass at length into English pauperism, as has been abundantly manifested, both in our large towns and border parishes, is in itself a proof that somewhat of that unsoundness may be detected in the former, which has come forth so palpably upon the latter. To make the practice of the one country a model for the other, would be to commit back again the pauperism of England to that whence it might germinate anew, and so add one failure more to the many experiments which have been devised for its reformation. And yet the parochial charity of our land need not be extirpated. It is in the power of a wise and wholesome administration, to impress upon it a high moral subserviency—to turn it, for example, to the endowment of schools, or the establishment of parish libraries, or the rearing of chapels for an unprovided population; who, by one and the same process, could have their moral wants supplied, and be weaned from all that sordid dependance on charity, by which their physical wants have not been abridged, but rather aggravated, both in their frequency and in their soreness.

CHAP. XIV.

ON THE LIKELIEST MEANS FOR THE ABOLITION OF PAUPERISM IN ENGLAND.

IT might be thought, that, as a preliminary to our views of English pauperism, we should again expound those principles of our nature on which we mainly rest the solution of this much-agitated problem; and in virtue of which, we deem it not only safe, but salutary, to do away all legal charity for the relief of indigence. But this is a topic on which we, by this time, have amplified enough in the course of our argument;* nor could we again recur to it, without laying upon our reader the burden and the annoyance of a reiteration, into which we fear that our anxiety for the clearest possible elucidation has already too often betrayed us.

But we not only forbear a recapitulation of those principles on which we rely for the eventual cure of English pauperism; we shall, furthermore, be studious of the utmost possible brevity in our narrative of facts, when adverting to the present and the actual condition of it. More particularly, shall we abstain from the unnecessary multiplication of instances, in proof of such affirmations as

---

* See Chap. X. p. 53—66.

are abundantly certain, and familiar to all who take
any interest in the subject. This is a question on
which we feel that we are addressing a conscious
public, who need not to be awakened as to the existence of the evil, or made more intelligent than
they already are, as to its leading modifications.
It were a vain and idle parade to come forth with
a copious induction of parishes, with a view to demonstrate the reality of any practice, or the fla-
grancy of any abuse, that is of undisputed notoriety in all parishes. There are many occasions
on which there is a sort of common and recognised
ground between the author and his readers—when
much may be affirmed without proof, on the one
side, because instantly responded to by a prior and
independent knowledge, upon the other. It is of
no use to overload with evidence, where there is
already a settled and experimental conviction.*

---

* In the preface to a very able pamphlet on the Poor Laws, by the Rev.
Mr. Davison, there are the following judicious remarks on the quotation of
facts and examples :—

" All reasoning on the subject of the Poor Laws must be idle, which is
not supported by a real knowledge of the state of things in the country, as
it stands under these laws; and existing facts must shape the anticipated
experience by which any given alteration of them is to be judged of. Instances and particular cases therefore, commonly make a figure in the pub-
lications which treat of them. The author of these remarks has his facts
and examples in view, such as his opportunities of observation have afforded :
but he has not brought them forward to justify his notions by them. He
has declined doing it, as well because particular cases, unless they are strong
and aggravated, make little impression in the recital, and, in proportion as
they are aggravated beyond the common average, though they catch exceedingly the popular understanding, they are of less real value ; and also,
because his assumptions will either be justified by the general experience of

This supersedes much of that detail on which it had else been necessary to enter; but with this

---

those who may happen to read them; or, if they are not so justified, the facts from which they have been drawn would be equally met and opposed by the reader's own contrary experience."

In this work of Mr. Davison, which evinces both great taste and great judgment, there is about the nearest approximation to the true system of charity that we have yet met with, in any recent English writer who treats specifically on the subject of the Poor Laws. In some of our subsequent numbers we may take occasion to controvert one or two of his positions; and, more especially, that part of his argument where he contends for the necessity of a legal support in certain cases of helpless and hopeless indigence. We do not think that he goes far enough in estimating the power and the readiness of Humanity, to meet every occurring circumstance of necessity; and, thinking as we do, that Benevolence is paralyzed in her efforts, as well as stript of her essential character, when made the subject of a legislative enactment, we cannot but feel the utter erroneousness, while we admire the eloquence, of the following beautiful passage.

" The humanity, which it was designed, by the original text of the main statute upon this subject, to infuse into the law of the land, is a memorial of English feeling which has a right to be kept inviolate; and its just praise will be better understood, when it comes to be purified from the mistake which either a careless abusive usage, or an impartial and inexperienced policy in the extent of its first enactment, may have combined with it. It is the page of mercy in a book which has to deal much of necessity in severer things; and there is a spirit of Christian kindness in it particularly fitted to recommend the whole authority of law as a system framed for the well-being of its subjects. I would, therefore, as soon see the best clause of Magna Charta erazed from the volume of our liberties, as this primary authentic text of humane legislation from our statute book. And if, in the course of a remote time, the establishments of liberty and humanity, which we now possess, are to leave us, and the spirit of them to be carried to other lands, I trust this one record of them will survive, and that charity by law will be a fragment of English history, to be preserved wherever the succession of our constitution or religion shall go."

Had there never been any charity by law in England, charity by love would have both had less to do, and done her office with greater alacrity. The law has both augmented human want, and it has enfeebled human sympathy. After all, it has not so overtaken the field of indigence as to supersede the need of individual humanity, while, by its very nature, it has stifled the

reservation, that there are many facts so replete with inference, or in themselves, so characteristic, that, by a minute and circumstantial exhibition of them, we take the most effectual method both to prove and to picture forth the evils of the system, and the process by which it may be rectified.

And it is not the heavy expense of it* that we hold to be the main evil of English pauperism. We should reckon it a cheap purchase, if, for the annual six or eight millions of poor rate, we could secure thereby the comfort and character of the English population. But we desire the abolition of legal charity, because we honestly believe, that it has abridged the one, and most wofully deteriorated the other. Under its misplaced and officious care, the poor man has ceased to care for himself, and relatives have ceased to care for each other; and thus the best arrangements of Nature and Providence for the moral discipline of society, have been most grievously frustrated. Life is no longer a school, where, by the fear and foresight of want, man might be chastened into sobriety— or, where he might be touched into sympathy by that helplessness of kinsfolk and neighbours, which

---

principle of humanity. Had there been no law of pauperism, the unimpaired economy and relative virtues of the people, would, on the one hand, have kept the territory of want within its proper limits—and, on the other hand, would there have been a more alert and vigilant benevolence in society, for the discharge of that function, which the legislature has so unfortunately taken into their own hands.

* The whole money expended for the maintenance of the poor in England and Wales, on the year ending 25th March, 1821, was £6,958,445 2s.

but for the thwarting interference of law, he would have spontaneously provided for. The man stands released from the office of being his own protector, or the protector of his own household—and this has rifled him of all those virtues which are best fitted to guard and dignify his condition. That pauperism, the object of which was to emancipate him from distress, has failed in this, and only emancipated him from duty. An utter recklessness of habit, with the profligacy, and the mutual abandonment of parents and children, to which it leads, threatens a speedy dissolution to the social and domestic economy of England. And instead of working any kindly amalgamation between the higher and lower classes of the land, the whole effect of the system is to create a tremendous chasm between them, across which the two parties look to each other with all the fierceness and suspicion of natural enemies—the former feeling, as if preyed upon by a rapacity that is altogether interminable; the latter feeling as if stinted of their rights by men whose hands nothing but legal necessity will unlock, and whose hearts are devoid of tenderness.

This is not the doing of Nature, nor could it have so turned out, had not Nature been put into a state of violence. So soon as the violence is removed, Nature will return to her own processes—and a parish in England will then exhibit, what many of the parishes in Scotland do at this moment, a population where there is neither dissatisfaction nor unrelieved want, and yet, with little of public charity. All that is required, is simply to do away that artificial stress which the hand of legislation has laid upon the body politic—and a healthful state of things will come of itself, barely on those disturbing forces being withdrawn, wherewith the law of pauperism has deranged the condition of English society. It is just as if some diseased excrescence had gathered upon the human frame, that stood connected with the use of some palatable but pernicious liquor, to which the patient was addicted. All that the physician has to do in this case, is to interdict the liquor, when without further care or guardianship on his part, the excrescence will subside, and from the *vis medicatrix* alone, that is inherent in the patient's constitution, will health be restored to him. It is even so with that disease which pauperism has brought on the community of England. It is a disease originally formed, and still alimented by the law which gives access to a compulsory provision—and precisely so soon as that access is barred, there is a *vis medicatrix* that will then be free to operate, and which, without any anxious guardianship on the part of politicians or statesmen, will, of itself, bring round a better and happier state of the commonwealth. There might an unnecessary shock be given by too sudden a change of regimen. There might be an inconvenient rapidity of transition, which had as well be avoided, by wise and wary management. This consideration affects the question of policy as to the most advisable mode of carrying the cure into effect. But it does not affect the question of principle, either as to the cause of the disease, or as to the certainty of a good and wholesome result when that cause is done away. It is very true, that by a summary abolition of the law of pauperism, a sore mischief may be inflicted upon society—and yet it may be equally true, both that the alone remedy for the present distempered state of the lower orders, lies in the abolition of this law, and also, that there do exist, throughout the mass of English society, the ingredients or component principles of such a *vis medicatrix*, as would greatly alleviate the present wretchedness, and more than replace all those dispensations of legal charity which would then have terminated.

And surely it cannot be questioned, that all those principles of our Nature, which taken together, make out the *vis medicatrix*, are just as firmly seated, and would in fit and favourable circumstances, be of as unfailing operation in England, as in any other country on the face of the earth. There is much, no doubt, in its present system of legal charity, to counteract and disguise them. Yet even under this pressure, they are still to be detected in manifest operation. And they only need to be delivered from that artificial weight wherewith they now are overborne, in order that they may break forth, and be prolific of a most abundant compensation to families, when the supplies of pauperism are withdrawn from them.

For first, what malignant charm can there be in the air or in the geography of England, which should lead us to conceive of its people, that they are exempt from that most urgent principle of our nature—the law of self-preservation. There is certainly much in its public charity, that is fitted to traverse this law. Yet still, and in the face of this counteraction, manifold traces are to be found, even among the labouring classes, of a prudent and prospective regard to their own interests. These it is the undisputed tendency of pauperism to extinguish; and, therefore, any remainder of a prudential habit which may yet be observable, form so much the more decisive proof, that Englishmen are originally and constitutionally alike unto their other brethren of the species in this great characteristic of humanity. And, accordingly, in spite of their pauperism, and of its efficacy to lull them into a careless improvidence, do we find that the prudential virtues, even of the lower orders, are enfeebled only, and not destroyed. The Saving Banks, and Benefit Societies, which are to be met with in almost every district of the kingdom, are strong ostensible indications of a right and reflecting selfishness, which, if only kept on the alert, and unseduced from its own objects, by the promise and the allurement of public charity, would do more for the comfort of our peasantry than all the offerings of parochial and private benevolence put together. There is nought that would more revive or re-invigorate the impulse to accumula-

tion than the abolition of the law of pauperism.
Saving Banks would be multiplied;* and this,

---

* It must be admitted, however, that there is something delusive in the
returns made by Saving Banks, and that they may lead us to infer a
much greater degree of an economic habit among the people than actually
obtains. A very large proportion indeed of the deposits is made by household servants, and by contributors in easy circumstances. It were most desirable, that operatives could find their way in greater numbers to these institutions. Could they merely afford to slacken their work in a season of depressed wages, or to cease from working altogether, the overstocked
markets would be far more speedily cleared away, and the remuneration for
labour would again come back to its wonted or natural level.

The operation of public charity, in lessening the deposits, must be quite
obvious. The following anecdote illustrates this. To prove it is not necessary. A poor woman at Clapham, near London, whose daughter had
begun to put into the Saving Bank, said to her, " Why, how foolish you
are! It is all a contrivance of the rich to save their own pockets. You
had much better enjoy your own money, and when you want, they will take
care of you." The daughter *did* withdraw from the Saving Bank. My
friend Mr. Dealtry, who is rector of the parish, and from whom I obtained this information, adds, that the woman's remark did not apply so directly
to the poor rates, as to a charitable fund, which was first raised by contribution, and then distributed in charity. But the principle is the same.

There is, perhaps, no parochial history in England that more demonstrates
the inefficacy of poor rates, or that would better demonstrate the efficacy
of an economic habit among the people themselves, than that of Darlaston, in Staffordshire. Its population in 1821, was 5585—and of its thousand
and eighty families, one thousand and sixty were employed in trade, handi-
craft and manufactures. Comprehending only about 800 acres of land, it has
almost no agricultural resources. So that the rate falls almost entirely on
those householders who are not paupers themselves. The chief occupation
of the people was mining, and the filing of gun locks, which latter employment failed them at the termination of the war. The distress began to be
felt in 1816, at which time the poor rate amounted to £2086 15s. 7d. It
was now, that the resource of a compulsory provision arrived at its limit—
for the continued occupation of the land would have ceased to be an object,
had the holders of property been compelled to provide for the whole emergency. All would have been swallowed up had the distress continued; and
the householders who were liable to the rate, would, on a farther augmentation of it, have done what is often done in the heavily assessed parishes of

though the most palpable, would not be the only
fruit of that sure and speedy resurrection that

England—they would have made their escape to a residence in some near
parishes, that were less burdened. So that the grand legal expedient of
England, was, in this instance, tried to the uttermost, and its shortcomings
had just to be made up by methods that would be far more productive, as
well as far less needful, were there no poor rate, and no law of charity whatever. Mr. Lowe, the humane and enlightened rector of this parish, succeeded, by great exertion, in raising the sum of £1278 14s. 8d. from the benevolent, in various parts of the country; besides which, there was the sum of
£1157 10s. contributed by a society that was formed, we believe, in London, to provide for the extra distress of that period. In all there was distributed among the poor in 1816-17, the sum of £4523 3s. The parish
workhouse was quite filled with them. Its rooms were littered down for
the reception of as many as could be squeezed together. Some were employed at work upon the roads—and in the distributions that took place of
soup, and potatoes, and herrings, the gates were literally borne off their
hinges, by the pressure of the starving multitude. At length, after an interval of months, there was a return of demand for work. One American
trade sprung up for another that had failed. A large East India order gave
a great impulse on the occasion, and the idle hands were gradually absorbed
into other employments.

Now it would appear from this narrative first, that the poor rate did not
supersede the need of application to the benevolent, of whom, we may be assured, that on the abolition of legal charity, they would be still more prompt,
and with ampler means too, on every case of emergency. But, secondly,
and what is far more interesting, there is every reason to believe, that the
total distress without a poor rate, would fall short in its amount of the surplus distress with a poor rate. The truth is, and to this we have the distinct testimony of Mr. Lowe, that it lay within the means of the people in
good times, to have saved as much as would have weathered the whole distress. The prosperity of the place, was, in one respect, the ruin of it—and
there is every reason to apprehend that the dissipation and improvidence
which our public charities do so much to foster, make the same people who
are insolent in the season of affluence, proportionably wretched and abject
in the season of adversity. Mr. Lowe, whose judicious insight into all that
can affect the economic condition of his people, is only equalled by his un-
wearied labours for their spiritual well-being, writes thus : " That previous
savings might have enabled our manufacturing poor to meet the distress
of 1816-17, I feel confident, from many who have been thus carried

should then take place of an economic habit among the people. There would, in the privacies of do-

---

through it, and risen above it, who, a few years before, were in no better, nay, even in worse circumstances than others, who were completely overwhelmed by it. For example, our present overseer is actually administering relief, even in the workhouse, to some once in better circumstances, but less provident than himself. On this account, I have been anxious to make my people acquainted with the benefits of Saving Banks, against which so strong a prejudice prevails, especially among their masters, that I have to travel more than 10 miles with the little I can induce them to deposit there. And I much fear, it will not be until they have been some time established in the *midst* of us, that any extensive good will be done by them."

What an antagonist is a poor rate to this philanthropic scheme for the comfort and independence of the lower orders! We shall attempt, in a future chapter, to point out its depressing effect on the wages of labour, and the opposite effect of an acquired capital among workmen, permanently to elevate their condition, by upholding the remuneration of industry at a higher, or, at least, more uniform level. We believe, that this result is not only viewed without dismay, but would be hailed by our more enlightened masters and capitalists, as a state of things most favourable to the interests of both parties. The jealousy which the latter have of Saving Banks, is rare and occasional, and very much confined to manufacturers of low education, and limited capitals. It is to be hoped that, among these conflicts and varieties of sentiment, the working classes will, at length, attain to a clear discernment of the truth; and come to understand that they who advocate the overthrow of legal charity, and the fearless commitment of human indigence to the resources and the sympathies of individuals, are indeed their best friends.

I may here add, that in the accounts which I obtained of various Saving Banks, by inquiring on the spot, I found that the habit of depositing was more with servants, and people in easy circumstances, than with labourers; in Worcester, Gloucester, Clapham, St. Giles, and St. George in London, Bury St. Edmunds, and Sheffield—that there were also very few deposits by the latter in Westham, Essex; or in Playford, Suffolk; or in Acton; or in Turvey, Bedfordshire; or in Bedlington, Northumberland—and that the most cheering statements on this subject were made at Portsmouth, Gosport, Spitalfields, Whitechapel in London, Coggeshall in Essex, Nottingham, Hull, and Leeds.

This, we admit, to be a very limited induction; yet a sound experimen-

mestic life, be other effects beyond the reach of
sight or of computation.   A thousand shifts and

---

tal impression may be arrived at on this subject, from the average of a few
cases, taken at random, in distant parts of the country, and from neighbourhoods which exhibit the widest possible dissimilarity in the pursuits and
circumstances of the people.

My friend Mr. Hale, of Spitalfields, who is well known in parliament for
his vigilant and sagacious observation of the habits of the poor, has frequently affirmed, of those who have once been paupers, and been restored again
to a state of sufficiency, in better times, that they almost never deposit in a
Saving Bank.

We are apt to be carried away by too magnificent a conception of the
good that has been done through the Saving Banks, when we read of the
very large sums that have been deposited.   In Worcester, for example, the
total amount of deposits in June, 1822, during the four preceding years, was
£84,279 8s. 4½d. ; but then the number of depositors was only 2184, and of
these there were not many mechanics, but principally servants, minors, and
those of small limited capital.

Still, however, it cannot be doubted, that when a process for the extinction of its pauperism shall have been instituted in any parish, a Saving
Bank might, under a right influence and management, become a highly popular institution.   We do not think, that such a process should be attempted
any where at the first, without a security for the present rights of all existing paupers, and a very full concurrence on the part of those householders who are not paupers, in an application to parliament against the legal
necessity of providing for new cases.   Now we cannot imagine the concurrence of a large majority, without a very sincere and zealous disposition in
some, to do their uttermost in promoting every expedient by which the
virtues and resources of the people might be rendered available to their
protection from all the evils which are apprehended to accrue on the abolition of pauperism.   And there is many a manageable parish in England,
where one or two influential men could give a decided impulse in favour of
a Provident Bank, operating as they would, in a community where the
very general consent that had been obtained for their deliverance from a
poor rate, would be the best pledge of a very general co-operation in behalf
of an institution that was meant to supply its place.   The consciousness of
the people, too, that all right to a public or parochial aliment, was now sur-
rendered, would be a powerful auxiliary on the side of all that tended to help
or to husband their own independent means.   And while we should look
in the general for a wholesome effect on the habit and expenditure of fami-

salutary practices would come in place of the dispensations of pauperism. There would soon be a visible abatement in the profligacy of the land;*

---

lies, we should also expect a greatly more prevalent direction of labourers to the Parish Saving Bank, as one of the most striking and sensible manifestations of the good that is to be effected by the rescinding of the law of pauperism.

The parish of Ruthwell lies a very few miles from the English border, and its population of 1285, consist chiefly of husbandmen and the servants of husbandmen, with a few country artificers. There the inducement to economy is unimpaired by poor rates, and all the demands of indigence are met by an expenditure of forty-three pounds a year; a sum made up of free-will offerings at the church door, and small donations from non-resident proprietors. Its minister, the Rev. Henry Duncan, who is the patriotic inventor of Saving Banks, has fully exemplified, in his own neighbourhood, the efficacy of these institutions. In the Ruthwell Parish Bank the amount deposited is a fair experiment of the habit and capability of the lower orders; for it is by them chiefly, if not altogether, that the deposits are made. The total amount, on the first of June, 1821, was £1927 8s. 11d. and the number of depositors, at that period, was 134. It were questioning the identity of our Nature all over the globe, to doubt the possibility of a similar exhibition in any parish of like condition and circumstances in England; and if a process could be devised for the gradual deliverance of such a parish from poor rates, there can be no doubt that, by a single individual of ascendant influence, the doings of the parochial vestry might be altogether replaced by the doings of a parochial bank. This were possible, though not, we think, indispensable; for, apart from every public and institutional organ, we do believe, that by the private and unseen effect of a repealed pauperism on the habit of families, the parish would be in a more soundly economic condition than before.

---

* We hold it of great importance, in estimating the probabilities of any eventual reformation among the people, to distinguish between the virtues of direct principle, and the virtues of necessity. The former require a change of character: the latter may only require a change of circumstances. To bring about the one, there must either be a process of conversion which is rare, or a process of education which is gradual. The other may be wrought almost instantaneously, by the pure force of a legal enactment. It is thus that we feel disposed to meet the objection which is often urged against the reformation of English pauperism, as if the inveteracy of English

and, if there be any truth or steadfastness in Nature, there can be no question that, if legal charity were put an end to, this would at length be fol-

---

habits, and their total dissimilarity to the habits and character of the peasantry in Scotland, formed an insuperable barrier in the way of all amendment. There are many such habits that may be regarded as the immediate fruit of external circumstances, and that would quickly and necessarily give way when the circumstances were altered; and these are altogether distinct from other habits that essentially depend on the moral or the religious principles of our nature.

In the former class of habits, I should reckon all those to which we are prompted at the first, and in which we are led to persevere afterwards by the urgent dictates of self-preservation. It is thus that, with the decline of pauperism, there would be an instantaneous growth of sobriety; and we are further confident of a very great abatement in that species of profligacy which has deluged the parishes of England with illegitimate children. There is nought which more strikes and appals the traveller who is employed in a moral or philanthropic survey of our land, than not the gradual, but really instant transition which takes place in regard to this habit, when he passes out from the unassessed parishes of Scotland. The mischief done by the allowances of pauperism, is not merely that they hold out to crime a refuge from destitution, but that they, in a certain measure, shield it from disgrace. A family visitation, that would otherwise be felt as an overwhelming calamity by all its members, falls lightly upon their feelings; and one of the greatest external securities to female virtue is demolished, when the culprit, protected by law from the need of bringing a bane and a burden upon her relatives, is thus protected from that which would give its keenest edge of bitterness to their execrations. There can be no doubt that, if you withdraw the epidemic bounty which is thus granted to vice, you would at least restrain its epidemic overgrowth, which is now so manifest throughout the parishes of England—that you would enlist the selfishness of parents on the side of the purity of their own offspring. The instant that it was felt to be more oppressive, would it also be felt more odious: and as an early effect of the proposed reformation, should we witness both a keener popular indignation against the betrayer of innocence, and a more vigilant guardianship among families. As it is, you have thwarted the moral and beneficent designs of Nature—you have expunged the distinction that it renders to virtue, because you have obliterated the shame and the stigma affixed by it to vice—you have annulled the sanctions by which it guards the line of demarcation between them.

lowed up by a better succedaneum, in the improved
habit and management of families.

But, secondly, the law of relative affection, in

Accordingly, in all parts of England, the shameless and abandoned profligacy of the lower orders is most deplorable. It is perhaps not saying too much to say, that the expense for illegitimate children forms about a tenth part of the whole expense of English pauperism. We do not deduct, however, the sums recovered from the fathers, our object not being to exhibit the pecuniary burden that is incurred, but, what is far more serious, the fearful relaxation of principle which it implies. Looking over the accounts that are before us at random, we find one year's expense of Sheffield, for this head of disbursements alone, to have been £1388 3s. 10d.; for Leeds, £1062 12s. 3d.; for Bedford, £141 2s.; for St. Mary's, Nottingham, £1043 14s. 2d.; for St. Mary le Bone, £2865 5s.; for Hulme £83 17s. 6d.; for Stockport, £764 5s. 6d.; for Manchester, £3378 5s. ½d.; for Salford, £761 7s. 2d.; for Liverpool, £2536 6s. 4d. But it may serve still more accurately to mark the dissolution of morals, that we present the number of such cases in certain parishes. In the parish of Stroud, Gloucestershire, whose population is 7097, there now reside sixty-seven mothers of illegitimate children, who are of an age or in circumstances to be still chargeable on a Poor Rate. In the In parish of St. Cuthbert, Wells, with a population of 3024, there are eighteen such mothers. In St. Mary's within Carlisle, a population of 9592, and twenty-eight mothers. In the parish of St. Cuthbert's Within, of Carlisle, there is a population of 5884, and also twenty-eight mothers of illegitimate children now on the parish. In Horsley, Gloucestershire, there is a population of 3565, and, at present, twenty-nine illegitimate children regularly provided for. In St. Mary le Bone, the number of these children on the parish is four hundred and sixty. But it were endless to enumerate examples: and perhaps the far most impressive evidence that could be given of the woful deterioration which the Poor Laws of England are now working on the character of its people, is to be gathered, not from the general statements of a political arithmetic on the subject, but from the individual displays that are afforded either in parish vestries, or in the domestic habitations of the peasantry; the unblushing avowals of women, and their insolent demands, and the triumph of an imaginary right over all the tremors and delicacies of remorse which may be witnessed at the one; and, in the other, the connivance of parents, and sisters, and natural guardians, at a prostitution now rendered creditable, because so legalized as, at least, to be rendered lucrative. Instances do occur, of females who have so many illegitimate

a natural state of things, we should imagine to be just of as powerful operation in England as in any other country of the world. We do not see how

---

children as to derive a competency from the positive allowance given for them by the parish.

There is a sensitive alarm sometimes expressed lest, on the abolition of legal charity, there should be no diminution of crime, while the unnatural mothers, deprived of their accustomed resource, might be tempted to relieve themselves by some dreadful perpetration. It might serve to quell this apprehension, and to prove how Nature hath provided so well for all such emergencies, as that she might safely be let alone, to consider the following plain but instructive narrative, from the parish of Gratney, contiguous to England, and only separated from it by a small stream. The Rev. Mr. Morgan, its minister, writes me, that " To females who bring illegitimate children into the world we give nothing. They are left entirely to their own resources. It is, however, a remarkable fact, that children of this description with us are more tenderly brought up, better educated, and, of course, more respectable, and more useful members of society, than illegitimates on the other side of the Sark, who, in a great many instances, are brought up solely at the expense of their parishes."

This comparison of parishes lying together in a state of juxtaposition, and differing only in regimen, proves with what fearlessness a natural economy might be attempted; not, we admit, in reference to cases which already exist, but certainly in reference to all new cases and new applications. The simple understanding that, in future, there was to be no legal allowance for illegitimate children in a parish, would lay an instantaneous check on the profligate habits of its people. The action of shame, and prudential feeling, and fear from displeased, because now injured and oppressed relatives, would be restored to its proper degree of intensity,—would be surely followed up by a diminution of the crime—and as to any appalling consequences that might be pictured forth on the event of crime breaking through all these restraints, for this too nature has so wisely and delicately balanced all the principles of the human constitution, that it is greatly better to trust her than to thwart and interfere with her. She hath provided, in the very affection of the guilty mother for her hapless child, a stronger guarantee for its safety and its interest, than is provided by the expedients of law. This is forcibly illustrated by the state of matters at Gratney, and might help to convince our statesmen how much of the wisdom of legislation lies in letting matters alone.

this can be denied, without mysticism. It cannot well be proved; for it worketh in secret, and does not flash on the public eye through the medium of philanthropic institutions. But it may very safely, we think, be presumed of this home principle, that when once free from disturbance, it will settle as deeply, and spread as diffusively through the families of England, as it is found, on an average, to do through the species at large. It is unfortunate for the character of its people, that the fruits of this universal instinct are not so conspicuous as are its aberrations. To meet with the former, we must explore the habitations of private life, and become familiar with their inmates. The latter are blazoned forth in the records of crime, or have a place in the registrations of parochial charity. The advertisements which daily meet our eye, of runaway husbands, or abandoned children, and those cases of aged parents who have been consigned, by their own offspring, to the cheerless atmosphere of a poor's house, mark not the genuine developments of nature in England, but those cruel deviations from it, to which its mistaken policy has given rise. There can be no doubt, that after this policy is reversed, nature will recover its supremacy. Those affections which guarantee a mutual aid in behalf of kinsfolk in every country of Europe, will again flow here in their wonted currency. The spectacle of venerable grandsires at the fireside of our cottage families, will become as frequent and familiar in this as in other lands :　And a man's own children will be to him the best pledges, that the evening of his days shall be spent under a roof of kindlier protection than any prison-house of charity can afford. Let pauperism be done away, and it will be nobly followed up by a resurrection of the domestic virtues. The national crime will disappear with the national temptation ; and England, when delivered therefrom, will prove herself to be as tender and true to Nature, as any other member of the great human family.*

---

* We have not met with a testimony more universal throughout the whole of England, than that which relates to the perfect unconcern wherewith the nearest kinsfolk abandon each other to a poor's house. In most parishes, there is a great preference on the part of paupers for a place on the out-pension list, though it be only a partial maintenance which is afforded, to an entire support within the walls of the workhouse. I was informed, however, at Bury in Lancashire, that some very old out-pensioners, who had been admitted as inmates with the families of their own children, often preferred the workhouse, because, on purpose to get altogether quit of them, their children made them uncomfortable. This is very much of a piece with the general depositions that are to be had every where on the subject. We have seen whole columns of Manchester, and other provincial newspapers, filled with advertisements of runaway fathers, and runaway husbands, in which they are described with all the particularity that is employed for the discovery of felons, and outlaws, and deserters from the army. And yet we are not to infer from this an utter negation of all the relative feelings, on the part of these desperadoes. They know that their wives and children will not be permitted to starve—and in by far the greater number of instances, had this been the alternative, they would have remained at home. They do not leave them destitute, for they leave them in possession of a right to subsistence. The affection which they have to their own kindred, is still a rooted principle in their bosoms ; and what might appear, at the first view, an act of unnatural cruelty, is often an act of collusion and good understanding between the fugitives and their families. The very prosecution by children, for a legal aliment in behalf of their aged parents, instead of being an unnatural surrender of duty on their part, is often urged

And, thirdly, who can doubt, from the known
generosity of the English character, that nought

---

forward by the same filial regard that would prompt them to the defence or
prosecution of any other legal interest which belonged to them. So that
however unkindly the influence of pauperism is on the duties and affections
of relationship, there is nothing exhibited in England which can lead us to
deny to its people the same instinctive virtues that are to be found throughout the other tribes and communities of our species—and we may be well
assured, of as good a constitutional basis there, as in any country of the
world, on which all the charities of home, all the sympathies of blood and
of kindred, might be reared.

We have already said, that the virtues of principle require to be nurtured
by a slow process of education, while the virtues of necessity are of as immediate growth as is the necessity itself. Now this property of immediate-
ness is not confined to those habits which are imperiously demanded by the
urgencies of self-preservation. It is true, that a man who would not be
lectured into an abstinence from intoxication, though subjected to the discipline of moral and religious advice for many years, might be starved into an
abstinence from intoxication in a single day. And it is conceivable, that
were a piece of money given to him, by which he might either purchase the
bread for which he was famishing, or the liquor to which his propensity, in
an ordinary state, is altogether ravenous and uncontrollable, he might deny
himself the latter, by an act of preference that led him to the former. But
it is just as conceivable, that he would make the very same sacrifice in behalf
of his infant child in the agonies of hunger before his eyes. The truth is,
that it might be as painful to the individual to deny a strong instinctive affection, as to deny a bodily appetite. And we have no hesitation in affirming
our belief, that under a law not for the dismissal of existing paupers, but for
the non-admissal of new ones, the habit of kindness among relatives would
grow in England, with the growing necessity for its exercise; and that much
of what should else be squandered in carelessness, or low dissipation,
would have the wholesome direction of a virtue impressed upon it.

It is but fair to add, that in Gloucester we met with one testimony to the
care and guardianship that relatives, even in humble life, continued to exert
for each other, a still stronger in Portsmouth, and a slight one in Turvey,
Bedfordshire. Mr. Hale, who is so singularly versant in the habitudes of
workmen, vouches for two distinct classes, with equally distinct characters,
and affirms, that he knows a number of instances, where the children of
those who have never become paupers, will make a conscience of upholding
their parents; and thus confer on them the most gratifying reward of their

but scope and opportunity are wanting, in order to evince both the force and the fruitfulness of that sympathy which neighbours in humble life have for each other. That this is greatly less apparent in England than in other countries, is altogether due to its establishments of legal charity. We are not to expect so prompt and sensitive a humanity among individuals in those parishes, where the cares and the offices of humanity have been devolved on a public administration. Nor will acquaintances be much more ready to stretch forth a helping hand to him who can present a claim of poverty at a court of supply, than to him who can present a claim of property at the bank, where a treasure of his own is deposited. Yet even as it is, that beautiful law of our nature, whereby a busy, spontaneous, and internal operation is up-

---

independence. " I have known," he writes, " very many instances, (among my own workmen and others) of the children of those who have never been paupers, making conscience of supporting their parents in old age—they will even submit to many hard and severe privations, (much more so than paupers will submit to) to maintain their resolution and their promises, that their parents never shall become paupers." On the other hand, it often happens, that even when parents are living under the same roof with their children, there is no community of aid or of interest betwixt them. Mr. Ranken from Bocking in Essex, writes, that " it is very frequent for young people to live under the same roof with aged parents, and leave them to be wholly provided for by the parish, while they are fully employed, and at good wages; although, until they have been able to provide for themselves, they, in common with the whole family, have been receiving parochial assistance. Such is the want of proper feeling, that the parents, as soon as the children have attained the age of manhood, in but few instances, under any difficulties, think of assisting them more; nor do the children, after they have been emancipated from their fathers, pay attention to the wants and difficulties of their aged parents."

held throughout every aggregate of human beings,
is only weakened in England, by the operation of
the poor rate, and not destroyed. Like the law of
relative affection, it is not capable of being verified from the records or the registers of a general
and combined philanthropy—and can only be
witnessed to its full extent, by those who are thoroughly conversant with the habits of the poor, and
have had much of close and frequent observation
among the intimacies of plebeian fellowship. There
is not one topic on which the higher orders of
England have so crude and unfurnished an apprehension, as on the power and alertness of mutual
sympathy among the working classes. This, in
some measure, arises from its being in part stifled
throughout the whole of their land, because in part
superseded by their public and parochial institutions. But still it may be abundantly recognised.
We have heard it more particularly affirmed, of those
who have no legal right in the town or parish of
their residence, yet who rather choose to remain,
than be removed to the place of their settlement.
These form a pretty numerous class in large
towns; and, among the other virtues of industry
and carefulness, and good management, which
are ascribed to them in a superior degree, have
we also heard of their mutual liberality as one
striking characteristic which belongs to them.
There can be no doubt, that this would break forth
again throughout the mass of English society, on
the abolition of pauperism; and that by the re-

vival of a great popular virtue, all the evils which are now apprehended of a great consequent dis-tress among the people, would be completely done away.*

---

* I was so fortunate as to meet with a very good illustration of the principle affirmed in the text, in the very region of pauperism. I first learned of it at the house of Mr. Gurney, in Westham, Essex, who, in con-junction with his sister, Mrs. Fry, is so honourably signalized by his bene-volent attention to the comfort of prisoners. He has politely answered my further inquiries on the subject, in the following words: "In our work-house we have found it needful to order deprivations, as a punishment for its refractory inmates; and, amongst others, we have ordered that such females should be debarred the use of tea, which they much value. It has been continually so ordered, but it has always been reported as wholly nu-gatory, as the companions of such cannot see their neighbours without it, during their own enjoyment, and have always, in consequence, shared their small pittance with the delinquent. I use the expression of 'small pit-tance,' because we *so* distribute what we look upon as a comfort, and not a necessary of life. The same may, with nearly equal truth, be related in re-spect of the *men,* in their allowance of meat."

It is likely enough, however, that a spirit of hostility to the discipline of the workhouse, might be as active a principle here, as sympathy with those on whom the deprivation had been laid. But no man familiar with humble life, can at all question the strength of that mutual sympathy which obtains among the members of it; in whom it operates with all the power of a con-stitutional feeling, and is not dependent on a slow process of culture. There is no doubt, that it is in readiness for immediate service, on the abolition of pauperism, though it may lie dormant, so long as the imagination lasts, that under the provisions and the cares of a legal charity, it is wholly uncalled for. It is by no means extinct. It is only in a state of imprisonment; superseded, for the time, into a sort of inaction, rather than stifled into utter and irrecoverable annihilation. It is not dead, but sleepeth; and the repeal of the law of pauperism would effectually awaken it. The charity of nature would recover her old vigilance and activity, on the removal of that arti-ficial charity which has so long kept her in abeyance. Next, perhaps, to the pain of hunger, is the pain of witnessing its agonies in another: and this, of itself, is a sure and sufficient guarantee for the dispensations of legal charity being replaced by timelier and better dispensations. There is not a neighbourhood where the horrors of extreme want would not be anticipated;

But this disposition of the lower orders to befriend each other, were of little avail, in this question, without the power. There must be a *materiel*, as well as a *morale*, to constitute them those effective almoners, who shall come in place of that legalized charity which we plead the extirpation of. On this point too, there is a world of incredulity to be met with;* and it is difficult to find

---

and with all the promptitude of any other virtue of necessity, would the instinctive compassion of our nature spring up at the moment, with the occasion of its exercise. We believe, that even though the present allowances of pauperism were to be suddenly withdrawn, there would, to meet the instant distress, be a breaking forth upon it of our compassionate feelings, with somewhat of the force and recoil of elasticity; and much more are we confident, that were a simple interdict laid on its future allowances, the consequent rate of unrelieved want that might arise, from one year to another, would be met by a corresponding rate of perennial and unremitting supply, from the then liberated sympathies of our nature.

* As a specimen of this incredulity, we offer another extract from the interesting work of Mr. Davison on the Poor Laws.

" It is not fit that the poor should subscribe for the relief of one another. Pecuniary charity is not their duty; it is out of their province. Their own real wants forbid the exercise of it; and they have not the feeling which such a sacrifice requires. In no way are they made for it. And to try to make them generous, when they have more necessary, and more attainable virtues to acquire, is to misplace the attention we bestow upon them. Benefit Societies, among the lower classes of the poor, are vicious on this account. These Societies profess to offer a mutual guarantee against the calamities and contingencies of life, as well as its more extraordinary wants, out of a property too small to be exposed to the risk of other men's fortunes. The poor man's endeavours can hardly extend any further than his family. His capacity of feeling and exertion fills his little circle; more is too much for him."

A full arithmetical refutation of these statements is perhaps unattainable. The produce of those plebeian associations which have been instituted for religious objects, gives only a faint and distant approximation to it. There is a busy, though unseen circulation of aid, and sympathy, and service going

acceptance for that arithmetic which demonstrates the might and the efficacy of those humble offerings, which so amply compensate, by their number, for the smallness of each individually. The penny associations which have been instituted for objects of Christian beneficence, afford us a lesson as to the power and productiveness of littles. Even the sums deposited with Saving Banks and Benefit Societies point to the same conclusion. But perhaps the most impressive, though melancholy proof that can be given of a capability in humble life, greatly beyond all that is commonly imagined, may be gathered from the vast sums which are annually expended in those houses of public entertainment, that are only frequented by people of the labouring classes in society. We are most thoroughly aware, that the abolition of pauperism in England will never act by an instanta-

---

on throughout every vicinity where an aggregate of human beings is to be found. Its amount is great, because made up of offerings, which, though small, are manifold—of rills, which, though each of them scanty, are innumerable, and constantly flowing. We are aware that pauperism has laid a freezing arrest on this beautiful economy of nature: yet even where she has wrought the greatest mischief, she has still been unable to effect a total congelation. And many are the poorest districts, in the most crowded cities of our land, where yet more is rendered to human suffering by the internal operation of charity within themselves, than by all the liberalities which are imported from abroad. We do not at present contend, however, for any thing being done to call forth their subscriptions; but we do contend for nothing being done which shall deaden or reduce their sympathies. These, in fact, amid all the parade and speculation of a more ostensible philanthropy, form their best securities against the miseries of extreme indigence. Their means are greatly underrated; and their feelings and virtues still more ungenerously so.

neous charm on the moral habits of her peasantry. But, however slow it is that the virtues of principle come forth to their full and practical establishment in a land, yet this is not true of the virtues of necessity; for these latter do arise promptly and powerfully, to meet every new occasion that has been created for their exercise. There is no legislative enactment called for to compel such an attendance on funerals, as to secure that all the dead shall be buried; but at the expense often of much time and convenience, we find this habit to be sustained, as the established decency of every neighbourhood. That any who die should be permitted to remain without burial, would not be felt as a more intolerable nuisance, than that any who live should be permitted to starve without food. There would just be as painful a revolt against the one spectacle as the other; and without the artificial regulations of law, men would have found their way in England, just as they have done in all the other countries of the world, to the sure defence of every neighbourhood against a catastrophe so horrible. Were the law of pauperism suspended in any parish or county of England, a greater liberality, both among neighbours and kinsfolk, would instantly spring up as a kind of epidemic virtue there: just as we fear that a cold-blooded indifference to the comfort even of nearest relatives, might now be charged as the epidemic vice of England, in reference to the other nations of the world. But this is altogether a forced and unnatural appearance; and, were the causes of it removed, it is not to be doubted that England, on the strength of her people's native generosity, would nobly redeem the imputation that has been cast upon her.

The fourth and last counteractive against the evils that might be apprehended to ensue on the abolition of pauperism, is the freer and larger sympathy which would then be exercised by the rich in behalf of the poor. This we have placed last in the order of enumeration, because we deem it least in the order of importance. This, however, is a comparative estimate, on the soundness of which there might be the utmost diversity of opinion, while there can only be one as to the blasting effect of legal charity, on the warm and genial kindliness of nature. The door of the heart will ever remain shut against the loudest assaults of a legal or litigious applicant, while to the gentlest knock, from one who implores, but does not challenge, it will be sure to open. We have almost everywhere in England heard the farmers stigmatized as the most hard-hearted of men; and never, on the north of the Tweed, have we met with such a charge against them. But when once our farmers have become the administrators of a large compulsory poor rate in their parishes, then Nature, true to herself, in all quarters of the globe, will work the very callousness of feeling amongst us, that she is said to have done amongst our neighbours in the south. And yet, in spite of her freezing, artificial system, how manifold are the liberalities of England! Even under her present bondage to a perverse and unfortunate policy, what an earnest does she give of those still nobler liberalities that might be confidently looked for, after that policy had been done away! How exhaustless are her devices and her doings for the good of our species! and how prolific in all sorts and schemes of a benevolence which, it would appear, that the poor rate has not wholly superseded. There are subscriptions and philanthropic societies innumerable. There is not a parish of any great note or population in England without them; and they prove how surely we may count on a kind and copious descent of liberality, over all those places from which the dispensations of pauperism shall be withdrawn.*

---

* It were quite endless to enumerate the local benevolent associations that have been formed in the various parishes of England, and which are in constant operation, such as Lying-in, and Dorcas, and Destitute Sick, and Stranger's Friend Societies, and many other institutions of the sort, which at once demonstrate the inefficacy of legal charity, and the readiness of spontaneous charity to suit itself to all the varieties of human wretchedness. Another proof of the same two positions, is the toleration of a sort of secret and underhand begging in many parishes, and the affirmative answer, given almost everywhere, to the question, whether, after all, there is not much of private benevolence resorted to by the poor, and actually discharged upon them by the rich. So that when the inquiry is made, How is it possible that we can do in Scotland without a poor rate? the obvious reply is, that we do without a poor rate, just by those very expedients wherewith in England they meet all that want and distress which, even with a poor rate, they are not able to overtake; and which surplus of unprovided want is, in all probability, as great as the whole would have been, had no poor rate ever been instituted.

There are two inferences which may fairly be drawn from this contemplation. First, it would

---

It has been imagined by many, that a poor rate is particularly called for in those manufacturing towns where the people are so exposed to ebbs and alternations in their circumstances. We may afterwards try to demonstrate, in the course of a separate argument, on the relation that subsists between pauperism and the wages of labour, that the poor rate aggravates all the inequalities to which a manufacturing population are exposed. But meanwhile, it is instructive to perceive, that so far from a poor rate being a sufficient remedy against vicissitudes of this sort, there never occurs a season of distressed trade, and reduced wages, when the heavily assessed towns of England have not recourse to the very shifts that are practised in other places, for meeting the adversity of the times, and when the symptoms of distress are not, in every way, as flagrant and appalling as they are any where in Scotland. In the calamitous winter of 1816-17, subscriptions were resorted to all over England—and soup kitchens were kept in busy operation —and urgent appeals were made to individual benevolence—and, in a word, as much of helplessness, under their ordinary regimen for the poor, and as much the need of a supplemental and extraordinary effort, were felt in the very centre of pauperism, as in those towns of Scotland where the compulsory method had scarcely begun to be acted on, or was altogether unknown. To quote examples were altogether superfluous. The thing was about universal in great towns, and very general even in populous villages. So that, in reference to the fluctuations of trade, pauperism has been also tried and found wanting; and that country which has tasted longest of its dispensations is, in seasons of commercial embarrassment, also put upon its shifts, and is on a perfect level with other countries, as to its distresses and its temporary plans.

Now it must be quite obvious, that though the necessity should be as great for an additional effort, in such a season of extraordinary distress, yet that the ordinary burdens of pauperism must affect very sensibly both the means and the disposition of those on whom the effort and the sacrifices are laid. But the worst circumstance attendant on these extraordinary subscriptions, is that they leave behind them a permanent addition of ordinary pauperism. In places where there is no legal charity, they may leave no permanent depravation of habit behind them. After the last shilling is expended, the people are all remitted back again to their wonted independence; and not till the recurrence of a similar visitation, do they look for the supplies of charity from abroad. But the uniform experience of places where there is a compulsory provision is, that in every instance of a sub-

appear that England has not, by her expedient of
a poor rate, overtaken the whole field of human

---

scription made for the people, in bad times, there are so many thereby in-
ured to the habit of receiving, and who thus find a readier way to the supplies of ordinary pauperism; and that there cometh thence a distinct accession on the poor rate, from which even the return of prosperous times never
has the effect of altogether relieving them. So that nothing can be more
unsuitably assorted the one with the other, than occasional subscriptions
for seasons of extraordinary distress, and a regular pauperism at all seasons.
Wanting the latter, the former might with greater safety be raised more frequently and more abundantly, and so as to meet the varying circumstances
of the people: or, in other words, let there be no regular pauperism in a
manufacturing town, and fewer obstacles would exist to that peculiar
method which is generally resorted to, for meeting those vicissitudes in the
condition of the working classes, to which it is peculiarly liable.

I feel very grateful to that distinguished philanthropist, Mr. Hale, for his
permission to publish the subjoined narrative, relating to that magnificent
subscription which was raised in 1816, for behoof of the distressed families in
Spitalfields. The sum raised for this object amounted, I understand, to
somewhere about £30,000; and I have Mr. Hale's distinct testimony as
to its mischievous effect on the parish of Christ Church, which is one of the
Spitalfield parishes, in having left there a permanently increased pauperism.
The Committee of gentlemen who superintended the distribution of this
money were of the greatest respectability. There was a numerous attendance of them every morning, during a great part of the winter, as early as
eight o'clock. They were indefatigable in their exertions every day, devot-
ing almost their whole time to its duties. They were unremitting in their
investigations, from morning to night, to guard against cases of imposition.
And in these circumstances, therefore, it is a most instructive lesson, of the
vanity and perniciousness of all public charity for the relief of indigence, to
know, that much of this money was given away to unworthy objects—that
a great many of the applicants relieved were impostors—that many of
Mr. Hale's own workmen, earning from 15s. to 20s. per week, received
from this subscription, and that a great many of them had from 3s. to 4s.
a-week from the fund—that, when this was discovered, the workmen alleged, in their vindication, that to get from this fund was a general thing—
that discoveries like these induced the Committee at length to break up the
distribution—and that, at this period, they had a surplus left of about £7000.
A thousand pounds of this money were given to the " Spitalfields Soup
Society," and the remainder, at various periods, to the " Spitalfields Bene-

wretchedness. There is a mighty surplus of unrelieved want which remains to be provided for;

---

volent Society;" and the money has only been got through about a twelve-
month ago.

Now, from this important narrative we not only gather the fact, that
a subscription fixed many cases of permanent pauperism on the parish of
Christ Church, where the burden of it is still felt—but we may learn what
a world of delusion exists among the higher orders, in regard to the whole
habits and capabilities of the poor. It might lead them to suspect, that
after all there may be a great deal too much of machinery raised for the
purposes of public and proclaimed charity; and, more especially, that the
great national apparatus of a legalized pauperism, is, perhaps, a thing wholly
uncalled for. More especially does it demonstrate how easy it is for a great
general management to be led astray; and that the only way of proceeding
with judgment and efficacy in the administration of relief, is through the
medium of small independent jurisdictions. Were Spitalfields broken
down into moderate parishes, we venture to affirm, that each could, on its
own separate resources, uphold itself in comfort and independence through
every season of fluctuation; and that there is no insuperable obstacle even
there, in the way of committing the charity of law back again to the charity
of nature.

We have been much gratified with the testimony of one so soundly experimental as Mr. Hale, in favour of the local system, and of its power,
when once established and proceeded on, to resolve even the most difficult
cases in the much agitated problem of pauperism. I find, from a publication
of his about ten years ago, that he had then imbibed the very spirit of locality, and appreciated the importance of the principle in its application to
questions of police. I wish much that he could be prevailed upon either to
republish his pamphlet entitled, " Considerations on the Causes and Prevalence of Female Prostitution"—or, at least, that he would extend his
valuable remarks towards the conclusion, on the power of the existing parochial machinery in London; and so give his thoughts to the world, on this
part of the subject, in a separate form. It is highly creditable to the liberality
of Mr. Hale, that though himself a dissenter, he has abundantly recognized
the moral and economical benefits to which the territorial divisions of an
establishment are subservient. There are some of his brethren in the
north, who have manifested no small impatience and dislike towards this
principle in the tactics of philanthropy—and who have chosen to interpret
the explanation which has been given of it, into an affronting reflection
against themselves. It is the more refreshing, to witness in Mr. Hale so

and the charity of law has fallen so far short of her
undertaking, as to have left the same ample scope
for the charity of love, that we behold in other
countries where pauperism is unknown. This, if
any thing would, might open the eyes of our statesmen to the utter insufficiency of a legal provision;
and might demonstrate to their satisfaction, that
let pauperism stretch forth her allowances, and
widen her occupancy as she may, there will constantly, over and above the whole extent of her
operations, be as interminable an outfield as before
for the duties and the services of a gratuitous
philanthropy. The question is thus forced upon
us, What service has been rendered to humanity
by the poor rate? It has obtained for England no
discharge from the calls of a benevolence, which
might even have had a lighter task to perform,
had no such economy been instituted.

But, secondly, the task would not only have

---

thorough a practical devotion to it—and, while not a member of the church
of England, that nevertheless he goes hand in hand with the most zealous
of its functionaries, in working along with them at the established mechanism of one of its parishes.

I shall only add, that the testimony of Mr Hale, in regard to the effects
of the Spitalfields subscription on the ordinary pauperism, is corroborated
by Mr. James Holden, relieving overseer of the parish of St. Leonard,
Shoreditch, who states, that " when the relief by the subscription ceased;
a number of those who had been partakers of it, became paupers on the parish, who had not before applied for parochial relief," and that " he believes it
had the effect of increasing their pauperism."

It is also found in St. Giles, that these occasional subscriptions bring on
an increased pauperism, which they are never able afterwards to reduce.

been lighter, but there would have been greater ability and greater alacrity for the performance of it. It is unnecessary to expatiate on a topic so obvious, as that without a poor rate the means of benevolence would have been less exhausted. But what is of more importance, its motives would have been greatly more animating. As it is, benevolence meets with much to damp and to discourage her; and, more especially, in a certain hardness and unthankfulness among its objects, which it is the direct tendency of the reigning system to engender. That the good will of the one party be kept in vigorous play, it would require to be met by the gratitude of the other—but how often is this utterly put to flight among the people, by the shrewd imagination, that all which is done for them by the rich, is only done to lessen the burden of the poor rate—or, in other words, that what is rendered in the shape of kindness to them, is only to relieve themselves from the weight of their own legal obligations. This whole business of charity never will be put on its natural foundation, till the heterogeneous ingredient of right be altogether detached from it—till a distinct and intelligible line of demarcation be drawn between the two virtues of justice and humanity— and this is what the law of pauperism has done every thing to obliterate. While that law subsists, every nascent feeling of generosity on the one side, is in constant danger of being stifled by most galling and ungenerous suspicions on the other—and

not till the *right* of the poor to relief be taken
away, will the humanity of the rich be in fair circumstances for the development of all its fruit,
and of all its graciousness.

It is out of these various elements, then, that on
the abolition of pauperism, we would confidently
look for a sounder and happier state of the commonwealth. At first sight, it might appear that
were a legal provision swept away from the face of
English society, it would leave a fearful territory of
helpless and unrelieved misery behind it. But
there would first be a mighty abridgment upon
this territory, by the resurrection that would ensue of providential habits among the people: and
secondly, by the revival of their kindred or relative duties: and, thirdly, by the new excitement
that would be given to those mutual sympathies
which operate to a vast and unknown extent
throughout the mass of the community: and,
lastly, by the generosities of the affluent, who,
going forth spontaneously, with ampler means,
and on a field of charity now rendered more
manageable, by all the antecedent limitations,
would, at the same time, earn the reward, and be
upheld by the encouragements of charity, in the
gratitude of a people, then divested of legal jealousy, and of all that bitterness wherewith the
imagination of a rightful claim has tainted the
whole of this ministration.

And it would be wrong to conceive, that ere
there could be any sensible approach to such a

state of things, we must wait the tardy and laborious culture of many generations. The principles which guarantee a much quicker recovery of the nation to this state, are not instilled, however much they may be strengthened by a process of education—but rank with the strong and uncontrollable instincts of our nature. They are now, it is true, in part overborne by an artificial stress—but, on its simple removal, they will rapidly, and as by an elastic spring, assume a tone and vigour that shall give them instant efficiency. Even under the whole weight of those adverse and chilling influences, whereby the law of pauperism has so greatly enfeebled the antecedent laws of Nature in the human constitution, yet are the laws of self-preservation among individuals, and of sympathy among relatives and neighbours, still in manifest activity. They are cast down, but not destroyed—and when again set at liberty from their present unnatural bondage, they will replace all the dispensations of pauperism, with a tenfold blessing on the comfort and virtue of families.*

* Mr. Davison says well, that, " the actual progress of the harm, in contaminating the hearts and habits of our people, is, I am persuaded, very far short of all that overflowing measure of it which might have been let in upon us if it had not been powerfully resisted: and, if this persuasion be well founded, there is the firmer hope of our being able to retrieve ourselves, and make a successful turn, under those better energies, when they shall be more left to their own action, and disengaged from the counterpoise which has been hung upon them. The harm not yet produced, shows they have been strong at the bottom ; and it is, therefore, a most substantial encouragement. The soundness of the constitution has been tried by the malignity of the poison, which has not proved mortal to it. For that a great de-

It might seem somewhat ridiculous to hold a
lengthened and laborious argument—and that, for
the purpose of showing that the people of England have the same urgent appetite for the interest
and preservation of self with the rest of our species ; and that withal, there may be further detected in their hearts the same instinctive affection
for offspring and kinsfolk—the same prompt sympathy with the wants and sufferings of their fellow-
men. But, they are the parliament of England
who first set the example of this strange incredulity. That act of Elizabeth, which has been ex-
tolled as a monument of English feeling, and

---

gree of the bad influence of this system has not yet made its way among
our people, is, I think, most apparent. We have examples among our
lower classes, of sobriety, diligence, good conduct, and patient contented
labour; many cheerful, thriving, independent working families, though
they have been pitched upon the very edge of the precipice which the law
has cut away under their feet; and every such example is in derogation of
the natural tendency of the mistaken method in which they have been
treated. Perhaps, the sketch of our history is this : that a religious, free,
active, and enterprising people, have a depth and solidity of resources within
them, not easy to be exhausted. Even the poor laws have not exhausted
them. For had we not stood on some such ground of more than ordinary
strength ; had our people not had a conscience, a spirit, and a staple of honest feeling within them, to withhold them from accepting with unchecked
avidity, the corrupting overtures of eleemosynary maintenance, and to
qualify the partial and constrained acceptance of it to which they have yielded ; had they not had a sober religion continually recalling them to their
obvious duties; and a breed of character naturalized among them, by the
greater virtue and efficacy of many of our other constitutional laws themselves ; what is there in the nature of these parochial laws, as they are now
applied, which could have saved us from the degeneracy and degradation of
having become one great national poor-house, overrun with the infection
of a Spanish or Neapolitan leprosy of mendicancy?

" The evil, however, must be expected to be progressive, &c."

English wisdom, is a monument of the legislature's fears, that neither feeling nor wisdom were
to be found in the land. It is, in fact, the cruellest reproach which the government of a country
ever laid upon its subjects. It is an enactment
founded on a distrust of the national character—
or, an attempt to supplement by law, an apprehended deficiency in the personal, and the domestic, and the social virtues of Englishmen. And
never did an assembly of rulers make a more unfortunate aberration across the rightful boundaries
of the province which belongs to them. Never did
legislation more hurtfully usurp the prerogatives
of Nature, than when she stretched forth her
hand to raise a prop, by which she has pierced the
side of charity, and did that with an intent to foster, which has only served to destroy.

Before that we state, and attempt to justify our
own opinion of the best way by which a retracing
movement might be made, we shall shortly consider the two leading expedients—one of which has
been partially acted on; and the other of which
we shall advert to, not for the purpose of urging
its instantaneous adoption, but to prepare the way
for arguing those modifications upon it, which we
shall venture to recommend. The first of these
expedients is a more strict administration of the
law of pauperism—the second is the abolition of
it.

There has, of late, been a decided impulse felt,
in many parts of England, towards a more strict

administration of the law, founded both on the distress of the times, and on the unexampled height to which the expense of pauperism had arisen. And a very important facility has been rendered to this undertaking, by the Select Vestry Act, whereby the power of the justices, in summoning overseers to show cause why relief should not be granted, has been greatly limited or impeded—and the whole matter has been placed more absolutely than before under the discretion of the Parish vestry.* There are many towns and parishes in England, where this act has been proceeded on, and a good many more where of late paid and permanent overseers have been

---

* The act referred to in the text, is that of 59 Geo. 3. c. 12, and is better known by the name of Sturgess Bourne's act. England is much indebted to this enlightened senator, for the attention that he has bestowed on far the most interesting question in her domestic policy. He has, perhaps, done as much as human wisdom can possibly effectuate for arresting the mischief of a compulsory provision in behalf of indigence. But there would appear to be an inherent mischief in the very principle of such a provision, which baffles every expedient that falls short of extirpation. In the meantime, however, legislators must feel their way as they can, through the prejudice and the practical obstinacy that might still withstand the application of a radical cure—and so it is, that the parliamentary measure which has been devised and carried by any individual, might not be a fair exponent of his whole mind and principle on the subject to which it relates. The greater number of those philanthropists who restricted their endeavours, in the first instance, to the abolition of the Slave Trade, were, at heart, and from the very outset, the determined enemies of all slavery. It is natural to expect, that all palliatives and superficial treatments shall be put to the proof, ere the method of amputation is resorted to—and it does appear pretty evident, from a Report, drawn up with admirable judgment, of the Committee of 1817 on the Poor Laws, to the House of Commons, that the necessity is at length becoming obvious of a change far more systematic and fundamental than any which shall ever be achieved by a mere improvement in the way of administration.

employed, who soon acquire a habit and an experience that qualify them for the business of rigid
investigation. The expedients which have been
used either to reduce the claim of the applicant,
or to repel him altogether, are exceedingly various
—and certain it is, that under the energy of a far
more active and watchful regimen than wont to be
exercised, there has been a very marvellous reduction of expenditure in many parts of England.*

---

* We are not aware, whether the supplemental appendix to the Report
from the Select Committee on Poor Rate Returns, ordered by the House
of Commons to be printed 15th July, 1822, has yet been published. This
will exhibit the sum expended for the relief of the poor in every parish of
England, for each of the six years which follow the 25th of March, 1815;
and from it, therefore, we shall gather a precise estimate of the reductions
that have been accomplished in those places where select vestries, or assistant overseers, have been appointed. The immediate appearance of such
an authentic document as this, supersedes the necessity of any details that
may have been collected on the short and rapid survey of an individual. It
might, therefore, be enough to say, that very great reductions have been
made in St. Mary's Within, Carlisle, Liverpool, Manchester, and the township of Pilkington in its neighbourhood, Salford, Stockport, Birmingham,
Worcester, Minchinhampton, Wells, Westham in Essex, many of the
London parishes, and Nottingham. In general, the reduction has been
greatest in those towns or populous parishes, where there was the greatest
command of an agency for strict and careful management—and this has
proved available in many intances, where a select vestry has not been
adopted at all.

In St. Mary's Within, Carlisle, the expenditure of the year 1819-20, was
£3039 19s. 6d.; and in 1821-22, was £1436 1s. 11d. Its select vestry
was established in June, 1820. There must be a sum of from two to three
hundred pounds deducted for other expenses than those of mere pauperism ;
but this rather increases the proportion of the saving on that head of expenditure. At all events, the reduction in two years was considerably below the half of the cost for the poor in 1819-20.

In Manchester, the whole expenditure of the money raised, in name of
poor rate, was, in 1816-17, £66,525 18s. 6d. and, in 1821-22, was
£39,044 6s. ; but, of this latter sum, more than £15,000 was for other

In some instances, it has suddenly subsided to one third of what it was before—and in far the greater

---

purposes than those of pauperism: and should a similar deduction be made from the former sum, the expenditure, for the poor alone, has been reduced more than one half in Manchester, in the space of five years.

Mr. Marriot writes me, that in the township of Pilkington, of the parish of Prestwich, near Manchester, " the gross disbursements, under the poor rates, were from five to six thousand pounds; they are now reduced to about twelve hundred." This is one of the most remarkable cases that we have met, of a great reduction having been effected by a firm, yet mild, and friendly, and, on the whole, popular administration.

In Stockport, the whole expenditure, in 1816-17, was £11,377 12s. 1d. and in 1821-22, it was £5,446 4s. 9d.; and the cost, for the poor alone, has been nearly reduced to one third.

In Worcester, the reduction has been very great, as may be seen from the following statements. The highest sum paid by the Worcester house of industry to the out-poor, was in February 1817, when the weekly allowance was £83 11s. 4d. The lowest sum paid to the out-poor, in November, 1822, per week, was £20 2s. making a reduction of one fourth, in this department. And again, the amount of one week's maintenance for the poor, in May 1817, was £54 2s. 5d. and in November 1822, was £12 16s. 8d.; which is as great a reduction in this second department.

Mr. James Sherrin, the assistant overseer of the In parish of St. Cuthbert, in Wells, writes that the poor rate there has declined, in three years, from £1,820 to £900, and the expenditure from £1,830 to £795; being considerably more than a half.

In Minchinhampton, the number of inmates was very soon reduced from sixty to twenty-eight, and that, by unremitting exertion on the part of the overseer to get work out of doors for them.

In the parish of St. Peter, West Cheap, London, the expenditure has been reduced from £478 19s. 4d. in 1818, to £161 10s. ¾d. in 1822.

In St. Vedast, which is now under the same excellent management of Mr. Twinch, as the former, the rate has been reduced from 1s. 6d. to 9d. in the quarter. In 1815-16, the expenditure, for the poor alone, was £1022 1s. Mr. Twinch began to act as overseer the year thereafter, which was the one of heaviest expenditure all over England. Yet under him, the cost of the poor was reduced to £790 12s. 2d. and has since been gradually brought down to £566 16s. 10¼d. This is one of the small city parishes, and its population is only 398.

From the parish of Westham, Essex, Mr. Gurney writes, that " the rate

number of cases that were investigated by us, the
saving has been ascribed to the improved manage-

---

in 1818, for one whole year, was 8s. in the pound, amounting to £11,846, at which our expenditure may be reckoned, or very nearly so; and that, in the year 1821-22, the rate amounted to £5,818, with our expenditure equal; and that the reduction is mainly due to strict and judicious management."

The following is extracted from the last Report of the Select Vestry for that parish:—

" The Select Vestry having now finished the third year of their labours, and the new system having been fairly tried, the present seems a favourable occasion to point out some savings which have occurred under their management. In the year, ending Lady-day, 1819, the year previous to the appointment of the Select Vestry, (in April, 1819,) the payments made to the out-door poor amounted to..£4,652 0 9

In the year ending Lady-day, 1820, being the first of the
    Select Vestry, to.. 3,406 9 7
In the year ending Lady-day, 1821, being the second of the
    Select Vestry, to.. 2,988 2 10
And in the year ending Lady-day, 1822, being its third year, to 2,788 8 3
Making the expenditure of 1820 less than that of 1819, by............ 1,245 11 8
And that of 1821, less than it by.. 1,663 17 9
And that of 1822, less than it by.. 1,863 12 6
Making a saving, in three years of £4,773 1s. 11d. or £1,591 0s. 7d. per annum; and this in the department of out-door poor alone. And in the expenses of the workhouse establishment, a very great reduction has also taken place; for while, in 1818-19, its expenditure was £3,201 4s. in 1821-22, it is only £1,534 17s. 1d."

In the parish of Broadwater, in the county of Sussex, the expenditure on account of the poor, was, in 1817, £3,383 19s. 5d. At the end of this year, a Committee was appointed to assist the parish officers, and, under them, the expenditure has been so far reduced as to have amounted, in 1822, only to £1,641 8s. 2d.; and the rate in the pound was reduced from 14s. to 5s.

In the parish of St. Mary's, Nottingham, the occasional relief for the year 1819-20, amounted to £7,032 5s. 11d. and its permanent, to £2,242 9s. In the next year, the occasional was reduced to £4,240 12s. 1d. and the permanent to £1,763 7s. 6d. This is a great reduction in one year.

The following narrative not only presents us with the amount of the reduction effected, but also explains to us the means by which it was brought

ment more than to any improvement which may have taken place in the circumstances of the people.

---

about. It is the copy of a letter from the overseers of Walcot Parish, in reply to another from the parish of Chester, requesting a statement of the plan of economy they pursued, by which an actual saving was made of £4,025, in the year's expenditure, beginning March 25, 1820, and ending March 24, 1821. The extract is from a newspaper, and it may be right to state, that in a written account from that neighbourhood, the saving in one year is only represented to be £2,650 16s. 3½d.

" *Walcot Workhouse, Bath, April* 16, 1821.

" Gentlemen,—In answer to yours, requesting some information concerning our improvement in the management of the Poor for the last year, I have to inform you, that in the first place, when we came into the office of Overseers (March 25th, 1820), we began by closely adhering to the principles laid down in the Act 59 Geo. III. cap. 12. commonly called the Select Vestry Act; that is, strictly to inquire and " examine into the state and condition" of all our paupers—about 925 families, besides 186 bastard children, and 98 individuals in the poor house ; and this was done by our visiting them, every one at their own habitations, and inquiring into the means they possessed, and their ability to contribute to their own support; also by an inquiry in the neighbourhood, of those persons who were best acquainted with them and their circumstances ; then striking off the book all those who could support themselves without parochial assistance, and providing work for all who were in any way capable, but who complained they could not get it for themselves. Though the work was unproductive *(as work)* to the parish, it was the means of getting rid of numbers from the books. As we paid but low wages, the paupers soon got employment for themselves ; for we made it a rule never to give relief but by work (except in cases of sickness, extreme old age, and infancy); and on all new applications for relief, the same system of inquiry and work is pursued, and we find numberless instances of a downright refusal to do our work; and if accepted, two or three days is in general the longest time we have to employ them, before they quit and provide for themselves; we thereby prevent the increase of our pay list, which has been, and is now, decreasing every week, instead of increasing weekly, as it had done for years past. Next, with regard to bastard children, all cases where the reputed fathers were dead, or absconded (which last is generally the case with us), if the mother is in service, or other employ, we refuse her all assistance from the parish, considering it nothing less than giving a bounty from the poor rates (by giving her any

It was most gratifying to learn, that even after the many dismissals, and reductions of allowance,

---

thing) for the encouragement of prostitution, vice, and wickedness of every description, and laying contributions on the honest and industrious, for the support of the licentious and profligate. In cases where the mother is in bad circumstances, and, perhaps, the father also, and where he is absconded or is dead, we never allow more than 1s. or 1s. 6d. per week, and by calling on the Magistrates to commit some mothers (who have had two or three bastards) as lewd women, we have greatly reduced this head of expenditure; and although in some cases an order of filiation had been made on the reputed father to pay the overseers 2s. 6d. per week in relief of the parish, we very seldom pay the mother so large a sum, but place her on a level with other illegitimate mothers; we being determined never to give encouragement to prostitution. But the above system has not been carried into effect without the greatest opposition being made to it by the paupers, which was only overcome by the firmness and determined resolution of the overseers. In the beginning, we had almost insurmountable difficulties to encounter, as you may well imagine. The paupers left no manœuvre unpractised—no scheme untried—no art, which they were capable of, unattempted—no source unapplied to, which had the smallest chance of giving success to their object, namely, obtaining *money without working for it.* They had constant recourse to the select vestry, to the Magistrates, and to Ladies or Gentlemen, who, they thought, were humane, to get them to advocate their cause; this was followed day after day, and week after week; but the manner in which they were met by the select vestry, and the Magistrates in general, reflects the highest credit on the good sense, discernment, and determination of those Gentlemen to stop the progress of vice, prodigality, improvidence, and idleness. We have no doubt, that if the same system were pursued through the whole kingdom, the expenses of maintaining the poor would soon be reduced to a very inconsiderable sum, and the number of prisoners confined in our gaols lessened; for nothing tends more to encourage crime, than giving money to keep persons in idleness, while industry promotes health, competency, and happiness.

" Thus, Gentlemen, we have given you a brief outline of our plan of management, by which the most happy effects have been produced; and with pleasure we state, is still likely to operate to the general benefit of the parish, not only in the reduction of the poor rates, but in checking the growth of pauperism and crime.—I remain, Gentlemen, Yours, respectfully,

" (For J. Allen and J. Wilkinson, Overseers,)

"JOHN CURRY, Assistant Overseer."

which had taken place, the people were, to all sense, in as great comfort and sufficiency as before.   This

---

We shall conclude this lengthened detail by the following notices of what has been recently done in the parishes of Bingham and Southwell, in the county of Nottingham, extracted from a pamphlet on the management of their poor, by an overseer:—

" The money collected for, and expended in aid of the poor, in the parish of Bingham, in the year ending at Lady-day, 1818, was £1,206; and it had been considerably more in some preceding years.   This enormous expenditure among a population, ascertained at the last Census to amount to 1,574 persons, a considerable portion of whom are employed in agricultural pursuits, has, by judicious management, been lessened in the last year, 1821-22, to the sum of £400 1s. 9d.   The total expenditure for the preceding year, 1820-21, amounted to £495 10s. 4d.

" In the year 1817, there were fifteen bastard children supported entirely by the parish of Bingham, at a weekly expense of £1 14s. 6d.   Now, the sum of 2s. only, is paid weekly by the parish towards the support of two bastard children.

" No allowance from the parish of Bingham is now made to labourers in aid of wages.

" Should it be asked what effect this important reduction in the amount of the poor rates has had on the general appearance and conduct of the inhabitants of Bingham, I am authorized in stating, that here too, the result is precisely what accurate reasoning would have led us to expect.   The people appear to be more happy, more comfortable, more respectable, than they did, when such large sums were disposed among them, in the form of relief; their attendance at church is more regular; they are more industrious, orderly, and sober, than they were before; in short, the parties who have been the greatest, if not the only losers by the change, are the publicans, with whom a considerable portion of the money, which used to be paid to the poor by its parish, was spent.

" The means by which all this good has been accomplished at Bingham consisted chiefly in the provision of a poorhouse, into which all persons belonging to the parish, who could not, or who would not maintain themselves, were received and maintained: but then, the regulations which were formed for this poorhouse, or workhouse, by the magistrates, (conformably to the power given them by the 50th of Geo. III. c. 50.) were so strict; there were so few indulgences permitted in it, and so small a portion of those comforts, which but too frequently serve to lure people into such abodes, were found within its walls, that its inmates were generally glad to

is a fact pregnant with inference. Every negation of a claim, and every abridgment that is made

---

quit it, and return to a reliance on their own endeavours, after a very short stay; and they were, moreover, observed to exert themselves afterwards with redoubled energy, rather than expose themselves and their families to the danger of again encountering its privations and restraints.

" The amount of relief actually disbursed to the poor of Southwell was, for the year 1820-21, £2,069; its population being 3,051. The amount of relief disbursed in the year just ended, at Lady-day, 1822, has only been £1,311.

" In cases of bastardy, wherever the parish is actually put to expense, by the parents not maintaining their illegitimate offspring, lists of the father's and mother's names are publicly exhibited, and showing the sum that each is in arrear to the parish. On every second offence, the overseers apply for the committal of the mother to the house of correction; and even for a first offence, if it be attended by circumstances glaringly offensive.

" A residence within the walls of the workhouse at Southwell, is now regarded as an evil by the lower orders; and they will speedily find that the readiest, indeed the only way, to avoid this evil, will be for them to become industrious, sober, and economical."

Besides these, there are numerous testimonies to the effect of an energetic administration all over England. Most of the select vestries which have been formed, have entered upon their duties with a spirit, and been rewarded with a success, that for a time has suspended the desire of all further reformation. Those who have long been accustomed to a yoke, will, on the removal even of a small part of its weight, feel an ease and a deliverance, that might serve to reconcile them to the existing laws, and lead them to look no further than to a right and vigorous administration of them. Accordingly, it is not to be disguised, that, to the question, Whether the reformation wrought by select vestries, and permanent overseers, had lessened their desire of a still more radical reformation, and served to reconcile them to the existing laws? the reply was very frequently an affirmative one. And we instance this more particularly of the following places, where, in the triumphs of their recent success, and the confidence of still greater achievements in future, there was a decided conviction, on the part of able and intelligent men, that no change in the law of pauperism was requisite:— Kendal; Liverpool; Bury in Lancashire; township of Pilkington; Salford; Birmingham; Leamington; Wells; St. Peter, Westcheap, London; and Sheffield.

on a former allowance, is, in fact, a commitment
of the people back again, either in whole, or in

On the other hand, an utter hopelessness of any permanent good under
the present system, or, at least a desire for its radical abolition, was expressed in Darlaston, Gloucester, Bristol, Portsmouth, Mary le Bone, Clapham, Westham in Essex, and generally, though not universally, in the agricultural parishes.

To Christopher Wilson, Esq. of Abbothall, near Kendal, I have been
much indebted for the valuable facts and suggestions wherewith he has furnished me upon this subject. The expedient of a select vestry has been
carried into beneficial effect; even in some of the smallest country townships
of that extensive parish. And in reply to the apprehensions which I expressed, lest in defect of a good and vigorous agency, the measure would be
altogether fruitless in the agricultural districts, he writes, that " in his
opinion the country townships will be better managed than the others; because, there the select vestry will nearly be permanently composed of the
same individuals, some of whom born in the township, and occupying
their own lands, will be intimately acquainted, even from their infancy, with
the character, conduct, and habits of almost all those who make application
to them. Whilst the probability is, that in large towns the select vestry
will be changed annually, and the habits of the applicants, in a dense population, cannot be so well known.

" The wisdom of the people of Scotland in rejecting all legal interference
towards the maintenance of their poor, cannot be sufficiently admired, when
we see the misery resulting from such provisions enacted in this country.
May we copy your example by retracing our steps. The first step has been
taken by the legislature, by removing (through the select vestry act) the
interference of the magistrates."

It is our part respectfully to wait the evolutions of time and of experience
upon this subject—though we still feel strongly persuaded that by no device
and no modification whatever, the mischief which lies in the very principle
or system of a legal charity, can be effectually stemmed. The right of
maintenance from a public and compulsory fund, will be sure to create a
pressure of demand upon that fund, and a certan degree of resistance must
ever be held up for the purpose of causing it to recede, or even of keeping
it stationary. Now, our fear is, that the requisite energy for this is not to
be found in all places, nor that we can count upon its continuance in all
times. It may subsist with the impulse of the occasion which called it
forth. And though both in towns, where an agency is to be had, and even
in rural districts, where some individual of power and of patriotism happens

part, to the antecedent resources of nature, whether these resources should lie in their own thrift and industry, or in the kindness of relatives and neighbours towards them. It is of no consequence to the reasoning, what the instrument has been by which they have been displaced from the region of pauperism, and either their entire or partial support has been devolved on capabilities which exist elsewhere. It may have been an obstinate refusal on the part of the vestry.* Or it may have been a decision of theirs, founded on a strict investigation, that may have led to the discovery of means of which they had not been previously aware. Or it may have been the offer of work, which the applicant disliked.† Or it may have been the threat

to come forward, we may have the guarantees for a strict and efficient administration, yet do we much apprehend, that in reference to the whole empire, there will be found, after perhaps a slight temporary reflux in the amount of pauperism, as oppressive a load of it as before on the resources of the country, and fully as injurious a blight along with it on the happiness and virtue of families.

* It of course often happens in the higgling that takes place between a pauper and the vestry, or even between a pauper and the justices, that the refusal is altogether arbitrary, a determined commitment of him back again to his own resources, without any clear or specific apprehension of what these resources are. We have been credibly informed, that of late, when young men without employment, have applied for relief to magistrates of the western division of the county of Suffolk, they have refused to succour them, telling them that in times like these, they must provide for themselves. They have gone away in consequence, and when thus put upon their own shifts, did not find it necessary to repeat the application.

† It was so, the reader will perceive, in Bingham and Southwell; and it is so in many parts of England. The workhouse is often employed as a scarecrow, by which to distance or to deter applications. Is this fair treatment

of an exposure, that he would have been ashamed
of. Still the conclusion which may be drawn from

---

of a people? first, to instil into them the imagination of a right to subsistence, and then to counteract this by associating terror or disgrace with the
prosecution of it? Does not the very necessity of thus assimilating an
eleemosynary house to a Bridewell, prove that there is a fundamental error
in the whole system? Would it not be better, if instead of first giving a
wrong impulse, and then devising a force of resistance by which to neutralise it, that both the one and the other were dispensed with? Or, in other
words, that instead of first granting a right, and then guarding against it
by the severities of a prison discipline, that both the grant and the guard
were withdrawn; or, in other words, that the legislature would disencum-
ber the land at once from the invasion which itself hath made, and the defence which itself hath provided.

We recommend the following passage from Mr. Davison upon this subject, to the attention of our readers:—" I know that many persons consider
the terror of the workhouse to be a salutary check upon the poor; and are
not unwilling to press the alternative upon them of receiving their subsistence
in such an asylum, or of receiving nothing. The degradation of the asylum is to deter the approach to it. The hardship of it is to be the security
they would keep in hand against importunate claims. There is a certain
policy, no doubt, in this virtual correction of the wide and excessive en-
gagement of the law to take care of every body. And whoever considers
the growth of heavy demands upon the parish, to be wholly independent
of the constitution of the law, and believes it is to be ascribed solely to the
misconduct or the misfortune of the applicants themselves, neither originat-
ing in the public system, nor encouraged by it, he may vindicate the policy
on grounds of justice as well as expediency. But another who thinks that
the public system itself is, in some measure, a source of the evil which is
subsequently to be checked by such intimidation, must consider the law
as visiting its own mistake upon those whom it has misled, when it first
makes a promise of relief, and then tenders the relief in such a form as may
forbid the acceptance of it. For my own part, believing as I do, that the
Poor Laws themselves (in their practice, however, much more than by their
original enactment) have actually favoured the growth of pauperism, and
that they have loosened the motives of frugality, sober labour, and personal exertion in the country, I derive no satisfaction from the sight of those
equivocal establishments, intended to play off a double meaning of invita-
tion and repulse, of protection and abandonment; but would much rather
see the laws gradually retract the erroneous principle upon which they have
proceeded, than pretend to make it good in so exceptionable a manner."

a great and sudden contraction of the pauperism, in those places where a strict management has been entered upon, remains unaffected—and more especially, if there be the same visible aspect of sufficiency as before. There was much of the former pauperism wholly uncalled for. The sufficiency of the natural resources had been underrated, and there had been a delusion as to the need of a sup-

---

Nevertheless the Bingham experiment is a highly instructive one. It proves, that if instead of counteracting the law of poor rate by the discipline of a workhouse, both the law and the workhouse had been swept away, at least two-thirds of the existing paupers would have found refuge in the sufficiency of their own proper resources, and only one-third remained to be provided for. We do not plead, however, for any such summary abolition as this, but only for the withdrawment of the legal right from all new applicants. And if only one-third would have been behoved to be provided for on the event of an immediate extinction of the poor rate, we may be sure that a greatly smaller number than these will become destitute under that gradual process of extinction which we recommend—fewer by all who in a natural economy of things, will have the foresight and the frugality of which a poor rate had bereft them—fewer by all who shall be cared for by relatives, that would else have abandoned them—and, at last, so few, as that individual benevolence shall be delighted to succour and sustain them.

It is right to add, that in many parts of England, workhouses are regarded as by far the most odious and intolerable part of the whole system—and that such is their actual management both in single and incorporated parishes, as to have brought down upon them, in not a few instances, the reprobation of the wise and the good. But the very tendency of these establishments to corruption, is of itself an argument against them as a specific for the distempers of pauperism.

In seasons of commercial distress, the utmost benefit has accrued from work held out to those who allege a want of employment. It has proved a test by which both to ascertain the honesty of the application, and to get rid of unworthy applicants. Subscriptions will ever be had for providing such work on emergencies like these, and much more after the country is emancipated from pauperism, than at present. The offer of work, instead of money, has been known to effect marvellous reductions in Liverpool, Manchester, Birmingham, Nottingham, and many other places.

ply from the resources of artificial pauperism. So that, in some cases, the expenditure was three times greater than it ought to have been—and the discovery of a delusion to such an extent, might well lead us to suspect that, perhaps, could all the channels of aid, and employment, and sympathy, be traced throughout the mass of society, with all those hostile influences by which public charity has done so much to close or to obstruct them, then it might be found, that there exists a still deeper and more subtle delusion than has yet been ascertained.

We will lay no disguise on the whole amount of our convictions upon this subject. Under a lax administration, it would appear that instances have occurred of an expenditure three times greater than was afterwards found to be necessary. Or, in other words, the dispensers of legal charity were so far misled as to overrate, in this proportion, the call which existed for it. But even under a strict administration of pauperism, and when there is no misleading of the dispensers at all, still there is a most grievous misleading both of the recipients, and of society at large. The very existence of a public charity has misled them. It misleads many annual thousands from their own economy, who otherwise would never have been reduced to a dependence on charity at all. It misleads parents and children, and remoter kindred, from the exercise of their relative duties. It misleads the benevolent, of all ranks, from that sympathy they else would have felt, and that liberality they else would have exercised. On the part of the dispensers, the discovery of their error has occasionally been the saving of two thirds to the legal charity—but the correction of that error on the part both of the poor and of the public, into which the very existence of a legal charity has blinded them, would greatly more than cover the remaining one-third. Or, in other words, the good of the wholesome re-action that must ensue on the abolition of pauperism, would greatly overpass all the apprehended evils—and were the legal charity for indigence utterly swept away, there would be less of suffering, as well as less of sin in our borders.

But, it may be asked, if, under the operation of existing acts, the cost of pauperism really admits of so great an alleviation, might not the whole evil of it be reduced in the same proportion? And ought we not to be satisfied with this, rather than hazard a radical change of system throughout the land?—and see what can be done with a good administration of the laws that we have, ere any further innovation shall be thought of?

The select vestry act has been proceeded upon only in 2145 instances. There has no such vestry been formed in about six-sevenths of the English parishes. The number of permanent overseers, too, is only 1979.* The truth is, that in the country,

* And it proves how slowly the formation of select vestries is making

it is extremely difficult to find materials for the formation of an efficient vestry—and in this way the benefit of the act has been very much confined to towns. Throughout the great majority of the land, the business of English pauperism is moving on in its wonted order—and there is as strong a practical sense of its oppressiveness in the kingdom at large, as at any former period. The agricultural interest, in particular, was never more heavily burdened with it than at this moment—and were the whole present poor rate of England translated into quartern loaves, or estimated according to the price of the necessaries of life, it would be found, that in no past season of our history, has so much of the effective wealth of the country been expended upon its pauperism.*

progress, that though the Act for them passed in 1819, and on the 25th of March 1820, 2006 parishes had constituted select vestries, yet through the whole of the succeeding year there was only the small fractional addition of 139 to this number. From a possible misunderstanding of the question which regarded permanent overseers, it is not clear whether their number increased or diminished during that year. Certain it is, that the formation of a select vestry has been attempted without success in many parishes—that in some it has been given up after it had been established for a few months—and that there is the apprehension in some more of a speedy dissolution. In Darlaston and Ilkestone they are laid aside—and it is found that in Bedlington the very feeling of the relief which has been effected has induced a sort of unconcern. They are apt to think that they have done enough—and, should they let down their posture of vigilance, matters may soon revert to their old condition again.

* The reduction that has taken place in distinct parishes, and some of the most striking instances of which we have already quoted, is generally to be estimated from 1817-1818, which was the year of greatest expenditure all over England. We find that, in particular cases, the cost of the

And there is reason to fear, that even in those parishes where a select vestry has been most successful, there may be a speedy recurrence to the same lax and careless style of administration as before. There were a vigour and a strenuousness at the first which may, perhaps, subside with the novelty of the undertaking. Even the very relief that has been achieved, might lead to a satisfaction and a repose, that would soon call back as great a host of applicants as ever—for it is in the very nature of pauperism, that, at all times, there is the pressure of a tendency from without, which will

---

pauperism was brought down to a sum three times less than its maximum. But while this proves how much may be done by a very strenuous administration, it is of further importance to know how little has been done by this over the whole country. Through England at large there has not been a decline by the fraction of an eighth part from its maximum expenditure on the poor rates—that of 1817-1818, having been £7,890,148, and that of 1820-21, £6,948,445.

In reference to the present state of the agricultural interest, the burden of the pauperism has increased greatly beyond the proportion of the means, and that too in parishes where it were possible to state the thing in such terms as to impress the belief of a great reduction. Mr. Morton of Pud-hill, in Gloucestershire, writes me, that " in 1811 the poor rate in Horsley, a parish in that county, was 12s. in the pound—(the nominal rent in Horsley was then two-thirds of the actual or rack rent);—that in 1821 it was 7s.; and in 1822 it was 6s. in the pound. But the rack or real rent of the parishes, as well as of all the neighbourhood, being reduced at least one-third of what it was in 1811, and the rate in the parish-book standing the same, the 6s. in the pound paid in 1822 is on the rack or real rent, and not on a nominal rent as in 1811. The 12s. in the pound on the nominal rent of 1811, was in fact only 8s. in the pound on its real rent. So that the whole amount of the reduction estimated in money is only from 8s. to 6s. on the real rent. But further, the price of wheat in 1811 was 14s. per bushel, and in 1822 only 5s. Though the farmer, then, has only one-half of the money to pay for the poor that he had to pay in 1811, he has to pay more in wheat, and that in the proportion of 14 to 10.

instantly force admittance, so soon as there is the slightest relaxation from that vigilance, wherewith its approaches have been guarded.

The marvels which have been of late effected by a strict administration, have suspended, in some places, the desire that was at one time felt for a radical change of system in the public charity of England. But we do not think that this can last long, and have no doubt, that after various expedients have been tried and found wanting, the final result will be a stronger experimental conviction than ever, of something wrong in the principle as well as in the practice of the poor laws. There is, we believe, a possible rigour in the execution of them, by which, if put into operation, two-thirds of all the paupers now in the country, might be thrown back upon their own resources, and yet be landed in a state of as great comfort and sufficiency as, with their present allowances, they at present enjoy. This has been exemplified in some parishes, and we do imagine, that it might be exemplified throughout the vast majority of the land. But then this requisite degree of rigour will, in the first place, not be adopted in most parishes; and, secondly, in those parishes where under a strong temporary impulse it has been resorted to, and with great immediate success, it will not be persevered in. The very success will lull the administration into its old apathy. The pitch and the tension to which it has been wound up, will relax again.* The very humanity as well as indolence of managers, will gradually and insensi-

---

* It is not to be denied, however, that where there is a firm and consistent administration, the labour of it will come, in time, to be very much reduced, by the very hopelessness of success on the part of unworthy claimants. Lister Ellis, Esq. of Liverpool, who has conducted, for some time, the affairs of its pauperism with great energy and intelligence, tells me, that the whole attention which he now finds necessary, does not occupy more than two hours in the day.

And it is also true, that in those rare and occasional instances, where a gentleman of respectable station, and, withal, of humane, and conciliating, and kind manners, undertakes the labour of reforming the pauperism of a parish, he may not only at length reduce very much his personal trouble, but even earn a popularity, and a gratitude, from the objects of it.

Mr. Marriot, that active and intelligent magistrate, in the neighbourhood of the township of Pilkington, writes me, that " the extreme burden of the poor's rate then did bring forward very successful exertions on the part of the occupants, in the collection, as well as distribution of the rate." " The undertaking of retrenchment, and economical distribution, may, in the outset, have been attended with some degree of odium: at this time, I think, all parties are aware of the service that has been rendered to the ley-payers, as well as to the paupers. Mr. Weston, of Stand, has had a principal share of the merit, in the very great benefit his surrounding neighbours have experienced.

" In the years 1816 to 18, I had considerable trouble in attending to this part of duty. I acted a good deal in the capacity of superintendant overseer of the poor. I sat one day every week from ten till three, and sometimes near four o'clock; for Pilkington only, I have sometimes heard seventy pauper cases in a morning. I had a most cheering satisfaction in my labours: the poor were invariably respectful and thankful for a very moderate relief, and the superior inhabitants viewed my exertions in a manner most flattering to my feelings. At this time, I sit one morning in a month, and am seldom detained one hour by my duty."

We entreat that the reader will observe here:—First, how soon a consistent mode of treating the poor will lead them to accommodate their habits to the spirit of the system by which they are governed; and, if that be a spirit of retrenchment, how readily they learn to forbear their applications. And, secondly, how an economical administration may, at the same time, become a popular one, if conducted with a patient and obliging attention to the cases that are submitted to it.

bly lead them to admit of successive mitigations—
and nature, at length, tired out of that strenuousness which was assumed at the outset, will subside
into her old inertness. This has been the history
of many a philanthropic establishment, and more
especially, of many a parish workhouse. They
set out with amazing vigour and efficiency, but
at length relapse into the tame and ordinary style
that is averaged all over England. There must
ever be an equilibrium in pauperism between the
pressure of demand from without, and the force
of resistance from within. We hold it possible so
to increase that force as to throw back the pressure of at least two-thirds of the demand, which
has actually been yielded to. But we do not think
it probable, however, that such an increased force
of resistance will either be summoned into action
at the first, or upheld afterwards. And so soon as
it is again slackened to what it originally was, will

This experience of Mr. Marriot's is in perfect harmony with that of Mr.
Ashworth, of Turton, near Bolton, who affirms of the poor, that they are
very easily managed, if one treat them with civility, and *with a reason for it.*
It is very clear, that in the hands of intelligent men, and especially, of those
who add the influence of rank, to that of worth and talent, a great deal may
be done, *during the time* of their personal superintendence, to neutralize the
mischiefs of a system that is inherently and essentially vicious. It were
not to be wondered at, though the gentlemen now quoted, should all feel
inclined towards the side of the existing laws. But it must be recollected,
that it was the pressure of a heavy expenditure which first aroused these
various neighbourhoods to a more active management; and that, in many,
we fear, the most of instances, this management might almost insensibly
slip back again into a state of laxity, till the expenditure shall again accumulate, and the impulse be renewed as before.

the equilibrium be again adjusted by the re-admittance of as much pauperism as before.

But even though the force of resistance from within, was kept up in the utmost possible intensity—yet we cannot imagine a state of things more injurious to the virtue and peace of the commonwealth. Even though the discipline of a workhouse should at length be perfectly assimilated to the discipline of a gaol, we fear that like many other of the legal scarecrows which have been devised, its only reaction would be in working down the taste and character of the people to its own standard. In proportion as the law multiplied its severities, would pauperism acquire a stouter stomach for the digestion of them—and those regulations which at first might deter, will, at length, be got over, because of a now fiercer, and hardier, and more resolute population. We have, at all times, exceedingly doubted the policy of those expedients which are meant to operate *in terrorem*—and have ever thought of them as most fearfully hazardous experiments on the principle and feeling of the lower orders. They may repel some of those who are of a better and finer temperament than their neighbours ; but, in by far the greater number of instances, will they blunt the delicacies which are thus handled so rudely ; and the very instrument which they thought to lay hold of for driving applicants away, will vanish before their grasp. After a temporary subsidence of pauperism from this cause, there will be a reflux of it in its old force and abundance; and worse than the heavy expenditure which it brings back, shall we behold throughout the country a deteriorated *morale*, the hardfavoured aspect of a more sullen and impracticable population.

This holds eminently and conspicuously true of one set of expedients—those by which pauperism is made as affronting as possible. Every thing has been tried this way, and often with great temporary, but never we believe with permanent success. It is indeed a most mischievous ordeal—and never fails ultimately to degrade the poor, without any saving to the wealthy. The badges, and the publication of names, and the posting of them in conspicuous places, may all work a recoil from pauperism for a time, but only to come back with accumulated force, and with a more sturdy and unmanageable character than before.* This, in

---

* At Liverpool, the names of the paupers in each district are posted in the streets, near or at the places where they lived. This method has been recently adopted, and Mr. Cropper, who informed me first of the prodigious reduction that had taken place in the expenditure, ascribes much of it to this publication of the names.

The following extract of a letter from Mr. Sherrin, the assistant overseer at Wells, blends with information on this point, some other articles of importance. We give it entire, as the plain testimony of a practical man, whose narrative affords a very fair specimen of English pauperism. It is a series of answers to the subjoined questions.

" 1st *Question.* Has not the poor rate of the In Parish declined, in five years, from £1800 to £900?

1st *Answer.* The Poor Rate has declined in five years from £1820 to £978, and the expenditure has declined from £1830 to £795. There was collected last year £183 more than was expended, which sum was turned over to the present overseers.

fact, is one of the many demonstrations how ticklish the ground is on which the law of pauperism

---

2d Q. Is not this more due to a proper attention, than to the improved circumstances of the people?

2d A. It certainly is: and in the five years past that I have filled the office of Assistant Overseer, I have had many difficulties to encounter: but, in the last three years, I have found great assistance in the select vestry that has been formed.

3d Q. Do you not think the people who have been dismissed from parochial relief are now better off, since they have been thrown upon their own industry?

3d A. They are: and much better labourers and mechanics.

4th Q. Was it not by the offer of work chiefly you got rid of them?

4th A. It was partly, and partly by publishing their names.

5th Q. Did not the more careless management of former overseers give rise to much drunkenness and dissipation among the paupers?

5th A. It did: and I have been creditably informed, that many of the paupers were in the habit of spending the Sabbath-day in drunkenness, and then sending their wives with a large cloak on to the vestry, for more pay; and they generally succeeded: the payers not then attending, and but seldom more than one overseer at the vestry-room, and he only serving for the year, would give them relief to get rid of their abusive tongues.

6th Q. Has not the publication of the names of paupers a good effect in chasing away many applications?

6th A. It has: and when we published their names at first, a great many who were receiving pay, but not deserving it, came to the pay-table, and gave it up, and threatened to bring an action against us if we ever put their names again in the list of paupers; although they stated before the publication, they could not do without parochial relief."

At Wells, too, the practice of publishing the names is of very recent adoption, and is still of efficacy. But it had been tried earlier in other parts of the country, and is now, I understand, given up. I have now a paper before me, printed by order of the vestry, and containing the names of the poor belonging to the parish of Minchinhampton, in the county of Gloucester, with the sums by which they have been relieved, from March 25, 1817, to March 25, 1818, exclusive of house rents. The cases of illegitimate children are expressly specified—and at the head of the catalogue there is put down the following: " Whoever may see any of the persons in this list living idly, when work may be had, or drinking in public-houses, is requested to inform the overseer, who will report to the magistrates the

hath placed the whole of English society. It, in fact, may be regarded as a compound of temptations on the one hand, and of severities on the other; and with the latter it has awkwardly attempted to neutralize the mischief of the former. The practical effect of the whole has been to form two distinct classes or characters of population, which stand more widely and remotely contrasted in England, than they do, we believe, in any other country of Europe. The one is a pure, and a noble, and a high-minded class, who, of course, would be revolted by the severities of pauperism. The other yield to her temptations, and, by weathering the brunt of her severities, their meanness and corruption have only been rendered more inveterate. The spirit of education and of moral enterprise that is now abroad in England, must extend the one class. But while the law of pauperism continues, the other class too must increase and multiply. They are the in-field gipsies of the land; and they transmit their habit to their descendants; and this is the reason why pauperism is so apt to fix, as if by a hereditary settlement, in families. There is thus a mass of corruption, that never will be got rid of but with the extinction of

---

names of the publicans who harbour them; or who suffer this paper to be defaced or torn down, without applying for another, or who refuse to put it up in their kitchens."

We have since heard from the neighbourhood that this is not now attended to. And the overseer of Horsley, a contiguous parish, informs me, " that the publishing of the names had a great effect at first, but they soon became dead to it."

this boasted charity by law. Until a blow be given to the root of the mischief, it will be found, in the long run, that there is a noxiousness in its antidotes, as well as in its bane. Its severities, in fact, are alike hurtful with its temptations. It is not by playing the one against the other, that any substantial or abiding reformation will be gained. There must be a way devised by which to cancel both.*

---

* We have little doubt that ultimately this expedient will not lessen the expense of pauperism; while this serious addition will be added to its other mischiefs—that of being landed in a more hard-favoured population than before.

In a recent conversation with Baron de Stael, who appears to inherit the talent of his mother for observing the features and the discriminations of national character, we were much struck by the remark, that no where in Europe did he ever witness a people where the extremes of vice and virtue, of profligacy and good principle, stood out in bolder or more prominent relief than in England. Such a chasm in the scale of character is certainly not at all discernible to the north of the Tweed, where the gradation is filled up between the opposite extremes, and the extremes themselves not stretching far in either direction, leave a sort of decent and uniform mediocrity for the general habits of our Scottish population.

This may explain the reason why such contradictory answers are given by different individuals, to the question that relates to the improvement or decline of character among the people. From justices of the peace we should expect, and have gotten, an altogether opposite reply to that which is given by clergy or Sabbath school teachers. They come into contact with the two opposite species of character. At Stockport we had most distinct testimonies to the fact of pauperism settling in particular families; and in every place where the activities of Christian and philanthropic zeal are most abundant, may we recognise a marked separation of two classes in the widest possible diversity from each other. Mr. Lowe of Darlaston writes, that "here, more than in most places, are to be seen two entirely distinct classes of population, rendered so among the adults partly by the cause above pointed out, but principally by the influence of the Gospel; the reception or rejection of which divides my population into professors and

Still the fact of so great a retrenchment in the
expenditure of certain parishes, goes far to en-
lighten the question of pauperism. If the applicant for relief shall swear an inability for his own
maintenance, the burden of the refutation of his
plea lies upon the parish—and such often is the
difficulty of the proof, that, rather than undergo
it, his claim is admitted without the due investigation. The severities of a stricter administration
bring this matter more closely to the test—and accordingly we have seen, that, as the fruit of inquiry and discipline, a parish has sometimes been relieved of two-thirds of its expenditure, or the
pauperism has shrunk into one-third of its original
dimensions. But, under a gratuitous system of relief, the net amount of the distress would have
lain within still narrower limits. Much of it would
have been anticipated by the higher economy of
the people themselves—and much of it been met
by a higher sense of relative duty among the families of the land. There is not a parish, where the
remainder of unprovided want would not have
found an ampler and a far kindlier asylum in the
charity of good will, than it now finds in the charity of law. Indigence would not have been treated as a crime—nor humanity been so strangely
transformed out of its proper and original charac-

---

profane, with very little intermixture indeed of the devout or pharisaical.
But the distinction is especially observable among the rising generation, to
which, if I mistake not, your inquiry especially relates, and is the effect of
the introduction of general education."

ter. Each of its ministrations would have helped to sweeten the whole breath of society, and to cement more firmly together the materials of which its fabric is composed—instead of being so conducted, as to widen every year the disruption that now obtains between the higher and lower classes of the commonwealth.

Believing then, as we do, that no general or abiding good will ever be effectuated by a stricter administration of the law of pauperism, we feel our decided preference to be for the gradual abolition of it. We have no doubt, that greatly less of poverty would be created in the absence of a compulsory provision, than that which now comes forward and pleads a right and an interest therein. And we have as little doubt, that all the unavoidable or genuine poverty which might then be found, would be more fully, and far more gratefully met by spontaneous charity, than it now is by a legal dispensation. We even think, though we are very far from desiring it, that though a present and sudden arrest were laid on all the existing allowances of pauperism, there would be no instances of starvation throughout all our borders—but that, on this sudden transition to a natural state of things, nature would evince the strength and the promptitude of those better securities, which she herself hath provided against all the extremes of human wretchedness. But we again repeat, that confident as we feel in the sufficiency of nature, this is not the way in which we should

like that sufficiency to be proved—and that, however desirable the transition to her better economy
may be, it is not *per saltum*, but by successive
steps that the transition ought to be made. It is
our firm conviction, that England may thus be
made speedily to emerge from her present state
of pauperism; and that after its last vestiges have
disappeared, she will bear upon her surface a better and a happier people than before. The greatness of this result has led many to assign a spectral
or visionary character to the whole argument.
Yet surely it is not impossible, both that a result
may be great, and that there may be a smooth
and practicable avenue which leads to it.

It is only to mitigate the apprehension of serious
evils which might ensue, even on a gradual abolition of pauperism, that we affirm our belief of
human society being so well founded on its own
native and essential principles, as that, without any
appalling calamity, it were able to stand the shock
of an instantaneous abolition. And we rest this
affirmation on an experience which has been recently verified, and is still in process of verification all over England. By the Act of the 59th of
Geo. III. c. 12. which was passed only in March,
1819, power was given to the overseers of parishes
to follow up each application from a native of Ireland or Scotland, by the removal of him to his
own country. This power has been very extensively acted on. But the way in which it has

operated, is, that the great majority of Irish who had been in the habit of receiving parish allowance, on perceiving that each new application was followed up by a removal, simply ceased to apply, and remaining where they were, betook themselves forthwith to a dependence on their own shifts and resources. This act empowering their removal, either on their abiding, or on their proposing to become paupers, was virtually, in reference to them, an instantaneous abolition of pauperism. And yet, did a very small fraction of them indeed consent to be removed—but the interesting fact is, that, generally speaking, of the vast majority who remained, and who had been suddenly dismissed from their wonted parish allowance, there was the same aspect of comfort and sufficiency among them as before. They contrived to do without it, and, to all appearance, did as well. They were thrown, and that with a sudden hand, upon their own expedients—and these availed them for all of which they had been bereft. We doubt not, that all the four counteractives against the mischief of a repealed pauperism were pressed into the service on this occasion, and that these discarded Irish drew more from their own industry, and from the aid of relatives, and from the sympathy of acquaintances, and, lastly, from the liberalities of the affluent, than they else would have done. At all events, they have found their compensation—and so most certainly would English-born paupers too, if the same bold experiment were made upon them.*

---

* This remarkable fact with regard to Irish paupers first met us at Manchester, where the weekly amount of relief rendered to their families, at the beginning of 1817, was £275 13s. 6d.—and through the year ending March 25, 1822, was only £17 10s. 1d. Though under no legal obligation to aid or to maintain any Irish, yet they do from humanity still expend upon them about five hundred pounds a year. At one time the number of Irish upon their poor fund nearly approached to one-half of the whole. Very few of them were relieved—and of these a great part returned, while the great bulk of them remained, and are not sensibly worse off than before.

From Stockport I received, by the kindness of Mr. Marsland, who is a magistrate there, the following distinct statement.—" The number of Irish families chargeable to the township of Stockport, at the time of passing the Select Vestry Act, (March 1819,) was 53, only 5 of which were passed to Ireland; the remainder were willing to maintain themselves rather than be removed."

Mr. Hale of Spitalfields writes, that " there are many Irish paupers since the last act for facilitating their removal, fallen off from parochial aid, and who still remain with us. And there is to all appearance as much sufficiency among them as before. In this parish, (Christ Church, Spitalfields,) when the act was first passed, we sent home from five to six every week; and now we do not pass home an Irishman once in two months. Before the last act, our average of casual Irish paupers was from twenty to thirty in a week; and now we do not relieve above two in a month—and yet we have as many Irish constantly residing in the parish, and they are in more comfort, because they are now more economical. The parishes of Whitechapel, St. George in the East, and All Saints, Poplar, being near to the side of the Thames, have by far the greater number of Irish. Neither of the above-mentioned parishes have now so many Irish who apply for relief, or to be passed home, as they had when the act was first passed, but still they have as many Irish residing among them."

It should be observed, that the Irish who are passed now, are not, in general, those who at one time were on the lists of regular pauperism, but those who having occasion to travel back again to their own country, take this method of having their expense paid. They are aware that an application for relief will be followed by a removal—and it is the removal, and not the relief, which they want. It is thus that they have learned to serve themselves of the act. For instance, from the united parishes of St. George and St. Giles, London, they had to remove 250 Irish families upon

Yet we recommend no such experiment. We
only would draw from it the benefit of an *argu-*

---

one occasion within ten days. They apply in hundreds, and especially when
returning home from the hay harvest.

Mr. Gurney of Westham, however, thinks that this new act has increased
the distress of the Irish in his particular parish, though it has certainly
checked their disposition for dissipation and excess.

The general testimony on this subject is very much at one with those
testimonies which relate to the English paupers whom a stricter administration had thrown back upon their own resources. On this last topic we
omitted the instance of Worcester, from which place William Sprigg, Esq.
writes, " that, as far as his observation goes, the poor ejected from parish
relief, and obliged to provide for themselves and families, are better off, and
appear more cheerful and comfortable."

The number of poor in its workhouse in November 1817 was 306—and
the number in it in August 1822 was 128.

It seems to have been little adverted to in Scotland, and, more especially, by those who have discovered an inclination for the establishment of
the English poor rate amongst us, that, after all, this has not proved so unfailing a specific for human want, as to have, in the least, superseded the
very processes of charity, which are resorted to in a country where poor
rate is unknown. We shall, therefore, before concluding these Notes,
lay before the reader a few of those articles of information, upon this subject, which happen to be within our reach.

In seasons of great distress, the voluntary efforts of charity are found to keep
pace with the increase of the assessment: so that, in many places, the begging
is at its highest where the poor rate is at its highest, and the year of heaviest
expenditure by the vestry is also the year of largest subscription in the parish.

We have no other vouchers beside us, than the notes of conversations on
the spot, for the facts, that, upon occasions of this sort, there have been
subscribed, in one year, at Leicester, the sum of about £2,000; at Bury,
in Lancashire, from £800 to £1,000; at Salford, £1,000; at Birmingham,
about £3,000; at Minchinhampton, upwards of £200; in the small parishes
of Rodborough, £50, and Woodchester, between £70 and £80; at Bristol,
from £2,000 to £3,000 ; at Wells, from £150 to £200; at Clapham, £300;
in St. George's, London, £2,000, beside a distinct subscription of £1,800,
for the united parishes of St. George and St. Giles; at Westham, £600 or
£700; at Bocking, £300; at Loughborough, £400; at Nottingham,
£1,000; at Leeds, from £2,000 to £3,000, chiefly for soup; and, at New-
castle, the same sum for employment to the poor.

mentum a fortiore in behalf of that gradual emancipation from pauperism, which we hold to be so

---

These are given roundly, because given at the time, on a mere general
remembrance. The one at Leicester is distinct from the great and peculiar
subscription that took place there. We bring these forward merely to show
the universality of gratuitous expedients for relief, in England, to meet that
surplus distress, which their boasted poor rate either could not, or did not
overtake. The sums now given are only for one year; but these efforts
are of frequent recurrence. It is remarkable that the largest subscription
of the kind at Portsea, was not connected with the great transition from
war to peace, but arose out of such necessities as were general all over the
neighbourhood. In Portsmouth, too, there has been a subscription of from
L.500 to L.600 ; and, without specifying them, they are common at Gosport,
Halstead, Mary le Bone, and Coggeshall, where I was told that the subscriptions are highest when the poor rate is highest.

In Kendal, they have had large additional subscriptions in particular
years. They preferred this to an increase of the rate, because it would
have been hard on the poorer of those who pay rate, and it gave an opportunity of larger charity to those whose wealth exceeded the measure of their
leviable property. In 1800-01, there was subscribed L.732 ; in 1809, L.400;
and in 1817, L.400. The subscription for the Lying-in charity is L.43, and
for the sick poor, by a female society, L.82. The latter attend to all, whether legal residents or not, and whether on the poor rate or not. In the
years of extraordinary subscription for indigence, there was also a great increase of poor rate, and a permanent increase of pauperism afterwards.

The information that follows is more precise, and is taken either from
written or printed documents which happen to be within our reach.

" In Leicester, the greatest subscription for the poor, in one year, was in
the winter of 1816-17, where a subscription was made. amounting to
L.2130 8s. 9d. of which the sum of L.763 8s. was raised by an Association
of ladies, and consisted of subscriptions from ladies alone, a committee of
whom distributed it in articles of clothing, I believe, entirely; the remaining L.1,367 0s. 9d. was distributed in provisions, the whole to all the
parishes in Leicester indiscriminately."

" The subscriptions made for the relief of the necessitous poor in Manchester, during the winter of 1816-17, amounted to the sum of
L.6810 10s. 7d."

" The largest sum ever raised in the town of Stockport, by voluntary subscriptions, is about L.500."

" There was a great deal of begging around us, (at Darlaston) when times

practicable, and which has succeeded with ourselves in a way that has greatly outstript our fond-

---

were at the worst, when the improvident part of the population of the most distressed parishes, were scattered over the adjoining country, to the distance of many miles."

" Amount of voluntary subscriptions for the relief of the poor in the city of Gloucester, the whole expended in the months of January, February, and March, 1817, £600; 1820, £832; 1821, for coals, £28; 1822, for coals, £24."

The following is an extract from the report of the Benevolent Society at Westham, from October 1819, to October 1821:—

" The poor of the parish, however, are so numerous that the committee have to lament their inability to afford relief in very many cases of urgent distress. They therefore feel compelled to press upon their benevolent neighbours the great advantage which would result from a more enlarged and general subscription, and the experience of four years enables them to speak with confidence of the beneficial tendency of the plan; which affords an opportunity to relieve the really necessitous, at the same time that it renders it more easy to detect imposition, and discourage the system of begging from door to door."

Where hath been the efficacy of a poor rate, if the call upon the benevolent remains as urgent, as we find in other places where no poor rate is in operation?

" The following are the particulars of the sums raised at Liverpool, by voluntary contribution, at two different periods, for the relief of the distresses of the poor. They were considered, in both instances, the result of a stagnation of trade, which threw a number of labourers and others out of employ, and of very severe weather.

" Total Receipts, between Dec. 1816, and March 1817			£8914	4	0
Expended in Mattresses, given after being first legibly inscribed, to prevent their mis-appropriation	£229	10	0		
In Potatoes and Herrings, given	1040	11	0		
Bread, do.	1720	1	0		
Between Jan. and Sept. loss by gifts, and sale of Soup below Cost price	5120	4	0		
Sundries	446	0	0		
			£8556	6	0
Balance			357	18	0

est anticipations. Let every existing pauper continue to be treated as he would have been though

---

" Receipts from Jan. 1820, to April, including Balance of
    former contributions..L.1841 4 4
    Expended from 21st Jan. to 28th April,
        1820, in Soup, sold at reduced prices........ L.629 5 3
    From 22d Jan. to 21st March 1821, in do.   220 9 2
    Invested in government Securities.............. 1000 0 0
                                —————— 1849 14 5
" In this period there were 280,366 quarts sold at $\frac{1}{2}$d. per quart."

The following evidence, that after all which the poor rate does, it still
leaves much to be done, (as much, we think, as if there had been no poor
rate,) is taken from an account of the Worcester Institution for the Relief
of the Poor, in the year 1819. There may also be seen from it, how the
poor rate may fail of its endeavours to overtake the growing distress of a
country, by at length, reaching its limit.

" At the close of the last war, the labouring poor of this country, in
many instances, totally deprived of their accustomed means of support, were
entirely dependent upon parochial relief for subsistence, whilst, in others,
they were either restricted to a small portion of work in the week, or their
wages were so materially reduced, as to render their utmost exertions inadequate to procure even a scanty supply of the cheapest necessaries of life:
hence then, poor rates progressively increased, till, in many places, they
became absolutely insupportable, and no longer commensurate to the demands upon them. Local subscriptions for the relief of the distressed
were resorted to, and the liberality of the public, on these occasions, was
eminently displayed; but as the manufacturers, and persons in the middle
walks of life, were themselves involved deeply in the difficulties of the times,
it was not to be expected that these resources would be sufficiently ample,
in parts where the calls for assistance were the most urgent.

" To meet this deficiency, a society was formed in London, open to the
bounty of the opulent in all parts of the kingdom, for the express purpose
of relieving the distresses of the poor in the manufacturing and commercial
districts: to these districts large sums were occasionally remitted, as their
necessities, on strict and judicious investigation, appeared to require."

At Worcester, it is said, that " the expectation of a large subscription
was not sanguine"—" the ordinary calls on the public being heavy." But
it is gratifying to find, that workmen who were in employ " vied with each
other in their contributions to the general fund; and the domestic servants

the present system had been left untouched—and
let all that is new in the improved system, be

---

in several families, who were themselves strangers to the prevailing distress,
manifested a commendable disposition to relieve those, who were the peculiar objects of commiseration. By these accumulated means, the committee
had the satisfaction to find the sum of L.2,333 13s. placed at their disposal."

Who does not see, on the one hand, that the poor rate, which formed by
far the heaviest of the ordinary calls, tended to restrain the subscription;
and, on the other, that in spite of poor rate, and therefore, much more in
its absence, there is a prompt and a powerful sympathy for all actual distress,
felt by workmen, and servants, and the very humblest of society, which, in
itself, is a better guarantee for a nation being conducted in safety, even through
the darkest seasons of vicissitude and suffering to which it may be exposed?

This sum was expended chiefly on Coals and Soup, the preparation of
which latter article will be deemed a curiosity in this part of the kingdom.

The following is the receipt for 1650 quarts, being the largest of the
daily distributions:—

	lbs.	oz.		lbs.	oz.
Beef	360	0	Parsnips	26	0
Pease	244	0	Salt	28	0
Scotch Barley	92	0	Pepper	2	0
Rice	56	0	Celery	24	0
Onions	56	0	Powdered Ginger	0	9
Leeks	22	0	Flour of Mustard	0	9
Carrots	26	0	Dried Mint	0	6

The Scottish reader will be somewhat surprised at the manifold ingredients of a composition dealt out in public charity, and, perhaps too, a little
amused with the statement, that " a more convincing proof of the estimation in which the soup was held by the poor, cannot be adduced, than the
circumstance mentioned in the report, that although the summer was considerably advanced, the demand for it was greater the last day than on any
preceding one."

Doubtless, the quality of the soup is perfectly sufficient to account for
the applications being so well kept up; but what we should fear is, that the
same thing may be observed of any gratuitous ministration whatever.

It is a great mistake, however, to suppose that the surplus of distress,
over and above what the poor rate provides for in England, is only occasional, and created, for short and recurring periods, by some political or
commercial change in the circumstances of the country. There is, in fact, a

made to bear exclusively on the new applicants. The former of course preserve their right of ap-

---

constant surplus, which we verily believe to be as large as the whole would have been without any legal charity at all. There is a certain portion of the face of English society taken up by pauperism—and, beyond its margin, there is a belt, and a very broad and extended one too, that is occupied by suffering still unrelieved—and this is the ground on which private and free benevolence has to expatiate. In other countries there is no space corresponding to that which exists within this margin; and there, too, there is unrelieved suffering. But we imagine, that there is not a well-habited, or a well-educated people in Europe, where the whole of this suffering put together is not less in the amount, than that which occupies the outfield of wretchedness, to which the provisions of the legal charity have not extended: or, in other words, the poor rate of England has left her more to do, and that, too, after abridging both her means and her inclination for the doing of it.

The following we deem a very interesting survey along the margin of pauperism, almost with one foot upon this margin, and another without it. It is when so employed, that one finds the best materials on which to judge of the real efficacy of a poor rate. The extract is taken from a pamphlet, by Mr. Rutter of Shaftesbury, entitled " A brief Sketch of the Poor, &c." of that town.

" As the recital of individual cases of distress would be tedious, and does not appear to be absolutely needful, we shall confine our description to the visits recently paid by some inhabitants of this town, to two large houses occupied by a number of poor families and individuals. The rent of both these houses is paid from the parish funds, and they may be considered, in some measure, as the existing poor houses.

" In one of these houses, No. 1. Is an upstairs room, inhabited by a woman eighty-four years of age, bed-ridden and almost blind, and who receives four shillings and sixpence per week from the parish. The general appearance of this room is wretched, and the floor and staircase are falling in. No. 2. A tolerably decent room, with good floor but bad ceiling, inhabited by a man and wife and one child, who receive no parish pay. No. 3. A double garret, not inhabited; window out, scarcely any flooring, and that little falling in; the rain comes in through the naked tiles, upon the inhabitants in the room below. No. 4. A small room upstairs, completely in ruins, not inhabited, but a nuisance to those below. No. 5. In a little better condition than most of the others, inhabited by a man and wife and five children, who receive no pay from the parish. No. 6. On the ground floor, a room tolerably comfortable, inhabited by a widow and two children,

plication to the vestry, and their right of appeal
to the magistrate till death.   It is with the latter

---

who receive no parish pay.   No. 7.   By far the most comfortable room in
the house, inhabited by a husband and wife and eight children.   No. 8.   A
miserable hole, with part of the floor falling into a common sewer, inhabited
by two women and a girl, who are nearly naked, and much emaciated; they
have no bedding, and only one blanket to cover them; their general state
was excessively wretched and revolting.

" On the whole, the appearance of the inhabitants was marked by extreme
poverty and filth, and the place has long been notorious as a scene of great
wickedness.   The premises were almost entirely untenantable and require
a thorough repair; and the yard was filthy beyond expression.

" The visit to the other house may be thus described.   We ascended an
insecure staircase, to a room, which for the sake of distinction we shall call
No. 1.   Inhabited by a man and wife and daughter, and two others, who were
much distressed for want of food and firing in the winter, but received no
parish pay.   We perceived three bedsteads in the same apartment, covered
with ragged great coats instead of blankets; the roof was open to the tiles,
and every part hung with cobwebs, and darkened by smoke.   This description was pretty fully borne out by our after observation, and would be correct if applied to the other apartments, but as some shade of difference existed, we prefer giving our observations as we proceeded.   No. 2.   A small
apartment on the ground floor, about eight feet by ten, inhabited by a man
and wife and four children, who have only one bed in a small room adjoining.   No. 3.   Upstairs, ceiling open to the rafters, one miserable bedstead,
scarcely any bed or covering, inhabited by a widow and five young children,
and by a man and wife, all in one room!   The children are almost naked,
never taste any animal food, and were much distressed in the winter.
No. 4.   A miserable upstairs room, with a partially stopped hole through
the wall, just opposite an ill-covered bedstead, inhabited by a man and wife
and child, which appeared almost starved; they receive two shillings per
week from the parish, and live upon one meal of potatoes per day.   No. 5.   A
small miserable smoky room, inhabited by a man and wife, the former sixty-
eight, and the latter eighty-three years of age; no sacking to the bedstead,
and potatoes once a day.   No. 6.   On the ground floor; is inhabited by a
man and wife, a son about fourteen, and a young child.   The mother and
child appear extremely ill; the bed on which they sleep has ropes instead
of sacking, and the lad sleeps on the bare floor; they receive one shilling
a week.   No. 7.   Is one shade more comfortable; inhabited by a man and
wife and five children, two of whom have the hooping cough and no attendance; they receive no parish pay.   No. 8.   A small room upstairs, *with a*

alone, that we would try not the charity of law,
but the charity of discretion—and all our surest

---

clean floor; the rain comes in through the bare tiles, and there is only one
bed for the mother and her grown son! Such are the scenes which inquiry and personal inspection have opened to our view.

" It may perhaps be almost unnecessary to remark, that it is only in *recent*
times, that these buildings and their inhabitants have fallen into this extreme state of decay and misery, arising from various general and local
causes. Amongst these may be enumerated, the want of adequate employment,—the high price of provisions,—the present law of settlement,—the
increased depravity both of individuals and families,—*and he moral impossibility of regulation by any other means than a radical change of system.*"

Mr. Thomas Richardson of Bristol, the friend and intimate of the benevolent Reynolds, will forgive me for adverting to the very important testimony upon this subject, wherewith he has kindly favoured me in a recent
communication. It relates to those families who are hovering around the
margin of pauperism, without having entered it.

" It is indeed a matter of astonishment, how so many families who are
suffering the greatest privations, owing to the want of employment, or to
extreme low wages, and often from their chief support being laid aside by
sickness, many of whom furnish a picture of wretchedness of which no one
can furnish an adequate conception, but those who have been spectators;
I say, it is wonderful how such families can bear up under such burdens, and
can forbear from making applications to their parishes for relief. It is to
this spirit of independence that we are alone to attribute, that our parochial
rates have not grown more rapidly than they have done, amidst causes so
powerfully operating. Instead of its being a matter of surprise, that the poor
rates should have attained their present amount, it is to me much more so,
that pauperism should not have extended its baleful influence very far beyond its present enlarged bounds. I will advert to your remark respecting
the extent of the surplus of unrelieved poverty: I have no doubt but that
this surplus always marches ahead of whatsoever relief is afforded; and I
think we see this in Bristol, where, I believe, it is generally admitted that
the amount of the various sums, raised for the Infirmary, Dispensary, &c.
together with what is contributed to various public objects, and given in
private benevolence, exceeds the amount raised for the maintenance of the
pauper poor."

So truly it has been said that the poor rate of England has not lessened
the misery of its people, but only transferred it, and that, too, after having
gone far to exhaust the means, and to deaden the spirit of benevolence.

and strongest convictions are utterly belied, if it be not found, that without the raising of one compulsory sixpence in a parish, there shall be more of contentment, and greatly less of unrelieved want in it than before. Ere we enter on a more detailed exposition of the process, it will, at least, be perceived, from this general outline of it, that the existing pauperism of our land, instead of being forcibly put an end to, is suffered to melt away by the operation of death—that no violence is done to any individual who is now upon the roll—and that it only remains to be seen whether they who would eventually have constituted the next generation of paupers, are not better served and better satisfied, under another treatment that we shall venture to suggest for them. But the question now resolves itself into two parts. There is first the parliamentary treatment of it—and then the parochial treatment of it, after that the legislature has done its office. These two things are perfectly distinct the one from the other. The one is in contact with the law of the question, and the other with the human nature of it.

There is a stubborn incredulity, which, however widely it may appear to differ, is, in some respects, very much at one with sanguine Utopianism. It is true, that the same magnificence which captivates the latter, is that which is regarded by the former with derision and distrust. So that while the one is easily lured to a chimerical enterprise, and just because the object of it is great, it is this very greatness which freezes the other into hopeless and impracticable apathy. Yet both agree, in that they take a direct and instantaneous impression from the object itself, and are alike heedless of the immediate means by which it may be accomplished. It is thus, that the splendid visionary is precipitated from his aerial flight, because he overlooked the utter pathlessness of that space, which lay between him and the impossibility that he aspired after. But it is also thus, that the fixed and obstinate practitioner refuses to move one single footstep, because he equally.overlooks that continuous way, which leads through the intervening distance, to some great yet practicable achievement. But give him time—and the mere length of a journey ought not to repel the traveller from his undertaking—nor will he resign the advantage for which he looks at its further extremity, till you have demonstrated that one or more of its stages is utterly impassable. In other words, there is a blind infidelity, as well as a blinded imagination—and it is difficult to say whether the cause of philanthropy has suffered more from the temerity of projectors, or from the phlegmatic inertness of men, who, unable to discriminate between the experimental and the visionary, are alike determined to despise all and to resist all.

CHAP. XV.

ON THE LIKELIEST PARLIAMENTARY MEANS FOR THE ABOLITION OF PAUPERISM IN ENGLAND.

A GENTLEMAN who is now bestowing much of his attention on the poor laws, when informed of the speed and facility wherewith all its compulsory pauperism had been extinguished in a certain parish, replied, that it might be easy to effect the deliverance of one parish, but that it was not so easy to legislate for the deliverance of all England. But if an easy and applicable method can be devised for the parish, what is it that the legislature has properly to do? Simply to remove the legal obstructions that may now stand in the way of the method in question. Simply to authorise each parish that so wills to avail itself thereof. And should many, or should all of them at length go forth upon the enterprise, and succeed in it, then the extinction of this sore evil over the country at large, instead of being immediately referable to the impetus of that one blow, which has been struck against it by the lifting up of the arm of parliament—should be referred to a cause that is far more commensurate with the vastness of the achievement, even to the power of those multiplied energies that have been set at work, throughout the land, each of which, however, has only its own separate and limited object to overtake, and each of which acteth independently of all the rest.

However obvious this may be, yet we have often thought, that the overlooking of it, is one main cause of that despair and helplessness, which are felt by many of our legislators, on the subject of this great national distemper. There are many of them who would feel no difficulty, but for certain legal obstacles that stand in their way, in working off this nuisance each from his own little neighbourhood ; and are confident withal, that after this was done, there would, over the whole space which had thus been cleared away, be more of comfort among the families, and a higher tone of character than before. Now, this feeling is precisely that of thousands besides, each of whom, if free from one unfortunate restraint, could clear the mischief away from his own local territory, and thus contribute his own quota to the deliverance of the empire. But he who has a place and an authority in the councils of the empire, takes a wide and extended survey over the whole of it—and by a sort of fancied ubiquity, he brings himself into contact with all the struggles and difficulties of all the parishes—and he somewhat feels as if the weight and the labour of what is indeed a very operose concern, were wholly accumulated upon his own person—and, instead of regarding pauperism as that which can only be put to death by inches, and with the help of many separate hands, he sees it as standing forth in single combat, a hydra of dread and direful encounter, at the sight of whom every heart fails, and every arm is paralyzed.

And akin to this delusion, is the imagination on the part, we believe, of many, that the only way of proceeding against pauperism is by imperative enactments, which behoved to be instantly, and simultaneously followed up by a change of administration all over the country. It must be at once seen, that in this way of it a disturbing force would be immediately brought to bear upon each and all of the parishes, that all would feel aroused to a strong, because a practical interest in the measure—and that out of a conflict and variety of sentiment thus spread over the whole land, there might be formed a hostility greatly too fierce and formidable for the safety of the nation. It were the method for bringing into play the elements of a mighty agitation ; and spreading out the question on an arena wide enough, and conspicuous enough, for the great master demagogues of the land. Those writers who live upon the discontents of the people, would instantly seize upon it as the fittest topic for keeping up that fermentation, in the whirl and briskness of which all their prosperity lies. And so it is, that an attempt on the poor laws, is dreaded by many as the sure precursor of a revolution—nor is it seen what the possible way is, by which this question can be prosecuted with the same wisdom, and withal in the same calmness, and with the same happy results, as have oft been experienced in the treatment of other questions, and that, through a long era of peaceful and progressive improvement in the domestic policy of England.

We should, on this account, hold it to be highly advisable, that any enactment which might be made on the subject of pauperism, shall not be one that brings a certain force upon all of the parishes, but simply one that allows a certain freedom to any of the parishes—not one that puts forth a law, but one that holds out a leave; and a leave, too, only to be granted on such a free and extended concurrence of householders in the application for it, as to be itself a guarantee, that however odious a general movement against pauperism may be over the country at large, yet that each particular movement is, within the limits of its own separate parish, abundantly popular.

The process might be illustrated by the way in which the commons of England have been appropriated. There are general and public acts, not by which parishes are required to divide and enclose their commons, but by which they are empowered each to petition for a local act, or a separate enclosure bill, authorising the division of its own commons. In the general acts, the principles are laid down and defined, on which the local acts are to be granted. The consent of the parties interested, to the bill being passed into a law, is signified by the subscription of their names to it. And, though there is no fixed rule in this respect, yet it may be proper to state, that the consent of four-fifths of the proprietors in number and value, is expected by parliament.

Thus parliament has not made it imperative on parishes, to turn their commons into private property. But they have struck out a path by which this transition may be effected, and left it to parishes to make the movement if they will. Had so mad an impolicy been conceivable as that of attempting to overbear parishes into the measure, by a positive enactment, there would have been the reaction of a loud clamour and discontent all over the country—nor would any government have braved so formidable an encounter ; and that, for the sake of a reform principally intended for the benefit of those local districts where it was carried into effect. It was far wiser to break down the mass into fragments ; to do the business piece-meal, and to make the improvement of this branch of our domestic economy a successive process, and not a simultaneous one. The thing has now been in progress for years, and a great national improvement is going surely and quietly forward. Parliament has done its part by opening a practicable door—and it wisely leaves the country to do theirs ; and that, not by any general movement, but by the separate movements of separate parishes. And we do hear occasionally of a little parochial effervescence. But it is not such as to fill or to agitate the public mind, or to bring into slightest hazard the tranquillity of the state. A parish in the depths of

Cornwall or Yorkshire, will be all alive, of course,
to the interest of its own local arrangements ; but
it is wholly unfelt by the public at large; and it is
well that what might have been food and fuel for
the politics of a nation, has been thus fritter-
ed down into distinct portions of aliment, for the
politics of its thousand remote and isolated ham-
lets. The violence is dissipated and disposed
of, which might else have gathered into one wast-
ing volcano. The march, upon the whole, has
been as peaceful as it is beneficent—and a measure which, under one form, might have called
forth a great popular insurrection, has under another
been carried forward with sure and silent footsteps
over the kingdom. It has, for the time at least,
depressed the value of agricultural produce, and
so lessened the income of the landlord, who, perhaps, counted on being the chief gainer by it.
But it has also, for the same time, cheapened the
necessaries of life, and so added to the comfort of
the labourer, who perhaps felt himself to be the
chief sufferer by it. Meanwhile, it is clearing its
way through all the near-sighted and nugatory
apprehensions of the various classes—and whatever
be the temporary evils that are charged upon it,
its undoubted effect is to add to the abundance of
the country, and to make of it a wealthier and
more flourishing land.

Now, this we conceive should also be the order

of attack upon pauperism.* It is thus that this common, now a defenceless prey to the inroads of vice and idleness, should be gradually reclaimed, and placed within the secure limits by which all property ought to be guarded. We know it to be still a prevalent impression, that this were making an outcast, and an unprotected orphan of human misery; and though we hold this to be erroneous, yet it is an impression that ought to be most tenderly and respectfully dealt with. The benevolence of Englishmen must be satisfied; and it says much for that noble people, that burdened as they are, and mighty as the deliverance would be, could the

---

* It might serve to reconcile us the more to the process which is now recommended, that it is in the very order by which previous reforms on the poor laws have been attempted by Parliament, and responded to by the country at large. By the Select Vestry Act, or the act of 59 Geo. III. c. 12. it is declared, " that it shall be lawful for the inhabitants of any parish, in Vestry assembled, and they are hereby empowered to establish a select vestry for the overseers of the poor of such parish." And so of the Act 22 Geo. III. c. 83. commonly called Gilbert's act, which does not pass into effect in any parish, till called for by two thirds in number and value of the owners or occupiers according to their poor rate. Thus, under the authority of a general act previously passed, and by which leave is given to parishes on the consent of a certain number of qualified owners or occupiers to adopt certain arrangements, under which the affairs of the poor may be forthwith administered—parishes come forward, and on presenting the concurrence that is required, these arrangements are carried into effect. It is thus that Gilbert's Act has made a certain progress throughout England, and Sturgess Bourne's Act is still in progress. The Appendix to the Report of July last, from the Select Committee on Poor Rate Returns, contains many testimonies in its favour from the parishes that had adopted it. This, of course, will extend the range of its operation still more widely ; and thus it is that facts are multiplied, and experiment passes into experience.

poor rate be done away, yet the conviction must
first be done away, that the poor are not to suffer
by it. This surely is not a feeling which ought
to be rudely handled; and, therefore it is, that
throughout the whole business of reform, there
should not merely be the utmost tenderness to the
lower orders, but the utmost tenderness to the humanity of those who feel for them.

There are three distinct objects that should be
comprehended in the provisions of the General
Act, and each of which may be regarded sepa-
rately. The first relates to the act of concurrence
that should be required of any parish, ere that parish shall be empowered to make a radical change
in its management of the poor. The second relates to the nature of the change. And the third,
to the way in which the Parliament and people of
England are to be satisfied, both at the outset, and
through all the subsequent stages of this retracing
movement, that its effects are so beneficial, and
more particularly to the poor themselves, as to be
altogether worthy of a humane and civilized nation.

I. To grant allowance for the enclosure of a
parish common, parliament expects the consent of
four-fifths of the proprietors, in number and value.
To grant leave for the new-modelling of its pauperism, we should not object to the consent of a
larger proportion than this of all the parish householders, who are not paupers themselves, being

required by Parliament.* It is obvious, that the
larger the consent is that shall be required by the

---

* Gilbert's Act requires the consent to it of two-thirds in number and
value of those who pay poor rate. Sturgess Bourne's Act requires a majority of the inhabitants assembled in vestry; or, in other words, a majority
of those who are present, and pay the rate—it being provided by 58 G. III.
c. 69. " That no person who shall have refused or neglected to pay any
rate for the relief of the poor, which shall be due from and shall be demanded of him, shall be entitled to vote or to be present in any vestry of the
parish for which such rate shall have been made, until he shall have paid
the same."

We think that a larger concurrence than this should be required, ere a
parish shall have leave to adopt a change of system still more radical and
entire than that which is allowed by the acts either of Gilbert or of Sturgess
Bourne. A very large proportion indeed of all the householders who are
not paupers, should signify their previous consent to it—and the following
are my reasons for believing that even though their unanimity were held by
the first general act to be indispensable, still there are some parishes that
will be found to satisfy a condition, which wherever it can be realised, will
evince the utmost popularity of the measure, at least within the place where
it is to be put into operation.

The two opposite interests which are felt on the subject of the Poor
Laws, are the first by those who pay the rate, and the second by those
who receive from it. Now, practically, these two classes do not share between them the whole population of owners or occupiers. There is, in
many places, a very large intermediate class, who neither give nor receive;
but who so far from being neutral upon this question, will, of course, have
a leaning towards that compulsory provision, from which most of them perhaps look for some eventual benefit at one time or another to themselves.
Even apart from this expectation, their natural and generous inclination
will be towards the system as it is, so that in all places where this intermediate class is a very numerous one, a very large concurrence of householders
who are not paupers, may be next to impossible.

But it is to be remarked, that strictly and legally there is no exemption
from the rate, even for paupers themselves. The law is, that the rate shall
be made on every inhabitant who is an occupier either of houses or lands—
and so may it be carried down to the very margin of pauperism, nay, even
be brought within it, in either of which cases there could be no neutral or
intermediate class whatever. These exemptions from the rate are altogether at the discretion of those who make it, and accordingly the practice

general act, the fewer will be the parishes who can avail themselves of its provisions. It were far

---

varies exceedingly in different parishes, and different parts of the country. From out of twenty thousand assessments in Liverpool, for example, there wont to be about 13000 struck off; whereas, in Bury, in the same county, they stop the rate out of the pay of the pauper; and at Pilkington, the poor rate is levied on those whom even the overseers relieve at the same instant. In Manchester, the intermediate class forms nearly three-fourths of the whole population—there being 12,000 exempted of about sixteen thousand who are liable by law. I am informed from Stockport, "that none is exempted from paying of rates, not even the paupers themselves." The overseers are there made chargeable for all the assessments, while at Salford about 1,500 may pay the full rate, and about a thousand a portion of it through the landlord, a considerable number being still left, who neither pay nor receive. At Birmingham, there were at one time about fifteen thousand out of nineteen thousand, who did not pay; though the intermediate class there too is constantly diminishing. It were quite endless to enumerate all the arbitrary differences that take place in various parishes and townships. But certain it is, that the tendency all over the land is to carry the levy downward as far as it is practicable—and we should say, that the neutral class is perhaps narrowing into a more limited space and smaller number every year.

There is one clause, however, in the Select Vestry Act, by which this tendency has been counteracted. It is that by which a power is granted to rate the owners of certain houses, instead of the occupiers. Such houses as are let at a rate not exceeding £20, nor less than £6 by the year. We believe, that virtually this carries in it no relief to the occupier—for had the levy been exacted from him, he would have had his compensation for it in the diminution of his rent. We have no doubt, that the landlord is indemnified by a higher rent, for all that he must now pay to the poor rate; but the occupier is ostensibly freed from the burden of the rate—and thus may there always be kept in the intermediate class the tenants of such houses, as are occupied by industrious tradesmen, and well-conditioned operatives, and, in a word, all those who, taken together, form the better and more influential part of our working population.

We, therefore, on the whole regret this clause. There is substantially no relief yielded by it to the tenants; but it has withdrawn them from that ostensible place, in which, if they had been permitted to remain, they would have felt the hostility of a personal interest to the poor rate, and so have given additional force and power to that direction which even the popular mind of the country was beginning to take against it.

more difficult to obtain the requisite number of householders in a large and populous town, than in a small and manageable country parish; and it is therefore to be expected, that any movements which shall be made under the general act, will be made first in the agricultural districts of England. At the outset then, the more unwieldy parishes will have no interest in this regress from a legal to a free system of charity, unless in so far as they shall be the interested spectators of what is going on,—looking intently on the whole way of those adventurers who have slipt cable before them, and

---

Still, however, it is a matter of discretion to charge the rate either on the owners or the occupiers. Indeed it is more to facilitate the levy by laying it upon the one class, than to grant even the semblance of relief to the other, that this enactment is proceeded upon. On the whole, there is a far greater number of the community enlisted into the opposition against poor rate, than wont to be at former periods, and not a few are the parishes, therefore, where a nearly universal concurrence might be obtained for a radical change of system, on the part of all the householders who are not paupers themselves.

Before closing this note, it may be right to advert to the very great expense of a local act, obtained for a parish under the authority and according to the provisions of a previous general act. It would not be necessary, for the purpose of giving effect to the new legislative measures upon pauperism, that a parish should be at this trouble, or incur this expense. A simple certification to the justices assembled in quarter sessions, of any parish, having approven of the provisions of the general act, and being desirous to adopt them, might, from that time, entitle them to proceed upon it. It is precisely so gone about, for example, when a parish comes under the benefit of Gilbert's Act. By the 33 Geo. III. c. 35. § 1. " Whenever two-third parts in number and value, as required by the said act, of such qualified persons only as actually attended, or may hereafter actually attend at such public meeting, held in pursuance of the directions of the said act, have there signified or may hereafter there signify, their approbation of the provisions in the said act contained, and their desire to adopt them, such approbation and desire so signified, or to be hereafter so signified as aforesaid, have been and shall be a sufficient compliance with the said act."

perhaps waiting their arrival at a safe and prosperous landing-place, ere they shall have acquired the courage to think of an imitation. It is because we should like the whole process to be gone about surely and experimentally, that we should like, at least the first general act, to require a concurrence so very large in each parish, as that the number of parishes which it may actually set a-going, shall be indeed very small. It were well that this act was loaded, on purpose, with a condition that is not easily satisfied; and thus the trials will be restricted, in the first instance, to a few of the easiest and likeliest of the parishes. We do not want the whole of England to be thrown adrift, at the bidding of a yet untried hypothesis. But we want England to put herself to school. We think that she needs to go to school; and when looking attentively to those trial parishes, she is, in fact, learning the first lessons, and acquiring the sound rudiments of a sound education. Those parishes will be to her the alphabet, whence she may venture forward to achievements that are still more arduous; and at length be able to master those more complex and difficult results, which now lie far removed, on a distant and impracticable back-ground, from the eye of her understanding.*

---

* It gave me great pleasure to receive a letter from an English clergyman of talent and energy, and who has paid great attention to the management of the poor, in which the very idea that we have attempted to develop, is briefly but distinctly brought forward. " If power," he writes, " by a general bill, was given to vestries to make experiments and adopt mea-

There are many distinct advantages, in a very large concurrence of householders being required at the outset, ere any parish shall have liberty to enter on the new system of pauperism, and a few of these we shall barely announce, without expatiating on them.

First, it confines the operation of the proposed act to those parishes where the experiment is most popular; and so removes it altogether from those regions, where its very obnoxiousness to the community at large, would be a serious impedient in the way of its success. And it is evident, that the larger the requisite concurrence is made, the more effectually will this object be secured.

But, secondly, a large concurrence in favour of the new method, is our best guarantee for a resolute and powerful agency to carry on the execution of it. We should not despair of a most efficient vestry in any parish, for conducting aright the business of its gratuitous charity, where there had been nearly a unanimous consent to the abolition of its legal charity. There is no fear of any parish which has thus singled out, and made a spectacle of itself, that it will not acquit itself well, and at length demonstrate to all its neighbours, that without a poor rate, and without any painful

---

sures suitable to themselves, some materials might be furnished for a universal principle. I know a case or two, where the whole property of a parish is in the hands of one person, and that a person who saw and determined to meet the growing evil; and the poor rate has been reduced to a mere nothing, and that instantly. There is a case you may see of Mr. Estcourt, in the Report for Bettering the Condition of the Poor."

sacrifice at all, it can boast a happier and a better population than any of those who are around it. We prophesy a success to their undertaking that will be quite marvellous, even to themselves; and that they will very soon find, how nought is wanting but an energetic outset, to ensure the transition, both to the people's contentment and their own repose. But there is a better chance for the energetic outset where there has been a very extended concurrence—a surer warrant of success, where there is a wider responsibility. It is for this reason, that we would not have parishes to be selected for the experiment, by parliamentary commissioners, or any constituted body whatever. We would have parishes to offer themselves; and the single event of their doing so, with that full complement of names and signatures which the general act shall require, is, of itself, the best ground on which the selection of experimental parishes can be made.

And, thirdly, although the provision of a nearly unanimous concurrence on the part of householders, should, at the very commencement of this process, restrict the trial to a very small number of parishes, this does not eventually exclude the great body and majority of England from the proposed reformation. It only prepares the way for it. The truth is, that should so few as twenty parishes come forward, under the first general act, and should their experiment prosper, it will do more to assure the hearts and the hopes of the people of England than a thousand dissertations. It will be like the finishing of the first lesson that parliament has dealt out to the country, and will prepare both the teachers and the taught for a second. The next flight will be a bolder one; or, in other words, a second general act may be passed, whose conditions it shall be easier to satisfy, and under which as many hundreds may now come forward, as before there were tens of parishes. The success, in fact, of the first set of parishes will both embolden parliament to widen the door for succeeding parishes, which it does by lowering the terms of admittance, and it will also embolden these parishes to a readier, and more confident imitation. The simple expedient of reducing the extent of the concurrence would effectually answer. If upon the terms of an application from seven-eighths of the householders, so few as twenty parishes did adventure themselves on a yet untried project, and succeeded therein, then we may be sure, that upon the terms of a similar application from four-fifths of the householders, it is not too much to expect that two hundred parishes will soon feel encouraged to follow them. It is thus that by a series of general acts, as by a series of stepping-stones, England may emerge out of all the difficulties of her present pauperism. The very first footstep that she takes is on a firm basis, and all along she moves by a way that is strictly experimental. Throughout every inch of her wary progress, she never needs to abandon the light of observation;

and on the whole of this interesting walk over her provinces, and, at length, to her great cities, till she reaches her own mighty metropolis in triumph, is she guided from one achievement to another, and by the way that she best loves, because the way that is most eminently congenial, with the sober and the practical character of her under-taking.

II. In regard to the nature of the change, we should leave untouched the condition and the rights of all who, at the time of its being entered upon, are permanent paupers. There should be no dismissal of any who would not have been dismissed under the old regimen. It is, of course, quite fair to scrutinize their means and resources to the utter-most; and on any discovery of their being ade-quate to their own support, or on any actual im-provement that may have taken place in their cir-cumstances, by which they are enabled to provide for themselves, it is perfectly right that their names should be expunged from the roll. But this, in fact, is what always takes place under the present system, and should, therefore, take place under the new one: and ere they can be discarded, they may appeal, as now, to the magistrate,—a right which they should only forfeit, by the act of their being ejected beyond the pale of the existing pauperism. All, in short, who are actually pau-pers in any parish, at the time of its entering upon the new system, should, while paupers, have the very rights and securities which they now enjoy;

and the change of treatment, whatever it may be, should apply exclusively to those who apply for parochial relief, either for the first time, or apply for it anew, after they have been made to do without it for a period. In this last clause, a special reference is had, not merely to those who once, perhaps, were regular paupers, and were afterwards excluded, because of their means having grown better, or been better ascertained, but also to those who, alternate upon the parish from summer to winter, and, in general, those who, being neither the inmates of the workhouse, nor regular weekly pensioners on the out-door list, pass under the denomination of casual poor, or occasional poor.*

---

* We are aware that this might expose a trial parish to considerable trouble at the outset, for, in many instances, the casual poor form a very great proportion of the whole population; and, in some instances, there is a prodigious alternation of the pauperism from summer to winter. This might be remedied by the suggestion of an English clergyman, who proposed that all who had received, in any shape, from the poor rate, through the year preceding the time when the parish began to act upon the new system, might be treated as old paupers; and that those alone should be treated as new applicants who had never, prior to that, been in contact with the poor rate. This would certainly lighten, at the outset, the work of the parochial administrators, while it would only retard the ultimate accomplishment of an entire deliverance from the burdens of the old pauperism. For my own part, I do not think that, in the first instance at least, any such extended definition of the old cases is at all necessary. The trial parishes would be only those which were not encumbered with any appalling difficulties at the commencement of their undertaking; and ere the imitation parishes come forward, the legislature would have felt its way to all those nicer adjustments that might be deemed expedient. If a parish feel so oppressed either with its casual poor, or the fluctuations which they undergo from summer to winter, as that it could not adventure upon them with a gratuitous fund, it were better that it should wait the experience of such parishes

The first change then that we should propose in the parochial system, for the management of the poor, is that in reference to every new applicant, the special power of justices to order relief, should be altogether taken away. The parish vestry would, in this case, be the ultimate and the only place of application; and their decision, both as to relief, and as to the amount of it, would be final. There would, forthwith, cease all summoning by a justice of parish overseers, to show cause why relief should not be given. The thing, in fact, would be confided, as it practically is throughout the greater part of Scotland, to the humanity and discretion of the parochial court; and the thing to be ascertained in the trial parishes, is whether there would not be less of unrelieved poverty, as well as less of all profligacy and disorder under this regimen, than under the one that is now in force.*

---

as may have entered before it upon the new system; and we feel confident that this experience will be altogether encouraging. There are a thousand fears and difficulties in pauperism which vanish before the touch of personal intercourse; and, more especially, when that right has ceased on which the people wont to depend, and by which they wont to regulate their habits and their expenses.

* The following testimonies, however sound as to the evils which arise from the interference of the justices, must be taken with allowance, in as far as regards the personal worth and talent of an order of men, among whom are to be found many of the most exalted and estimable characters in our land. " First, the appeal to justices is a bad enactment. They are often weak men—men uninformed, and knowing little or nothing of business. They do not feel the burden they impose, but, on the contrary, a love of

The second change that we should propose relates to the fund out of which the new applicants

popularity and other passions often induce their determinations—and even
when this is not the case, it is impossible they should know a pauper's
real wants. His oath is received—the *onus refutandi* lies on the parish,
who often submits to imposition rather than take the trouble and expense
attending the necessary proof. I know the Select Vestry Act has put the
power in other hands—still with an appeal to justices. This is wrong. Is
it to be supposed ten or twenty respectable inhabitants in a parish *all* want
humanity? If they do, they have a character to sustain, and gross acts of
oppression would soon find their way to the public ear. If, then, the
power was solely in a select vestry, it being made imperative on the clergy
and a competent number of respectable inhabitants to form that vestry, I
am persuaded immense good would immediately be seen."

" Your statement respecting clerical magistrates is perfectly correct.
They universally favour paupers."

" I am thoroughly satisfied that the interference of magistrates does much
harm. It encourages the lazy, who are always thrown out of employment
and most clamorous, and often puts the good and bad upon an equal footing.
Overseers might, no doubt, sometimes be severe and even unjust—but
they are far the best judges of those immediately under their care—and
parishes would not submit to any flagrant acts of injustice towards a
pauper."

The Select Vestry Act has done much, in those parishes where it has been
adopted, to check the evils of this interference. That Act may be regarded
as a partial homage, to the sufficiency of the parochial court within itself
for doing its own business—and it were well, if the homage was at length
rendered complete and conclusive, by a progressive abolition of the power of
the justices in matters of pauperism throughout the land. There are adequate securities, in every parochial community, for the wants of the poor
being provided, and humanity attended to. It were at least well to submit
this to the test of experience.

On a recent excursion through England, however, we find a growing
disposition on the part of magistrates, to make common cause with the
parish overseers against the demands of idleness and profligacy—and the
heaviest complaints that we met against them, were in some parts of Dor-
setshire and Leicestershire, and in some of the London parishes.

" A great deal of vexatious interference on the part of magistrates."

" Many summonses, and the magistrates generally favourable to the
paupers."

shall be met. Of course, the poor rate, levied as
it is at present, upholds the fund out of which all

" You ask, Do not the magistrates often refuse to listen to the plea of
character, alleging they have to do with the plea of distress? Answer. Yes.
On one occasion I relieved a woman, who had an illegitimate child, with
2s. per week, when she summoned me before a magistrate, who ordered
her 7s. per week; and I refused to comply, and sent her into the workhouse,
when she discharged herself and child the next morning, and she did with
the allowance of 2s. a-week as before."

We in Scotland were approaching lately to this state of things, in some
parts of the country, where the practice had crept in of an appeal, on the
part of the applicants for relief, from the Kirk-Session to the Sheriff of the
County.   There has, however, been a recent decision against this, and the
appeal now lies from the Parochial Court to the Court of Session in Edinburgh—the analogous process to which in England, would be that of obtaining against the decision of the Parish Vestry, a mandamus from the
Court of King's Bench.   The apprehension is, that the poor might starve
before the court should determine—and, therefore, it is that in England a
nearer place of appeal is preferred to a distant.   In Scotland the more remote and operose method of redress has been preferred—and the experience
is, that the poor are never permitted to starve, and most assuredly never
would, though both the near and the distant places of appeal were alike
withdrawn from them.   On this account we regret the failure of Mr. Ken-
nedy's bill in Parliament.

It might be interesting to our English readers to perceive how it fared
with two parishes within a few miles from their own borders—first, when
our system was likened to theirs during the period of a nearer appeal by
the pauper to the sheriff, and afterwards when the right of appeal by its being shifted to a distant court, was made so operose as to become practically
void.

The Rev. Mr. Morgan of Gratney writes, " To avoid the expenses of
litigation, we have now and then judged it prudent to grant a trifling weekly allowance.   But since Lord Pitmilly's decision in an appeal case, relative
to the jurisdiction of sheriffs on cases of pauperism, we have not been so
pestered with letters and summonses.   We have, however, managed so
well hitherto as to incur no legal expenses, which has not been the case in
a neighbouring parish.   Owing to our vicinity to England, our poor imagine
that they have a right to be treated in the same liberal way, as their English
neighbours ; but our heritors and kirk-sessions have not allowed this idea to
have any weight with them.   In this parish, consisting of a population of

the expenditure of the old pauperism is defrayed,
—an expenditure that lessens every year by the

1945, for some years past the poor on our roll have averaged about sixty, and our subscriptions for their relief, for we have had no assessments, have not at any time exceeded two hundred pounds or guineas annually. At present they scarcely reach the half of that sum. We relieve the aged and infirm ones, who have no funds or relatives in ability to help them."

We likewise offer the following very instructive communication from the Rev. Mr. Monilaws of Kirkpatrick-Fleming, a parish, by the last census, of 1696 individuals.

" The amount yearly of the funds for the poor, before the assessment was resorted to, was about £30. This arose from collections. Inconsiderable as these funds were, I never heard a complaint from the poor, and their quarterly proportions of the above sum were received with thankfulness. An assessment was first imposed in 1813, for the support of a friendless young man who had lost his sight. The heritors sent him to the asylum for the blind in Edinburgh, and supported him there by a weekly allowance. The amount of the assessments during the years 1813, 1814, 1815, was about £10 10s. per annum for the support of the above individual; when after that period, in consequence of his being able to maintain himself by his own industry, he ceased to become a burden upon the parish. In the year 1817, in consequence of the almost total want of employment, among the labouring poor, the heritors saw the necessity of aiding this description of people, and assessed themselves to the amount of £114 for that year. Immediately thereafter, and about the month of July, a great number of other indigent people, seeing with what facility the labouring poor had obtained relief, and encouraged by writers, threw in their claims also for parochial assistance. Some of these claims were admitted, and the others refused, but the heritors being threatened with prosecutions before the sheriff, and actually in one case subjected to the expense of above £50, listened to the petitions of most of these claimants, and assessed themselves to the amount of £42 for their support also, for that half-year.

" In the year 1818, the amount of assessment was............£135
In the year 1819, do. do. was................ 149
In the year 1820, do. do. was................ 160
In the year 1821, do. do. was................ 140
In the year 1822, do. do. was................ 116

" It being found by a decision of Lord Pitmilly, that the sheriff is incompetent to revise the decision of the heritors and kirk-session regarding the application of persons to be admitted to parochial aid, has had a most benc-

operation of death on the old cases. Now we hold it essential to a sound and abiding reformation of the pauperism, that no fund should ever be raised in this way, for the new pauperism—that the power which the church-wardens and overseers have of *making a rate*, either with or without the concurrence of the inhabitants, for the purpose of meeting any fresh applications, shall henceforth cease—and that, if any fund be judged necessary, in order to provide for new cases, it shall, under a public and parochial administration, be altogether a gratuitous, and in no shape a legal or compulsory one. For the purpose of constituting such a fund, the minister and church-wardens may be empowered to have a weekly collection at the church doors ; or what is now gathered

---

ficial tendency indeed—for we have not been served with a summons to appear before the sheriff by a poor person, for two years past ; whereas in 1818, 1819, and 1820, we had many citations. Nor has a new applicant appeared at any of our meetings of heritors, for eighteen months past; and I sincerely hope that this system of assessments will be abolished altogether, when the poor on our present list dies off. I have only further to add, that the sum arising from collections, has never been mixed up with the above assessments, but has been managed by the kirk-session as formerly, and applied to the relief of a different set of poor, whom our kirk-sessions have always been in the habit of supporting."

We could not desire a better exemplification of the way in which pauperism advances under one system, and may be made to recede again under another. Could some such voluntary fund be provided in an English parish, as that to which the pauperism of Kirkpatrick-Fleming is now under the process of being recommitted, we have no doubt that the pauperism of the former too might at length be conducted to a similar landing-place—and that, simply by the operation of death on the old cases, and an uncontrolled treatment of the new cases on the part of the vestry.

in the shape of sacrament money, may be made over to it; or donations may be received from individuals—in all which ways the revenue of a kirk-session in Scotland is mainly upheld. The fund could be still further, perhaps, reinforced in England, by an act of parliament, empowering this new destination to those charitable donations which abound over the whole country, and to the extent of nearly half its parishes. We do not think this indispensable, though it might give a little more confidence at the outset, of a prosperous result. We think that many parishes might venture on their new cases without it; and we have no doubt, that under a kind, and moral, and, withal, an uncontrolled administration of the vestry, there would, from the free-will offerings of the parish alone, be found a landing-place, quite broad enough for the accommodation of the new pauperism, after that the old pauperism, and its corresponding poor rate, should have wholly disappeared.*

---

* We hold it nearly as indispensable, that the power of raising money by assessment, on the part of those who administer the parochial fund, should be taken away, as the right of an appeal to magistrates on the part of those who apply for relief from it. There are many parishes of England where, by local acts, this right is very much abridged, and yet the pauperism is often as oppressive with them as in other parishes. In those parishes of the south of Scotland too, where there lies no appeal from a pauper, but to the Court of Session—but where the practice of assessments has been introduced, there is, generally speaking, a very rapid progress of expenditure on the poor. The truth is, that the indefinite power of raising money has often as bad an effect on the dispensers, by slackening their management,

The third change that would be required, should be in the constitution of the vestry. Now, it is a certain amount of charge or assessment for the poor rate which entitles to a vote; and that, on the principle of those who pay the money having a voice and power in the administration of it. Perhaps it would not be deviating very widely from this principle, if, in respect of the annual sum yielded by the church-door collections, or the sacrament money, the ministers and church-wardens were made members of this vestry; and were the church-wardens of a parish only a more numerous class, there would, at this point, be a very near resemblance between the parochial courts of distribution and supply in England and Scotland. And when the old charitable donations of a parish have been transferred to the new poor's fund, it may be further right, that the legal guardians, or

---

as it has on the recipients, by corrupting them into habits of dependance. This is more especially the case, where the men who practically administer the fund, contribute very little towards the formation of it, as with the kirk-session of an assessed parish in Scotland; or, as it might often happen with the vestry of an English parish. We much fear that nothing will effectually stay the contagion in Scotland, but a law by which it shall be declared incompetent to raise a compulsory fund in behalf of any who shall apply for parochial relief after a certain specified date. This would both limit all new applicants to the kirk-session, and also limit the kirk-session to its own proper income—and we have the confident belief, that when both parties were so limited, there would, from the more moderate expectations of the one, and the more vigilant dispensations of the other, ensue a far more comfortable system of relief, than could possibly be attained with an ample command of means, and an appetency for absorbing them that was equally ample.

administrators of them, might be also members of vestry. And if a constitution still more popular were required, then the contributors of a specified annual sum might, for each year of such a contribution, be members. But we shall venture no farther upon such details of regulation; though we are quite sure that there are sound and obvious principles upon which, under the new system, a suitable constitution for parish vestries might be framed.

We are aware of the demand that there is for a *gradual* amendment of the pauperism, and that the change now recommended is of such an entire and revolutionary character, as might appear to be at utter variance with this wise and salutary principle in the practice of legislation. But it should be remembered, that there are two ways in which a process of improvement might be gradualized; either by a series of successive approximations, in the general law, to a state of it that shall at length be perfect and unexceptionable; or by the application, at once, of the best possible law, to a few of the simple and manageable parishes, and thence, the successive adoption of it by the larger and more unwieldy parishes. Now, our preference is for the latter way of it. Rather than experiment at large with a defective principle, we hold it better to seize, at once, on the right principle, and experiment with it on a few select and favourable territories, whence the light of experience may break forth, and gradually spread itself over the

land. We should far rather behold a sudden
change in the jurisprudence of the question, followed up by a gradual operation among the parishes, than a creeping and timid progress in the
former, but at each step of which there behoved
to be a general movement among the latter. The
law which enacted the abolition of all legal aliment
to the mothers of illegitimate children, or in aid of
defective wages, would raise a far greater ferment
in the country, and cause a more hurtful and hazardous jolt in the career of amelioration, than the
law which empowered the abolition of all legal
aliment whatever, but on conditions that would
ensure that safe and gentle progress, which should
not outrun the prejudices or the fears of any
neighbourhood. In one view of it, the process
that we recommend may be charged with a speed
and a suddenness. But then this speed and suddenness are all confined to the statute-book, where
we should like if there could be recognized at
once the true principle and philosophy of the subject. Practically, there would be no inconvenient
suddenness. In the inner department of legislation there would be a gigantic stride, but there
would not in the outer department of the kingdom. There, the march of improvement would
go on most smoothly and progressively; and far
better were it, therefore, that instead of feeling
our way, through a series of successive enactments,
to the pure and the rational principle, we should
lay hold of it *instanter*, and then find our way

with it through a series of successive parishes, till it was carried into full and practical establishment over the whole empire.

III. But what is this rational principle? Have we a right to fancy it, and to go abroad with the phantasy over the land? Is it not possible that after all, it may be a wrong outset that we make; and how are we to know, that under the operation of this boasted panacea, we might not add to the number, and sorely aggravate the wretchedness of our suffering families?

Now, to meet these questions, we affirm of the process, that it is strictly a tentative one. It is not the dictatorial imposition of a method on the part of one who bids an implicit acquiescence therein. It is the confident recommendation of a method, on the part of one who asks that it may be submitted to the touchstone of experience, and who is willing to submit himself to the guidance and the correction of this safe schoolmaster. There is all the difference in the world between rashly presuming on the truth, and respectfully feeling our way to it. A very few initial attempts will decide the question and set it at rest. It is a question between the free or gratuitous, and the compulsory or legal systems of charity. The latter has been tried all over England and found wanting. Let the former be fairly and fully tried, in a few parishes of England, and abandoned if they become sensibly worse, and do not become sensibly better. It is our own belief, that every year will witness an addition to her trophies and her triumphs—that she will accumulate her credentials, by each footstep that she takes along the varied line of her perambulations, and, at length, be welcomed as an angel of deliverance in all parts of the kingdom. But should her career not be a prosperous one, she will share the fate of her many predecessors,—she will vanish, with other expedients, into oblivion ; and the parliament of England can withdraw its sanction, when the people of England have ceased from their demand for her.

It is on this account, that to watch the progress of this new system, there ought to be parliamentary commissioners, not for the purpose of receiving appeals on the question of relief; for this would be reviving the present system in another form—but for the purpose of noting and reporting how it is that those parochial communities really do thrive, where the parochial managers have been left to their own unfettered discretion—how it now fares with the families—and whether the charity of law be so replaced by sobriety among the poor, and sympathy among the rich, that the charity of nature is more than enough to meet all those apprehended deficiencies which, in the distance, look so big and so fearful. If they can report any abuse more flagrant in the trial parishes than now occurs on the average throughout the parishes of England—if they can quote instances there of shameful neglect and cruelty, which under the present style of administration, would not have been realized—if they can speak adversely of the scheme, either because of the particular evils of it which it shall be in their power to specify; or, because of that darker aspect of misery, which stands visibly out on those parochial families that are under its operation—then let such a testimony to the effects of the gratuitous system be its condemnation. But if, instead of this, they can allege, as the fruits of it, an increased contentment, and cheerfulness, and good-will; a more manifest kindliness of heart on the part of the higher orders; and this returned by a confidence and gratitude on the part of the lower orders, that had been before unknown; a more frequent intercourse between the various classes of society; and withal, such an impulse on the side of popular education, as to be sensibly raising the mind and the habits of the peasantry; if they can further attest, that never had they been called to witness the spectacle of distress left to suffer for a season, except in the cases of guilt or of idleness, when it was wise that nature should be left to her own correctives, and her own cures; and that even then starvation was a bugbear, which, with all their most diligent search after it, they had in no one instance been able to embody—surely, if such shall be their testimony, the voice of parliament will soon be at one with the voice of the people, and both must unite in stamping their acceptance on a system so fully tried, and so nobly vindicated.

It is not wrong to demand proof for the soundness or efficacy of any expedient—but surely it is wrong to refuse the demand of him, who seeks that a proof shall be led. There is no error, but the contrary, in the paramount value that is set upon experience. But how can he be said to value experience, who obstinately shuts out the light of it? And every experiment lands in experience. An experiment may be just as instructive by its failure, as by its success—and if there be parishes in England that are sanguine enough to encounter its difficulties, or willing to brave the hazards of an eventual disgrace—on what possible grounds of reason, or of expediency, should the opportunity be withheld from them? It interferes with nothing. It hinders nothing. Those who desire it not, are not disturbed by it—and each corporation, whether of parish or township, is left to the repose of its own settled prejudices, till the light of ocular demonstration may chance to awaken it. Even the most incredulous may, at least, consent to the trial. And they who hold it in uttermost derision, should be the first to cheer it forward to the field of exhibition, that they might hold their delicious regale upon its overthrow. Meanwhile, all the other devices of reform and regulation, might go on as busily as before. This one does not elbow out any of the former from the parishes by which they are preferred. The act of Mr. Gilbert has been tried. The act of Mr. Bourne is in progress of trial. Other suggestions, we doubt not, will be made, and, perhaps, adopted for the purpose of mitigating the load of pauperism; for the purpose of arresting, and perhaps, turning the footsteps of this mighty destroyer. There is just one more that we should like were added to the number of them. We should like a radical change of principle, combined with a progressive operation—an entire revolution in the system of management, but carried into effect in such a way as should bring none of the anarchy or uproar of revolution along with it—a process no doubt, chargeable with the stigma of being altogether new, and which, therefore, should not be permitted to range over the land, till it has earned a credit by its actual achievements ; and a process, whose speed regulated only by its tried and ascertained safety, shall give no disturbance to other experimental processes, and bring no danger to the commonwealth.*

And nothing, it appears to us, can be more simple than how to suit the law of settlement to a parish which shall come under the new system. A stranger acquires no right in such a parish, though he should fulfil all those conditions on which a

---

* Should even the number of parishes that applied at the outset, be deemed too great by the Commissioners, they might have the power of limiting and selecting, and thus, of checking for a time, those parishes where there seemed to be a smaller likelihood of success, or a less degree of humanity and information among its householders.

settlement is acquired in other parishes. He may, or he may not, share with the other parishioners, in the gratuitous ministrations of the vestry; but neither he nor they should have any right to relief, after that the care of human want had been devolved on the free sympathies of our nature. It is thus, that a trial parish would not import any burden by the influx of strangers from the country at large, and the fair reciprocity therefore is, that the country should not be burdened by any efflux from the parish. As there can be no right acquired by one removing to a trial parish, neither should there be any right acquired by one removing from it. And let us not, therefore, look upon him as an unprivileged outcast from the securities of civilized life. He moves at his own choice, and with his eye open to his circumstances; and he is richer far by trusting to his own resources, and by knowing that he has nothing else to trust to, than he, who, along with the rights, has also the temptations of pauperism. Such a man will find his way; and it, on the whole, will be a way of greater sufficiency and comfort than any which law provides for the nurselings of her artificial charity. The emigrants from a trial parish into any other part of England, will exemplify the general habit of those who have acquired no settlement in the place of their residence, yet choose not to leave it—a habit, it has oft been remarked, of greater industry and virtue than is averaged in the mass of the population.

CHAP. XVI.

ON THE LIKELIÈST PAROCHIAL MEANS FOR THE ABOLITION OF PAUPERISM IN ENGLAND.

THE first obstacle in the way of entering upon a process for the extirpation of pauperism in any parish, is, that the difficulty of it will be greatly overrated. The present and the palpable thing is a large annual sum that needs to be levied for the support of the existing generation of paupers—beside the very ponderous establishment that has been raised, and which continues to be required, for their accommodation. It is quite obvious what an unwieldy concern it would be, were the assessment forthwith to cease, and provision to be made on the instant for all those actual poor, from whom their accustomed supplies had thus suddenly been withdrawn. There is scarcely a body of parochial managers in England, that would not shrink from such an undertaking—and without reflecting for a time on the real difference that there is between this undertaking, and the one which we have suggested—they look upon both with the same kind of fearfulness, and almost with nearly equal degrees of it. They measure the weight and labour of the enterprise, by the weight of the present pauperism that is now before their eyes; though, in fact, there is not one fraction of it, with which the new system has necessarily any thing to do. The pauperism that has been already formed, so long as any part of it exists, may be upheld just as it wont; and as it gradually melts away by death, the levies will gradually decline, till both the poor rate, and the poor who have been admitted upon it, shall have altogether ceased to be. Meanwhile, it is only with new applicants for relief that the new system has any task to perform—not with the full-grown pauperism of the present generation, but with the embryo pauperism of the next. There are many parishes, and more especially if you rank all who have been casual poor with the old cases, where the fresh applications do not come in at the rate of one every month, and in the treatment of which, therefore, you can calmly and leisurely prosecute every right expedient for the right disposal of them. There can be no overwhelming labour at the outset of such an undertaking. With the management that provides for the existing pauperism, there is much business to attend to. But with the management that is set up to meet and to anticipate the eventual pauperism, the business comes on gradually. At first, there is none. It does not begin but with the first applicant who offers himself—and he finds you at perfect leisure to attend to him—to take up his case, and most thoroughly to investigate it—to calculate his means and his facilities—to make inquiry after his relatives—to ascertain what work might be provided for him—to arrange perhaps

some method with a neighbour, as cordially disposed against pauperism as you, for taking him
into employment, and making his industry available still to his maintenance—to shift away his
application by some temporary aid from the purse
of unseen charity—in a word, to ply every expedient for disposing of him better, than by admitting him upon the roll of your new pauperism,
under that new economy which it is now your
earnest concern to administer well. After the
first has been disposed of, a second comes at a
longer or shorter interval, and he finds you still
better prepared for him than before; more skilled
in the treatment of such applications; more intelligent about the resources of humble life; more
able to acquit yourselves prudently and even popularly, by every new act of intercourse with the
poor; more rich in experience and knowledge;
and withal, more dexterous in the talent, not of
so shifting the request away from you, as that your
petitioner shall starve, but of so shifting it away
from you as that he shall be in better condition
than if he had been made a pensioner of yours.
Let this be persevered in for a little—and if one
regular pauper was admitted upon the list every
month under the old regimen, one will not be admitted every half-year under the new regimen.
The thing which now looks so formidable in the
distance, will, on the actual encounter with it,
dwindle into a very moderate and manageable af-
fair. Both the facility and the success will very

much astonish yourselves—and by the time that the pauperism on the poor rate has all died away, you will find it replaced by a pauperism both so mild in the character, and so moderate in the amount of it, that out of free-will offerings, and of these alone, all its expenses will be cheerfully borne.

And there is a very important difference between the old and the new administration, the practical operation of which you are not able to appreciate now, but in which you will soon experience that there is really all the might and marvellous efficacy of a charm. What is now demanded as a right, will then be preferred as a request. It is just the difference between the claiming of a thing, and the asking of a thing. Now, the use which you ought to make of this difference is not to bid any one parochial applicant sternly away from you, because now you have the power; but to give courteous entertainment to them all. When a fellow-man comes into your presence, and tells you of want or of disease in his family, you are not to " hide yourself from your own flesh." It will always be your part, and more especially at the moment of transition to a system of charity which is yet untried, patiently to listen to every case, and calmly to investigate, and mildly to advise, and to mix up the utmost civility and temper with your wise and firm prosecution of the matter which has been submitted to you. Now it is when so employed, that you will come to feel, and that very speedily too, the breath of another spirit altogether in your intercourse and dealings with the poor, than that by which they wont to be formerly animated. At present there is a jealousy between the two classes, upholden by a sense of right upon the one side, and by a dread of rapacity upon the other. But very soon under the new regimen, will the one party come down from their insolence, and the other party from that distant and defensive attitude which they now think it so necessary to maintain. This single change in the law will act, and that instantaneously, with all the power of an emollient between them—the poor ceasing to distrust the rich, and the rich forthwith ceasing to be afraid of the poor. It will give a wholly different complexion to the proceedings of the parish vestry—who, now left to their own discretion, will use it discreetly; and who, in proportion as they feel relieved from compulsion, will resign themselves the more to the influence of kindness. They will soon discover, that a harsh and imperious manner to the poor, is not at all necessary for their own protection. It will be quite enough for their security, that they investigate, that they advise, that they suggest expedients, that they offer their friendly interposition with relatives, who might aid, or with neighbours who might employ them—that, on the discovery of a vicious or expensive habit, they address them in a tone of remonstrance which is at once meek, and moral, and affectionate. It is not known how soon the poor would be moulded and transformed into another habit, under the power of a treatment like this; and how, when once the imagination of a right was done away, the old ministration of charity, as if delivered of the wormwood that law had infused, would instantly take on its native temperament of love and liberty. The rich would have a comfort in being kind, when what they did was recognized as kindness. The poor would have a pleasure in being grateful, when they saw, in the attentions of the wealthy, the spontaneous homage of that sympathy, or that reverence which is due to our common nature. There would no longer be a jaundiced medium between them. The hearts of the affluent would not revolt, as they now do, from that misery which, instead of calling for pity, loudly challenges redress. And the plebeian mind would not fester, as it does now, with untrue and ungenerous imaginations of the upper classes of society. With such an improvement in the materials of the parochial community, would it become greatly more manageable than before; and the body of management, the vestry, the parochial court of influential men, to whom the public charity, now rendered wholly gratuitous, had been committed, would soon find such an adequacy in the better and previous resources that either their own strict investigation had disclosed, or their own active influence had created, as to demonstrate that public charity, in this best form of it, could either be most easily upheld, or even was very much uncalled for.

And it should be adverted to here, that agreeably to the scheme which we have ventured to recommend, no parish at the first can embark on this retracing process from legal to gratuitous charity, without a very large concurrence of householders in its favour; and that this, of itself, is the guarantee for an outset which shall be altogether safe and prosperous, and, at least, for several years being passed over without any oppressive weight of applications. For whence are these applications to come? Not from the old paupers, on whose condition or on whose rights no change, by the supposition, has been made—not surely in very great number, from the families of those who, by their concurrence in the new system, have expressed a hostility against pauperism, which is the best security for such sentiments and habits as will keep them permanently above it—and therefore, only from that small body of dissentients who were not paupers at the time of the new system being adopted, or from the descendants of the old generation of paupers. The applications which do come from these quarters will come very gradually: and there will be ample leisure for discriminating between the real or the deserving want, and that which is either pretended, or is the fruit of vicious indulgence; and it will be found a work of perfect lightness and facility, to devolve most of those cases which ought to be attended to, on other resources than those of public charity. So that the remainder, which must be taken on the parochial fund, will be met and upheld at an expense that is indefinitely small, or, at least, that bears no comparison with the poor rate, which, by this time, shall have nearly disappeared. And, as this old burden melts away, the new resources will be every year becoming more productive. With the *morale* of private benevolence, now more free and energetic than before, its *materiel* will be also more abundant. There will be more both of power and willingness among the rich. There will be less both of need and of expectancy among the poor. The vestry, in fact, might very easily so manage, as at length to find, that even their office, as the administrators of the parochial fund, shall be well nigh superseded ; and that in regard, at least, to the affairs of parochial indigence, the whole economy of a parish can be well and prosperously conducted, not only without any legal charity, but without even the semblance of it, in any public charity at all.

But another fear is, that however sufficient the means may turn out under the proposed system, the management will be so very laborious, as to leave no room for hoping, that it can long be persevered in. Now this too is a bugbear—and if possible, a still more airy and unsubstantial one than the former. The only strenuous management that is at all required, will be at the outset, where each case ought to be fearlessly met, and sifted to the uttermost; and every right expedient bethought of and tried, that, if possible, it may be shifted aside from the parochial fund, and devolved in a better way on the thrift and labour of the applicant himself, on the duty of his relatives, or on the charities of private benevolence. Let this method be acted upon but for a month or two—and here is the way in which it operates. When the people come to perceive, that this is the way in which their applications are met, they simply, in by far the greater number of instances, cease to apply. They who are conscious of means which they know that it is in the power of a careful scrutiny to detect, will forbear to offer themselves. They who are idly disposed, will shrink from the hazard of having their plea refuted by some employment being put into their hands, which they would rather decline. Some who have kind relatives or neighbours, will rather continue to draw from them in secret, than subject their private matters to the inquisition of a vestry. There are many securities against the vestry being overwhelmed with applications. Some they will have—and each of them it is their part to follow up, by the most elaborate process of examinations and expedients. But they may rest assured, that in proportion to the labour bestowed on each one, will be the smallness of the number of them. Their business will at length be very much confined to the relief of such unquestionable and genuine distress, as they shall find it a delight to succour and sustain—and often a matter of perfect ease to find enough of benevolence for taking it off their hands. It is thus, that from an outset of strenuousness, they will, at length, be conducted to a state of permanent repose. This style of administration acts by a preventive influence upon the people. Its genuine effect is, to keep each man in his own place—and many whom the old system would have seduced to the door of the parish vestry, will " study to be quiet, and to do their own business, and to work with their own hands, rather than be burdensome." Many who would have brought aged relatives there, will learn to show piety at home, and to "requite their parents." Many who would have thrown their children upon a poor rate, will in the absence of this ruinous temptation, " provide for their own, and specially for those of their own house." That fermentation of hopes, and appetites, and busy expedients which might be witnessed now in every parish of England, where so many families have been thrown agog by the very existence of a legal provision, will speedily subside, when such a provision ceases to be administered; and with the greater speed, that the vestry are more dexterous and diligent with their investigations. The people will, at length, settle down into a habit of most manageable quiescence—and the vestry, after having marvelled at the end of the first year, because, after strict inquiry, they have had so little to expend, will still more marvel at the end of their second year, because of the very few inquiries which they shall be called upon to make.

Now no investigation, however rigid, or however persevered in, under the present system, will ever conduct the population to this state. It may repress, for a time, the appetite for public relief, but will not extinguish it. If the right shall remain with the people, they will be on the watch to recover it—and on the first moment of relaxation by the vestry, there will be a set in of the pauperism as before. And besides, a vestry liable as they now are to the control and interference of magistrates, will often prefer a compromise with an applicant, though they know him to be unworthy of relief, to the labour, which is often impracticable, of proving this to the satisfaction of others. The right may be looked upon as the principle that gives all its elasticity to pauperism, which by an external force may be compressed within narrower limits, but which, on the removal of that force, will suddenly expand again to its former dimensions. Let the elasticity be taken away, and the compressing force will not be long necessary. All that is ungracious in charity will at length be done away. When freed from constraint, it will assume its natural character; and under its reign, we shall shortly behold a better served and a better satisfied population.*

---

* There is one way in which, even under the present system, an exemplification might be afforded of some of those principles which have been

Having now fully considered the fears which
might restrain many parishes at the first from the

---

adverted to in the text. Let an upright and benevolent magistrate, aware
of the mischiefs of pauperism, and anxious to reduce them, assume all that
care and superintendence which we have supposed, in the vestry of a trial
parish—and he, even under all the disadvantage of a conscious right, on the
part of the people, and a large existing fund that lures them from their own
resources, will still, as the fruit of his steady perseverance, greatly reduce
both the expense and trouble of the management—and earn, if at all kind
and reasonable in his dealings and conversations with the applicants, even
a certain popularity among them.

The experience of Mr. Marriot of Prestwich, at p. 278, is quite in point.
He accomplished very great reductions on the pauperism of the township
of Pilkington—and that, by a strictness and a patience of inquiry which ultimately reduced very much his own trouble. It tended gradually to relieve him, from the load of unworthy and unnecessary applications—insomuch,
that the hours spent by him in this business, at length, were twenty times
fewer than they had been at the outset.

Now, this will do so long as the township of Pilkington has the rare advantage of a magistrate in its neighbourhood, who has the ultimate power
of decision in the cases of its pauperism, and who uses that power intelli-
gently and popularly. But suppose this advantage to be removed. The
right of legal relief remains—and an indefinite fund is leviable for the purpose of satisfying it; and out of these elements, there will, at length, be a
reflux of the pauperism, which may speedily recover all the force and magnitude that it ever had.

But suppose again that instead of thus acting in the capacity of a magistrate, one were to act in the capacity of an active and ascendant member
of a parish vestry, upon the new system—that the poor rate, and its corresponding pauperism, were suffered gradually to melt away; and that the
new cases were to be met with the charity of free-will offerings. Who
does not see, that the very same result, of a quiet and satisfied population,
would ensue; and this inconceivably heightened, by the jealousies and heart-
burnings of an imagined right being detached from the whole ministration.
With the new habits of a new race, there is a moral certainty of a parish in
these circumstances being conducted, in a few years, to a state of quiescence, that will then be permanent under every change of administration—
for with the present law of pauperism abolished, in reference to that parish,
there will be nothing to seduce the people from those peaceful and primitive habits to which they have been recommitted.

adoption of the new system, let me advert to the mistakes and mismanagements which might be incurred in the prosecution of it.

First, then, if the experiment shall prosper, it will not be because of the great supplies which are raised, but because of the great care which has been observed in the administration of them. We should not hold it to be a happy conclusion of the enterprise, if the vestry, under the new system, enabled by the liberality either of the collection at church, or of private donations, were to expend as much in the relief of indigence, as it did under the old. This is not the way in which we should like compensation to be made for the loss of the poor rate. A far better equivalent would be, in the improvement that had taken place on the industry, and sobriety, and self-respect, and virtuous habits of the population. Let there be as profuse an expenditure as before, and there will be no-

---

There may be detected, in this little narrative from Pilkington, the operation of a principle which never, under the present economy, can have its fair or full development in England—and that is, the effect of a kind and patient attention on the part of the higher orders, in conciliating the affections of those who are beneath them. The poor rate creates a heavy deduction from this benign and beneficial influence; and, therefore, what good may be anticipated from it in a trial parish, when even now we see it exemplified. We should imagine that this must often have fallen in with the experience of those gentlemen, who have taken an active part in the business of select vestries. We are persuaded, that many of them will have found the poor much easier to deal with than they at first apprehended; and that their observation will agree with that of Mr. Walker in Bury, Lancashire, who takes a principal share in the now stricter management that is there set up, and has met with less grumbling than was anticipated.

thing to foster these habits, in the new change that has taken place, from the system of a poor rate, to the system of free-will offerings. Now, if this be not adverted to, there might be a grievous error at the very commencement of the undertaking. The truth is, that even though there should be moderate supplies, yet for the first months there may be a rapidly accumulating surplus in the hands of the vestry, from the very gradual onset of the new applications. Hence a temptation to liberal allowances, which might afterwards land them in an embarrassment—for even on the principles of a friendly society, they ought to husband well their capital at the first, that they may be prepared for the full weight of those cases, which shall not for several years have attained their maximum. But independently of this, the charity that is administered by the new vestry is public charity; and this ought always to be held out as the worst, and, therefore, as the last resort of human suffering. The whole management should be conducted upon this principle as its basis. To have one's name enrolled in the lists of a parochial almonry, should be regarded as a humiliation, from which there ought to be felt an anxiety that the humblest and poorest of the community should, if possible, be protected. Let this principle be acted upon in the spirit of truth and friendship, by the upper classes of a parish, and it will soon be caught, and spread itself, as if by sympathy, among the lower classes. Ere an applicant shall become a pensioner on the parochial fund, every right expedient of prevention ought to be tried, and it is, in fact, the successful prosecution of these expedients wherein the great moral and economical good of the new administration lies.

But, secondly, though the private liberality of the rich in a parish to its poor, ranks as one of those expedients, and is much to be preferred over that open and visible distribution, that is so fitted both to corrupt and to degrade the objects of it—yet may the rich also be, to a certain degree, the instruments of the very same mischief, that we have now charged on an incautious public administration. They ought never to forget, that the best economic gift which can possibly be rendered to the lower orders, is a habit of self-respect and self-dependence—and for this purpose, they ought not to disdain a free and frequent intercourse with them. This of itself will go far to elevate the mind and the manners of our peasantry; and it is a very great mistake, that the visit of rank or affluence to a poor man's cottage, is not welcomed, unless it be followed up by some beggarly ministration. Wherever a case of obvious and ascertained distress meets the philanthropist on his walk, it is his part to approve that his benevolence is real, by " willingness to distribute," by " readiness to communicate." But he should recollect, that there are also other topics than those of mere almsgiving, upon which he might most pertinently and most profitably hold fellowship with his humbler brethren of the species; and shortly earn the confidence and regard of all his neighbourhood. The education of their families; the good order of their houses; the little schemes of economy and management in which he requests their co-operation; the parish bank, for which he has to solicit their agency and their contributions; the counsel, the service, the little presents of courtesy, by which he does not sink but signalize them; the cheap and simple attentions by which the cottage children can be made happy, and their parents grateful; those thousand nameless graces and benignities, by which the accomplished female can light up a moral gladness, in the hamlet which she has selected as the theatre both of many duties, and of many friendships—there is a way of prosecuting all these without alimenting the rapacity or the sordidness of our labouring classes—a way that is best learned in the school of experience; and after, perhaps, the many blunders which have been committed, and the many mortifying disappointments which have been sustained, by the young practitioner in the art of well-doing. It is not by money alone that he is to manifest his kindness. There are innumerable other ways, and better ways of doing it—and in the prosecution of which he might, in truth, refine and heighten that delicacy which he else would overbear. Let there be but good-will in his heart; and this, amid all his forbearance in giving, nay, amid all his refusals, when he apprehends a cunning or a corruption in the object of them—this will, at length, shine forth upon the people, in the lustre of its own moral evidence; and will give for him an ascendancy, that might be convertible to the fine result of their permanent amelioration. Such a man will nobly clear his way, through all those initial suspicions or calumnies, that for a time may obstruct his best aspirings after usefulness. If he have failed in those petty and oft-repeated, while heedless liberalities, by which many an indolent sentimentalist scatters poison on every side of him—the season of his vindication will come round, when the endowment of a village school, or some costly yet unquestionable benevolence calls for his princely offering—and from the vantage ground of his now accredited worth, he can deal with efficacy among the people, his remonstrances both against the vice and idleness which impoverish, and against the beggary which degrades them. All that good, by the exhibition of which he might corrupt others, he doeth by stealth, or in secret—but the main good that he doeth, and by which he most emphatically acquits himself as the benefactor of the poor, is by working out this lesson in the midst of them, that their own resources are the best securities against want, and that they themselves might indeed be their own best benefactors.

There are many of England's most enlightened clergymen, who, each at the head of his own vestry, in the absence of poor-rate, that sore pestilence in the work of all reformation, could, after having seized the true principle for the management of the poor, speedily send a new pulse throughout the community over which he presides, and spread an aspect of moral healthfulness over the face of his parish. With this as the distinct object of their management, of which no secret ought to be made, that they were, as far as in them lay, to commit every applicant back again, upon his own expedients, and first to ascertain what his own industry, and the relative duties and sympathies by which he was surrounded could do for him, ere they would admit him as a pensioner of theirs —with this as their object, firmly yet feelingly prosecuted, they will at length be gratified to find how marvellously little is left for them to do. If benevolence to our kind, be the real animating spirit of a parochial court, then let it be as careful, and resolute, and moral as it may, nothing will withstand it. The opposition which it may excite, at the first, by its wholesome severities, will at length hide its head as if ashamed. All the right sense and feeling of the parish will speak for it and be upon its side. Even the popular mind will be at length gained over—and then every thing is gained. The families of the poor themselves will at length feel an atmosphere of goodwill around them which, under the reign of legal charity, they never once felt; and they will acknowledge themselves to be now the happier objects of an attention, and a kindness, and a directing wisdom on the part of their superiors, under which they breathe a new moral existence. They will at length make common cause with their vestry—and whenever their innumerable sympathies are unlocked by the abolition of that system which has congealed them, it will be found, that apart even from the now increased aid and succour of the opulent, there is throughout the plebeian mass such a busy circulation of mutual help and liberality from house to house, as to leave the ministrations of the parochial charity very much uncalled for.

A more unfettered vestry, acting as it ought, in the spirit of a moral and ecclesiastical court, will, by the discouragements which it lays on profligacy, protect itself from the inroads of that which, in fact, is the main feeder of our existing pauperism. They will then have the power of doing so in their own hands; and they need be under no apprehension, lest by the putting of it forth, they should prove the occasion of such crimes, or such consequences as are shocking to humanity. They will, in fact, make no violent departure from such principles as are already recognized. In refusing the application of the mother of an illegitimate child, they will have the sanction even of English precedents. When they rest a denial on the idleness or drunkenness of the applicant, the trial vestry will just do what the select vestry are already warranted to do by act of parliament, which empowers them to have respect unto his character, as well as to his circumstances. Even when they forbear to act on the event of a run-

away parent, and that, because, as a body, responsible for the virtue of the parish, they are fearful
of the slightest countenance to a habit, by which
the ties of natural relationship have so woefully
been broken,—even this seeming cruelty to one
family, will turn out a blessing and a kindness to
many families. Nature will re-assert her supremacy, after that temptation is withdrawn by which
her feelings and her principles had been enfeebled.
Let it be the invariable practice of the vestry never
to interpose for the purpose of repairing the consequences of crime. The habit will be found as
safe as it is salutary. Many will be restrained
from evil, and a whole century may roll over a
parish thus purely and rigorously conducted, without one guilty mother being tempted to an act of
unnatural violence,—without one deserted family
being left by its neighbourhood to starve.

It is because of the mighty retrenchments which
may thus be effected, that we hold it quite safe for
a trial parish to meet, upon its now voluntary fund,
both the casual poor, and those who alternate from
summer to winter. At least there are many parishes, that might well hazard the treatment of both
these on the footing of new cases, instead of con-
signing them, along with the regular paupers, to
the compulsory fund. We should like it, in fact,
on account of the proof which it would afford of
the very great force of education that lay in circumstances, and of the speed wherewith a change
of habit followed in the train of a change of cir-

cumstances. In regard to the casual poor, their trivial and temporary applications to the parish are, many of them, founded upon some slight derangement that has taken place in their personal or domestic history—the illness of a few days of the father—or the confinement of the mother on childbed—or some short suspension of employment from the weather, or the cessation of demand for a week or two. Now, surely, to treat them as if they were incapable of foresight so very brief, is not treating them like rational creatures. It is most desirable that they should be trained to anticipation; and, by contesting these little demands with them, I should like to teach them this first and earliest lesson of it,—and so, carry them forward in this line of prudential habits, till even summer be made to provide for the deficiences of winter. The parish bank and parish vestry might thus be made to act to each other's hands; and the reason why I do recommend an encounter with the casual poor, and that, upon the voluntary income alone, is because I count on the most striking and immediate success with this part of the experiment, confident, as I am, of the very great facility wherewith a people may be made to suit their new habits to their new circumstances. It gives a hardier outset to the vestry, but with firmness and good management, the difficulty will be got over, and the greater will be the triumph.*

* We are quite aware that many parishes have been accustomed to deal so largely in casual relief, that unless all who have been the objects of it

The truth is, that under a good management,
though with very slender means, the first difficulty

---

shall continue under the operation of the old system, they would not adventure, with such a weight of demand and of pressure, upon the new ones.
This might be made a matter of discretionary adjustment at the outset; or
if they waited the event of the trial in smaller and more manageable parishes, they might then feel encouraged, and on the solid ground of experience, to make the attempt in this completer form.·

What we anticipate of many of the trial parishes is, that their success
will, in a very few months, so far outshoot their first expectations, as not
only to warrant their fullest confidence of the final result being prosperous, but as will lead them to hasten that result by the application of voluntary means, even to the whole of the old and regular pauperism ; and
so bring about an immediate extinction of the poor rates. There might be
a rashness in this, and it is altogether unnecessary for ultimate success ;
seeing that by the operation of death on the old cases, the poor-rate must
surely, though more slowly be done away. Still however the eclat of such
an achievement may beget an impatience for it ; and such is our faith in
the energies of the new system, that we hold them, in most instances, fully
commensurate to this.

The following is a specimen of what might be done, in the way even of a
sudden reformation, and may serve to illustrate how likely and how practicable is that smoother and more gradual reformation which we have ventured to recommend. The population of White Waltham is 795. Its expenditure for the relief of the poor, in 1820-21, was £480. But this, of
course, includes the cost of the in-door paupers also.

" *A simple Statement of the Manner of Relieving the Poor of White Waltham,
Berks.* By J. SAWYER, ESQ.

" The conduct of the gentlemen and farmers of the parish of White Waltham, in the county of Berks, in attempting to abate the evils arising from
an injudicious administration of the poor laws having lately been much the
subject of conversation in the neighbourhood, and of course, as might be
expected, approved of by some, and censured by others, it is thought advisable that a simple statement should be made, to enable their neighbours
to form a correct judgment of their proceedings. The heavy pressure of
the poor laws, in this period of agricultural distress, is severely felt : no one
denies this plain fact, while the benefit to the poor themselves, by the extent of relief lately given, is very much doubted ; greater misery it is sup-

which shall meet the vestry will be a very different one from that which is now apprehended. It will

---

posed being produced from the destruction of their provident cares and fore-thought, than the relief afforded from the poor rates counterbalances.

" Another point of view offers itself very strongly to the reflecting mind, whether sufficient, or at least equal relief, would not be given from motives of benevolence, which is now extorted by the hands of the law indiscrimi-nately; and whether the relief so given would not act very beneficially upon the mind of the receiver. To say that no misery shall exist, is beyond the power of man; all we can attempt is to lessen the quantity of it as much as possible.

" I do not attempt to conceal that, with the farmers, an abatement of the poor rate was the first object in view, but this was not the principal object with the gentlemen, who sincerely wished to improve the situation of the labour-ing classes; and while they acted in concert, there was not a well-grounded fear that the poor would be oppressed.

" At their first meeting the first thing proposed was, that the weekly pen-sioners, who were generally old and infirm, should be taken off the parish books, and supported by private benevolence, where necessary. One or two cases occurred, where it was stated that the relations would come for-wards, if the parish gave nothing, and this principle seemed so fair and just, and so desirable, that a brother, sister, or son, should do all in their power to assist their relatives, that it was acted upon; and the result proved that the widow was not left without assistance. In all the other cases, the gen-tlemen and farmers present voluntarily agreed each to support a poor pen-sioner; or where their occupations were small, several were joined toge-ther. The smallest occupiers cheerfully assented, and, in two instances, the widow's pension was made up from four and six contributors, and the only complaint which has been made on the part of the widow, was the necessity of applying to several instead of to one, namely, the overseer. And this has been occasionally remedied by the contributors agreeing to pay their quotas to the overseer, who would give to the pauper. No hardship has consequently been experienced by them.

" The actual expenditure of the parish in giving relief, from the 30th of July to the 3d of December, being a period of nineteen weeks, has been only £14 6s. 1¼d.; other sums have been paid, but for other purposes, such as county rates, allowances to paupers not resident in the parish, and some old bills incurred in a preceding period; while in former periods of a similar duration, more than six times the amount has been expended."

It might be necessary for the purpose of explaining, and, perhaps, of jus-

not be how to find the adequate supplies, but how
to dispose of the unappropriated and accumulating

---

tifying the tone of confidence wherewith some of our predictions are uttered,
to state it as our feeling that we speak experimentally. The parish of St.
John's in Glasgow, we now deem, by certain criteria which have recently
come to our knowledge, to be the lowest in the scale of natural wealth of
any in the city; and from its population, which consists of more than 8,000
individuals, is of more unwieldy management than are nine-tenths of the
parishes of England. The process which we have recommended there, for
trial, in the first instance, by the smaller and more manageable parishes in
that country, we might well pronounce upon with some degree of sanguine
expectation, when it is the very process that not only has succeeded with
ourselves, but that, in less than four years, has reached a more perfect state
than we looked for at the outset, even after the disappearance of a whole
generation of pauperism. We now find, that with means greatly more
moderate than our own, we could have described all that is essential in this
process onward to a final extinction of the old pauperism; that is, we could
have met the new cases; and suffering the old to remain on the fund by assessment, would at length have been delivered from these also by the operation of death. This sure method of getting rid of the assessment, we have
hitherto found to be practicable on means so exceedingly small, that we hold
it competent for any one parish in Glasgow, even upon its existing collec-
lection, however slender that collection may hitherto have been, to form an
arrangement by which the very same result might eventually be arrived at.
Our means have been greater than was at all necessary for this achievement;
not, however, it is of importance to remark, because our means have increased, for the collection at the church-door has become smaller than at
first, but because, such is the power of an independent management, that
our burdens have marvellously decreased. And what we have done with
the excess of our means, are the very things which we promise may be
done in the parishes of England. The truth is, that such is the power of
the system as to have landed us not in an under, but an over-sufficiency
for what we undertook at the outset. And, accordingly, instead of waiting
for the disappearance of the old pauperism by death, we have now relieved
the fund by assessment of it altogether, and defray the whole expenses of it
out of our voluntary fund. Still, however, there was a large unappropriated surplus, which, had it remained with us, and had we been under the
legal necessity of restricting it to the public relief of indigence, would have
embarrassed us. The only anxiety that we have all along felt was not, how
to make up a deficiency of income, but how, in a right and salutary way, to

surplus. Instead of a pressure on the voluntary fund, which it cannot hold out against, there will,

---

get rid of an excess. We honestly think, that had it gone to augment the allowances of our ordinary pauperism, this would have been a deleterious application of it. And, accordingly, we devised that very use for it which we now recommend to the trial parishes of England. We were enabled to vest £500 out of the produce of our collections, with the city corporation, for the perpetual endowment by salary of a parochial school: and we take this opportunity of repeating our grateful acknowledgments to the magistrates of Glasgow, for their concurrence in a destination, which at once proves, that the economy even of a city parish may be conducted without a compulsory pauperism, and also provides, in the education of the lower classes, an additional security against that low and crouching spirit of pauperism, wherewith a contagion from the south was beginning to taint our Scottish population.

It will be interesting to mark the future state of this parish. Should our successor in office, or the city rulers, overthrow the present arrangement, and bring the people of St. John's again into contact with the Town Hospital, there will then be a speedy re-ascent of its pauperism up to the average of that of Glasgow. The phenomenon will be quite analogous to that of a parish in England, whose pauperism has been repressed, for a season, by the energies of a strict administration, but which, on the moment of these energies being withdrawn, must resume its wonted magnitude, because the law remains, and the legal or compulsory provision remains, and the natural appetency of men for as much of this provision as it can seize upon remains. But should the existing arrangement continue to be protected and upheld both by the parochial and the general authorities of the place, then this is the outline of the history of its future pauperism. At present the whole yearly expenditure is a little above £300, whereof £250 is the produce of the old system, and less than £80 has been created, under the new, in the space of three years and a half. This sum will decline, for still the old pauperism is dying much faster away than the new is growing: so that, with the very moderate collection of £200 a-year in the church, and the still more moderate collection of £100 a-year in the chapel, the whole pauperism of St. John's can be nearly met now, and may, under the ordinary sessional management of Scotland, be equally well met for ever. And there is no fatiguing strenuousness of management called for now, on the part of the agents, for our people (and every other will manifest the same thing under the same circumstances) cease to disturb us by their applications, when we cease to have disturbed them by those lying promises of sufficiency which

from year to year, be a progressive enlargement
of it. The vestry will not be put upon their devices
to recruit their exhausted treasury. They will be
put upon their devices to find out a safe and salutary
absorbent for its overplus. In these circumstances,
the clergyman who is aware of the mischiefs of
public charity, might be tempted to lay an arrest
on the liberality of his parishioners and hearers.
But better far would it be, that he kept this liberality agoing, nay stimulated it the more, and
then impressed such a direction on the produce of
it as went not to corrupt the people, but to elevate
and to moralize them. He might do them harm
by a large public distribution for the relief of indigence, whether the means of it were provided
by a poor-rate or free-will offerings. But there is
no harm in thus meeting certain of the helpless
and involuntary sufferings of our nature. There is
none in so signalizing the dumb, and the blind, and

---

pauperism holds out, but can never realize. Our experience will just be
the experience of a trial parish in England, which, after having been conducted to a habit of quiescence, will never again break forth from it, provided that the legal provision, after which all are now agog, is conclusively
withdrawn.

We shall only add, further, on this subject, that we also speak experimentally, when we promise to a trial parish of England a greatly more
satisfied population under the new system than under the old. This has
clearly been our experience, as may be arithmetically proved by the movements and changes of residence that take place among the paupers of
Glasgow. The truth is, that the poor of all the parishes in the city are yet
interchangeable; and we suffer by it. There has been an efflux of fifteen
of our paupers to other parishes. There has been an influx from them of
twenty-eight to the parish of St. John's. Here is a balance of thirteen
against our funds, and in favour of the popularity of our management.

the lunatic of a parish.*   There is none, but quite
the contrary, in bestowing of this spare and super-

---

* If the expense of the parish lunatics, in the county asylum, be defrayed
from the county rate, it might continue to be so under the new system. If
it be defrayed by a separate charge on the poor rate of the parish, then the
new cases of it which occur may be taken upon the voluntary fund. At all
events, after the old pauperism is extinguished, that part of the assessment
which is still kept up for other purposes, should instantly change its name;
and it should then be felt, as the proud distinction of a parish, that it had
no poor rate—that it was subject to no other parochial assessment than that
of a county and constable rate.

For a fuller exhibition of our ideas on the right disposal of the surplus of
a parochial fund, see Chap. xiii. of this work; and a fuller statement than
what we have now given of the Glasgow pauperism, is to be met with in
Chap. xi. and xii. and in a Speech delivered upon the subject before the
General Assembly, in May, 1822.

Since the earlier of these sheets passed through the press, we have been
favoured with a sight of the Supplementary Appendix to the Report from
the Select Committee on Poor Rate Returns, ordered to be printed 15th
July, 1822. It gives the sums expended for the relief of the poor in each
of the parishes of England for six years, beginning with 1815-1816. It
should be remarked, that these sums fall greatly short of the sums raised in
the name of poor rate—and that, not merely because county and constable
rates, and other expenses, not connected with the poor, are deducted, but
because there are further deducted sums paid for purposes connected
with the poor, but not for the direct and personal relief of the poor; such
as, expenses at law, removals, salaries, the erection and repairing of workhouses, and several other expenses.

It is thus that the sums exhibited in this document are considerably beneath, not merely the sums raised in the name of poor rate, but also the
sums which express the whole cost or expenditure on the poor.

At Stockport in 1817, the sum put down in the Appendix for the relief
of its poor, is £7126 17s. In the annual statement of Stockport, for that
year, the whole disbursements come to £17,367 12s. 1d. from which even,
after deducting old debts paid, the returns from the fathers of illegitimate
children, and from other towns for their poor, along with county and constable rates, and other expenses not connected with the poor, there remains
a sum considerably above that stated in the Appendix.

fluous revenue in the erection or the support of
village schools, and so adding still to your securi-

For the reader's information, we subjoin a few particulars taken from
this very important document.

The following are the names of a few parishes, with their expenditure,
for the relief of the poor only, for 1820-1, and their population for the same
year as taken from the last census.

	Expenditure.		Population.
Colmworth, (Bedfordshire)	£611	1	450
Eaton Socon	2102	19	2039
Renhold	362	0	340
Roxton	710	0	537
Battlesden	366	4	151
Bletsoe	546	8	383
Stagsden	1046	13	542
Foxton, (Leicestershire)	889	10	383
Frisby	45	13	18
Gumley	533	10	289
Lubenham	1633	11	533
Wigston Magna	3412	17	2089
Ford (Sussex)	150	18	83
Kirdford	3243	0	1602
Shipley	3069	6	1159
West Grinstead	2835	1	1229
Oving	1289	7	637

The following are the names of a few parishes that have increased their
expenditure since 1817-18.

	Expenditure in 1820.		Expenditure in 1821.	
Huish (Devonshire)	£35	2	£59	5
Tavistock	1492	6	2559	19
Chawley	555	0	653	0
Brampton (Huntingdonshire)	793	0	886	12
Allwalton	124	6	200	3
Elton	695	15	864	15
Adbaston (Stafford)	383	15	691	3
Colwick	592	7	827	6
Tixall,	53	17	116	3
Wetton	264	0	358	6

ties against pauperism, by widening, through education, the moral distance between the habits of

---

The following are a few of the more remarkable instances of a decreased
expenditure.

	Expenditure in 1818.		Expenditure in 1821.	
Thatcham, (Berks)	£3742	7	£1552	9
Englefield	596	19	200	16
East Hendred	1265	3	616	6
Cheadle Bulkeley (Cheshire)	1096	0	458	7
Macclesfield	5165	12	2686	18
St. Erth, (Cornwall)	1047	9	471	6
Melbourne, (Derby)	1727	11	811	4
Stanton and Newall	1133	14	418	16
Cullompton (Devon)	2075	8	836	2
Bourton (Dorset)	2273	13	477	1

We find on again looking over the documents in our possession, that we
have erroneously stated, in a preceding note, the expenditure of Stockport;
though the fact is undoubted of a very great reduction within the four last
years. The permanent poor of St. Mary's, Nottingham, which are there
referred to, are out-poor only.

We have recently obtained replies to the subjoined queries, from the
Rev. Mr. Bickersteth of Acton, in Suffolk, which we offer to our readers,
as a pretty fair specimen of the state and effects of English pauperism in
the smaller country parishes.

1st, Would not you find a great obstacle in the way of your usefulness
to be removed, could the wants of the poor be provided for by the charity
of good-will, rather than by the charity of law?

"Doubtless: could these wants be provided for as *certainly* : the legal
relief is usually both demanded and given in a manner very injurious to all
parties, and which cannot but create serious obstacles in the way of ministerial usefulness."

2d, Are not the inmates of your workhouse very wretched?

"Truly so: and, in some respects, avowedly and designedly on the part
of those by whom it should be regulated that the inmates may be the fewer;
and yet this receptacle is crowded to excess."

3d, And, do you find this part of your system very injurious to the morals of your parish, and particularly of the young?

"When not only the old and infirm, but young persons of both sex-
es, and these generally orphans, and of the worst class, are brought together under one roof, the effect must be in the highest degree dangerous to

the people, and a condition so degrading. And there is something more to be taken to account

---

the morals; and, in fact, nothing but the callousness induced by habit, would render the place tolerable to one of better dispositions."

4th, Is there not very little of control or confinement in your workhouse?

" Control and confinement are, at present, terms unknown in our workhouse: and this is one aggravating cause of the evils connected with it. Some years ago, at my desire, a governor was appointed, and the place was put under better management: but the additional expense of that appointment, in connection with the depressed times, was made the plea for dispensing with a governor; and after his removal, the system rapidly declined, and the whole fell into its present state of wretchedness and insubordination."

5th, Had you not six or seven supernumeraries in October last, and do you not expect to have more?

" Yes: and I fear there are even some unemployed at present."

6th, Do you not find that very few of your benefit society members are paupers?

" Very few, if any, and this only in case of the total want of employment. In various instances, this Benefit Society has totally prevented any application for legal relief, and the advantage of it, in this respect, has ₋een strongly felt, and thankfully noticed by the land occupiers, &c. who contribute to the rate."

7th, Had you not subscriptions in hard winters, over and above the poor rates?

" In hard winters, the benevolence of individuals has been called forth, or spontaneously exerted for the relief of the necessitous, and quite independently of the legal relief."

8th, Have you not a small missionary association?

" Yes: and which is evidently important, not only *directly* by interesting the minds of the poor, and suggesting a train of thinking profitable and useful in various respects; but *indirectly,* by promoting gradually a spirit of disinterestedness, economy, independence, industry, and self-denial."

9th, Are you not sensible of a great improvement in the habits and character of the people?

" Certainly: vices now shun the day, which formerly stalked abroad with an unblushing front in the face of the sun: and through the divine blessing, some have been turned from sin to righteousness, and many more reformed, and brought under wholesome restraint."

than the eventual good of such a destination. It lends a most important facility to your present

---

10*th*, But do you not find that Christianity, on the one hand, and pauperism on the other, have had the effect of forming your people into two distinct classes, extremely opposite to each other in character and spirit?

" I should hesitate in distributing the public into two distinct classes as formed by Christianity and pauperism: the *latter* being only *one* out of *many causes*, which produce a habit and character in contradiction to the *former :* while those under the influence of Christianity become more and more averse to apply for legal relief; others, apparently not under that best influence, from inferior motives, refuse to apply for a relief, which, to be obtained, must be extorted by clamorous importunity: and others again, of a worse stamp, *will have* what the law grants, not caring to what degradation they submit in receiving it. Usually this legal relief, without either charity or cheerfulness, is supplied grudgingly and of necessity; and thus a distressing alienation of mind is continually fostered between the giver and receiver, very destructive of the good-will and harmony which ought to subsist between the different classes of society."

11*th*, Is not education making progress among you?

" Yes: the poor, even those who have had no advantage of education themselves, are *generally* desirous to obtain instruction for their children, and often grateful to those who assist them in attaining this object."

12*th*, Have you not had occasion to observe the great kindness of the poor for each other, in those cases of sickness, and other extra necessities which do not lie fully and immediately within the scope of the poor rate?

" Frequently; and with much satisfaction. Indeed this kindness is sometimes so exuberant as to need, at least, regulation, if not restraint; that the services of the poor, one to another, may be afforded with the least expense of strength or time."

Our only remark on this very interesting document, is, that we are not aware of a greater practical obstacle to the abolition of pauperism in England, than the doubt which exists among its generous people, whether the poor would as certainly be relieved under the operation of a free, as of a legal system of charity. We can perceive this doubt in the first of the above replies—and yet, from the 6th, 7th, 11th and 12th of them, do we gather an assurance, which to ourselves is most satisfactory, that in the absence of a compulsory provision, there would be far less of actual and unrelieved want in a parochial community; and that, in the then augmented sobriety, and sympathy, and knowledge of the lower orders, there would be most abundant guarantees against all those evils which it is apprehended might ensue upon the extinction of the poor rate.

administration. It enables you to meet every applicant for relief, with an argument that will moderate the tone of his demand, and perhaps shame him altogether away from it. You can then tell him, that, by his forbearance, he leaves you in better condition for the relief of families still more helpless than his own; that he in fact will be a virtual contributor to the good of humanity, and to the interest of the rising generation, simply by shifting for himself, and leaving your fund entire and untouched for higher charities; that he ought, on this ground, to make common cause with you; and that he renders a most important co-operation, when he ceases to be burdensome, and ministers with his own hands to his own necessities. Such an argument tells with prodigious effect in many parishes of Scotland—and it will tell in England too, as soon as it is relieved from that artificial system, by which the worth and capability of the popular mind are now overborne. There will at length be a kindred spirit, between the aristocracy of a parish and its common people. Public charity will fall into desuetude. Instead of a now apprehended deficiency in the voluntary fund, there will be a now unlooked for surplus. The point will not merely be carried but overcarried—and the best auxiliaries on the side of this great reformation, will be found in that very class of families, out of which pauperism now draws its ravening myriads.

But we forbear the prosecution of these details,

and shall but slightly allude to the benefits of a management, which elsewhere has been fully explained by us, as bearing an important part in all those measures which might be set agoing through a parish, for the extinction of its pauperism. We refer to the subdivision of a parish, and the assignation of a given district to each member of the vestry, who may charge himself with all its pauperism, and be the medium through which the applications from its people are conveyed to the parochial court. It will be found an effectual management for crowded towns—and is even not inapplicable to country parishes. That member of the vestry does his business best, not who transmits the greatest number of applications from his local territory, but who intercepts the greatest number; and who intercepts them not by his stern and haughty negative, but by his patient inquiry, and his friendly argument, and his kind offers of work, or of interest in behalf of the family, and his affectionate persuasion with the husband who is profligate, or the children who are hard and unnatural to their parents, and withal his firm discountenance both to the artifices of low imposture and to the effrontery of vice. He will be astonished to find, in a few months, that all the fancied difficulties of his task have vanished into nothing; that the people, when thus frankly and naturally dealt with, forthwith betake themselves to the resources of Nature, and find them to be enough; that after perhaps a little storm of trials and con-

tests, which outlive not one short and fleeting season, there is a calm, and a calm not again to be
disturbed, because that angry spirit to which law
ministered its provocatives is now hushed for ever.
His work ceases, because now the *vis medicatrix*
works for him, with all that primitive liberty and
vigour which belongs to her. His office becomes
at length a sinecure, and should he choose to lay
it down, he may retire with the character of having
best done the duties of a vestry man, because he
gave the vestry nothing to do.

END OF VOLUME SECOND.

Printed by W. Collins & Co.
Glasgow.

CPSIA information can be obtained
at www.ICGtesting.com
Printed in the USA
LVOW12s0045040418

572228LV00001B/24/P